D0139954

Tourism Development and the Environment: Beyond Sustainability?

Tourism, Environment and Development Series

Series Editor: Richard Sharpley

School of Sport, Tourism & The Outdoors, University of
Central Lancashire, UK

*Editorial Board: Chris Cooper, Oxford Brookes University, UK;
Andrew Holden, University of Bedfordshire, UK; Bob McKercher,
Hong Kong Polytechic University; Chris Ryan, University of Waikato,
New Zealand; David Telfer, Brock University, Canada*

Tourism Development and the Environment: Beyond Sustainability?
Richard Sharpley

Titles in preparation

Tourism and Poverty Reduction
Pathways to Prosperity
Jonathan Mitchell and Caroline Ashley

Slow Travel and Tourism
Janet Dickinson and Les Lumsdon

Sustainable Tourism in Island Destinations
Sonya Graci and Rachel Dodds

Please contact the Series Editor to discuss new proposals at
rajsharpley@uclan.ac.uk

Tourism Development and the Environment: Beyond Sustainability?

Richard Sharpley

WITHDRAWN

I P F W

HELMKE LIBRARY

G
155
.A1
S473
2009

publishing for a sustainable future

London • Sterling, VA

First published by Earthscan in the UK and USA in 2009

Copyright © Professor Richard Anthony John Sharpley, 2009

All rights reserved

ISBN: HB 978-1-84407-732-8
         PB   978-1-84407-733-5

Typeset by JS Typesetting Ltd, Porthcawl, Mid Glamorgan
Cover design by Yvonne Booth

For a full list of publications please contact:

Earthscan
Dunstan House
14a St Cross St
London, EC1N 8XA, UK
Tel: +44 (0)20 7841 1930
Fax: +44 (0)20 7242 1474
Email: earthinfo@earthscan.co.uk
Web: **www.earthscan.co.uk**

22883 Quicksilver Drive, Sterling, VA 20166-2012, USA

Earthscan publishes in association with the International Institute for Environment
and Development

A catalogue record for this book is available from the British Library

Library of Congress Cataloging-in-Publication Data
Sharpley, Richard, 1956-
   Tourism development and the environment : beyond sustainability? / Richard
Sharpley.
      p. cm. – (Tourism, environment, and development)
   Includes bibliographical references and index.
   ISBN 978-1-84407-732-8 (hardback) – ISBN 978-1-84407-733-5 (pbk.)
1. Tourism–Environmental aspects. 2. Tourism–Economic aspects. 3. Economic
development–Environmental aspects. 4. Sustainable development. I. Title.
   G155.A1S473 2009
   338.4'791–dc11
                                                              2009007598

At Earthscan we strive to minimize our environmental impacts and carbon footprint
through reducing waste, recycling and offsetting our CO_2 emissions, including those
created through publication of this book. For more details of our environmental
policy, see www.earthscan.co.uk.

This book was printed in the UK by The Cromwell Press Group.
The paper used is FSC certified and the inks are vegetable based.

Contents

List of Figures and Tables

Figures

Tables

Series Preface

The relationship between tourism and the physical, socio-cultural, economic and political environments within which it occurs and upon which it impacts has long been recognized and considered within the academic literature. At the same time, the potential role of tourism as an agent of socio-economic development has also long been promoted and debated, although it is only relatively recently that a more critical and theoretically informed perspective on this role has been adopted. However, these two issues have been implicitly connected within the concept of sustainable tourism, a tourism development paradigm that, since the early 1990s, has dominated the tourism literature but which, to a great extent, has focused on prescriptive, managerialist or 'blueprint' approaches to tourism development. Moreover, it is now increasingly accepted that the sustainable tourism development debate has reached something of an impasse.

The purpose of the Earthscan *Tourism, Environment and Development* series, therefore, is to advance knowledge and understanding of the relationship between tourism and the environment at a time when not only is the environmental agenda in general, and climate change in particular, gaining increasing political prominence on the international stage, but also when environmental integrity is the key challenge facing the tourism sector. Collectively focusing on the tourism–environment–development nexus, books in the series explicitly relate the developmental role of tourism to its environmental consequences, critically reviewing and challenging contemporary approaches, and exploring new approaches, to managing and developing tourism within contemporary social, political and economic contexts. Each book presents a contemporary, succinct and critical analysis within a specific theme or context but, at the same time, contributes to a broader picture provided by the series as a whole whilst extending the debate beyond the contemporary perspectives of sustainable tourism development.

Introduction

Two decades ago, the concept of *sustainable tourism development* was virtually unheard of. More precisely, although the term 'sustainable development', initially proposed in the International Union for Conservation of Nature (IUCN's) World Conservation Strategy (IUCN, 1980) and subsequently popularized and politicized by the Brundtland Report (WCED, 1987), had already entered the language of development policy, it had yet to be applied to the specific context of tourism. This is not to say, of course, that there was a lack of concern about the scale, scope and consequences of widespread tourism development. Since the mid-1960s, the rapid growth of tourism, particularly international mass tourism, and the inexorable spread of the so-called 'pleasure periphery' (Turner and Ash, 1975) around the globe had been accompanied by increasing calls for restraint in its development. Numerous commentators had drawn attention to the potentially destructive environmental and socio-cultural effects of the unbridled expansion of tourism (though not in the apocalyptic terms that would later become popular), and, by the end of the 1980s, the 'alternative tourism' school was firmly established, as were concepts such as green, appropriate, low-impact, responsible and soft tourism.

By the early 1990s, however, the attention paid generally both to the perceived negative impacts of tourism and to alternative approaches to tourism development had become refocused through the specific lens of sustainable tourism development. It is unclear (and, most probably, unimportant) to what or whom the term can be attributed. One of the first published references to it dates back to Globe '90, an international conference held in Vancouver in March 1990 from which emerged, amongst other things, a 'strategy for sustainable tourism development' (Cronin, 1990). At the same time, Pigram (1990) explored policy considerations for sustainable tourism, whilst in November of the same year the 'Sustainable Tourism Development Conference', probably the first event to address the subject explicitly, was hosted by Queen Margaret College in Edinburgh – here it was stated that 'sustainable tourism is an idea whose time has come' (Howie, 1990, p3). The following year, the publication of the then English Tourist Board's *The Green Light: A Guide to Sustainable Tourism* (ETB, 1991) heralded the entry of the concept into the tourism policy arena, since when sustainable tourism or sustainable tourism development (terms that are used interchangeably but that refer, in fact, to two distinctive perspectives on tourism development) have occupied a dominant position in both the academic study of tourism and in tourism policy and planning processes. Indeed, by the mid-1990s, it was claimed that sustainable tourism development had achieved 'virtual global endorsement as the new [tourism] industry paradigm' (Godfrey, 1996, p60), a position that, arguably, it has maintained to this day.

From an academic perspective, sustainable tourism development has not only become firmly embedded as a subject within taught tourism programmes at all levels from secondary (high school) through to postgraduate study, it has also become an increasingly popular, if not the most popular, area of research within tourism. Numerous books address the topic either from a general perspective, within particular contexts, such as rural, island or community tourism development, or within the guise of 'ecotourism' as a more specific and, perhaps, rigidly defined sub-category of sustainable tourism development. At the same time, two dedicated academic journals, the *Journal of Sustainable Tourism*, first published in 1992, and the *Journal of Ecotourism*, dating from 2002, continue to provide a forum for academic research in the field. Moreover, articles addressing issues related to sustainable tourism development are regularly published in other tourism academic journals as well as in those from other disciplinary homes, such as development studies, environmental studies and geography. In fact, a quick search in Google identifies almost 115,000 results for sustainable tourism development, supporting the claim made by some cynics that the most sustainable thing about the concept has been academic research into it!

Tourism policy and planning, from the global to the local level, has also become increasingly defined over the last two decades by the objective of sustainable tourism development although, as will be noted shortly, the extent to which policy has been translated into practice 'on the ground' remains debatable. Certainly, the World Tourism Organization (now the United Nations World Tourism Organization, or UNWTO, to distinguish it from the World Trade Organization) has long published policies and guides for sustainable tourism development. For example, its *Sustainable Tourism Development: A Guide for Local Planners* (WTO, 1993) was followed by *Agenda 21 for the Travel & Tourism Industry*, published jointly with the World Travel and Tourism Council (WTO/WTTC, 1996). In 1993, the latter organization initiated 'Green Globe', which has since evolved into the world's principal certification scheme for the travel and tourism industry. It is now administered by EC3, a commercial organization wholly owned by the Sustainable Tourism Co-operative Research Centre (STCRC) in Australia. The WTTC also sponsors the Tourism for Tomorrow Awards, which recognize and promote best practice in 'responsible' tourism, although it should also be noted that, somewhat ironically, the WTTC's membership comprises the chairmen and CEOs of the world's top 100 travel and tourism businesses and, therefore, that the organization is committed to realizing tourism's growth potential! Other global organizations, such as the United Nations Environment Programme (UNEP), have also published policies and guides for sustainable tourism development (for example, UNEP/WTO, 2005), whilst innumerable policy and planning documents at the regional, national and local levels adopt a similar focus. The travel and tourism industry itself has, to an extent, also engaged with the concept of sustainable tourism development. For example, the European Community Model of Sustainable Tourism (ECOMOST) project was an early attempt, under the auspices of the International Federation of Tour Operators, to adopt an integrated, sustainable approach to tourism planning in Rhodes and Mallorca (IFTO, 1994). More contemporary schemes include the International Tourism Partnership, a leadership organization that promotes sustainable activity across the tourism sector, and the Tour Operators' Initiative, a non-profit initiative based in Switzerland and supported by UNEP, United Nations Educational, Scientific and Cultural Organization (UNESCO) and the UNWTO that, since 1992, has promoted sustainable approaches to tourism development amongst tour operators.

In addition to both public and private sector initiatives, the voluntary or third sector has also become involved in promoting sustainable tourism development. Pressure groups such as Tourism Concern, based in London, or Studienkreis für Tourismus und Entwicklung in Germany have long campaigned to raise awareness of tourism's potential negative consequences and the need for alternative, sustainable approaches to tourism development. At the same time, charitable organizations working within the relief and development sphere, such as the UK-based agency Tearfund, have also sought to promote sustainable development through tourism (Tearfund, 2002).

In short, sustainable tourism development has, since the early 1990s, re-presented the dominant tourism development discourse in academic, policy/planning and, to an extent, political circles. However, two broad observations can be made. Firstly, the academic study of sustainable tourism development has reached something of an impasse. Despite the extensive attention paid to it over the last 20 years, manifested in innumerable books, journal articles, conference papers and other publications, there still remains a lack of consensus over not only definitions and the theoretical foundations of the concept, but also the extent to which it can be translated into a set of practical policies and measures for the effective planning and management of tourism in the real world (Berno and Bricker, 2001). In particular, it is often claimed that the sustainable tourism development debate is disjointed, theoretically flawed and based upon weak or false assumptions (Liu, 2003), whilst it has long been suggested that the principles of sustainable tourism represent little more than a micro solution to a macro problem (Wheeller, 1991). Certainly, the typical 'blueprint' approach to sustainable tourism development, combining western-centric environmental managerialism with principles drawn from the alternative development school (i.e. 'bottom–up', community-based development), is only applicable to particular contexts or defined projects and of limited relevance to global tourism as a whole (Southgate and Sharpley, 2002).

Secondly, research some years ago found little evidence of widespread adherence to sustainable business and development principles within the UK outbound travel and tourism industry (Forsyth, 1995). Despite more recent initiatives, such as those referred to above, as well as undoubted growth in the supply of and demand for so-called ecotourism (Sharpley, 2006a), there is little reason to suppose much has changed, either in the UK or elsewhere. For example, a recent survey (again in the UK) found that only around one-third of travel agents and tour operators believe that 'the travel industry has a role to play in limiting global warming' (Taylor, 2008). In other words, other than in the case of a small number of specific projects and destinations (relative to the overall supply of tourism products and services), there is little evidence to suggest that the principles of sustainability or sustainable development have been adopted amongst individual businesses, sectors of the travel and tourism industry or, indeed, at the destinational level. Thus, with the notable exception of the activities of the STCRC in Australia, a gulf remains between the rhetoric and academic theory of sustainable tourism development and the reality of tourism development 'on the ground'.

In addition, a number of general observations can be made with respect to trends and developments in tourism over the last two decades:

- The demand for tourism has continued to grow. In 1990, just over 439.5 million international arrivals were recorded. By 2000, this figure had risen to 687.3 million, representing an average annual increase of 4.6 per cent (UNWTO, 2008a). Latest data (at the time of writing) indicate that in 2007 international arrivals reached 903 million, a remarkable growth of 6.6 per cent over the previous year; moreover, despite the deteriorating global economic climate, international arrivals grew at about 5 per cent during the first four months of 2008 compared with the same period in 2007 (UNWTO, 2008b). In short, it would appear that the UNWTO's long-standing and rather daunting forecast of 1.6 billion international arrivals by 2020 will be easily met, if not exceeded (WTO, 1998), although rises in the cost of oil and, hence, travel, may serve to dampen future demand.
- This continuing growth in tourism has underpinned or, perhaps, been stimulated by the emergence of new destinations around the world. Traditionally, the major flows of international tourism have been within particular regions, with Europe (as one of five tourism regions defined by the UNWTO) both generating and receiving the highest proportion of international tourists. This remains the case. In 2005, Europe attracted 54.7 per cent of total international arrivals, though this share has been steadily falling from 72.6 per cent in 1960 to 61.6 per cent in 1990. Conversely, the Middle East and Asia Pacific regions have enjoyed a rapid increase in the share of global arrivals whilst, in particular, a number of least developed countries, such as Tanzania, Cambodia and Uganda, have in recent years experienced growth rates in tourist arrivals well in excess of the global average. Moreover, the UNWTO currently publishes tourism statistics for a total of 215 states of which 71, or just under one-third, received at least a million international tourists in 2005. Whilst the 'big players' in Europe and North America continue to dominate (although the top ten destinations in 2005, accounting for almost 46 per cent of global arrivals, included China, Mexico and Turkey), countries that have joined the '1 million club'

since 1990 include Jordan, Syria, Cuba, Peru, Chile, Costa Rica, Vietnam and Cambodia, as well as a number of former USSR states, such as Latvia, Estonia and Azerbaijan.

- In addition to the growth in and expansion of tourism destinations around the world, more countries are becoming important generators of international tourism. The principal sources of international tourists (ranked by expenditure) remain Germany, the US, the UK, Japan and France. However, much of the increase in tourist arrivals in the Asia Pacific and Middle East regions, for example, is the result of intra-regional travel underpinned by economic growth in those regions. Not surprisingly, China and Russia have also become major tourism markets, whilst India's international travel expenditure, though still relatively small at 0.8 per cent of global expenditure (the same as Ireland's contribution), grew by a remarkable 70 per cent between 2002 and 2004. It is likely that the continued growth in international tourism will be enhanced by outbound tourism from these three rapidly growing economies.

- Significant factors in the continued growth of tourism, beyond economic growth in tourism generating countries, have been the related influences of the liberalization of international air transport and the emergence of low-cost airlines, particularly within Europe where increased freedom of movement of labour has also contributed to a growth in intra-regional tourism (Rosenthal, 2008). Thus, whilst the cost of air travel globally has declined in real terms since 1990, low-cost airlines have not only enabled more people to travel (or enabled people to travel more frequently), but have also played an influential role in the development of new destinations within their sphere of operations. Ryanair, for example, carried over 49 million passengers to 24 different countries in 2007 and was, according to the International Air Transport Association (IATA), the world's largest international airline (IATA, 2008), though these figures are dwarfed by the combined domestic and international operations of the major US-based airlines. With over 30 million passengers, Easyjet was the fourth largest international carrier. Evidently there are significant environmental considerations related to the expansion of low-cost airline operations, whilst the future of the sector (and of airline operations more generally) is uncertain given the dramatic increase in aviation fuel costs. For example, according to the UK's Civil Aviation Authority (CAA), jet fuel prices rose from US$320 per tonne in January 2004 to $900 per tonne in November 2007 (CAA, 2008). More recently, oil prices have fallen back, yet, as a consequence of the previously high cost of oil, as well as lower levels of demand resulting from the global economic downturn, not only are low-cost airlines rationalizing their routes, but there have also been some notable casualties. For example, Zoom, the low-cost airline operating principally between the UK and Canada, ceased trading in August 2008. Nevertheless, relatively cheap air travel is likely to underpin continued growth in international travel.

- Globally, the role of tourism as an agent of socio-economic growth and development has become more pervasive. Within the developed world, peripheral or economically disadvantaged regions are increasingly focusing on tourism as a means of stimulating economic and social regeneration whilst, for many less developed countries, tourism has come to represent a vital ingredient of their development policies. Indeed, although the less developed world as a whole accounts for roughly just one-third of total international tourist arrivals and receipts (a share that has remained largely unchanged since the early 1990s), the relative importance of tourism to many less developed economies has grown. For example, the WTTC lists over 30 countries in which tourism, though relatively small by international standards, contributes over 20 per cent of gross domestic product (GDP). Furthermore, in many cases this economic dependence is enhanced by the fact that tourism is an option of 'last resort' (Lea, 1988); that is, alternative, viable development options are not available to them. However, although tourism has undoubtedly contributed to the socio-economic development in a number of less developed countries, such as Thailand or Mexico, in many others such development is less evident, challenging the widespread belief in tourism's potential developmental contribution.
- One of the fundamental assumptions of underpinning the concept of sustainable tourism development is that there has been an increase in environmental concern on the part of tourists and, hence, growing demand for 'responsible' travel experiences. Certainly, the emergence of the 'new' tourist has long been predicted (Poon, 1993) and a number of surveys have suggested that tourists' travel decisions are increasingly influenced by environmental concerns. However, other research has consistently demonstrated that tourism is relatively immune to environmental concerns (or that 'responsible' tourist behaviour is motivated by factors other than environmental concern). For example, in a recent poll, just 1 per cent of tourists stated that their carbon footprint was an important factor when deciding on a holiday purchase, whereas cost is the most important consideration for 43 per cent of tourists (Skidmore, 2008). Even despite the growing awareness of climate change, research has shown that this is having little or no impact on travel behaviour. For example, one study found that the few people who expected to fly less frequently in the future would do so as a result of a change in personal circumstances rather than because of concerns over the environmental impacts of aviation (CAA, 2008, p49). Thus, despite the long-held belief that tourists are demanding 'greener' holidays, the evidence suggests that environmental concern remains low on their list of priorities when purchasing holiday or travel experiences.

Collectively, these trends demonstrate that, over the last two decades, global tourism has largely reflected the dominance of the market in the supply of and demand for tourism. Economic and political liberalization have facilitated increases in the supply of tourism services and experiences and reductions in the costs of travel, thereby contributing to an increase in the demand for tourism, which itself has also been stimulated by increasing levels of wealth and disposable income both in the traditional generating regions and in some emerging economies. Undoubtedly, some tourism operators, and indeed some tourists, are motivated by genuine environmental concerns; moreover, this admittedly simplistic analysis also overlooks a variety of influences and trends in the supply of and demand for tourism as a whole, such as an increased focus on quality and value for money, a growing demand for cultural tourism experiences and so on. Nevertheless, the important point is that, despite all the attention paid to sustainable tourism development in academic circles, despite the innumerable sets of sustainable tourism guidelines and policy documents, despite national and global accreditation schemes and despite the best efforts of pressure groups and others to encourage so-called responsible behaviour on the part of tourists, the sustainable tourism message appears to have had little impact on the overall growth and development of tourism.

Thus, in short, a significant gap remains between the idealism of the concept of sustainable tourism development as explored at length within academic circles and the reality of tourism development in practice. That is, it has proved difficult, if not impossible, to translate the conceptual principles of sustainable tourism development into a feasible, workable set of policies and practices relevant to the real world of tourism. Certainly, there are numerous examples of 'good practice', often recognized through accreditation or awards, yet these represent just a tiny proportion of the total supply of tourism. Consequently, more widespread sustainable tourism development remains elusive. At the same time, however, tourism not only remains a growth sector in the international economy but also is an increasingly utilized catalyst of economic and social development. Equally, the recent positioning of climate change high on the global political and economic agenda has brought the environmental impact of global travel into clearer focus, whilst the more localized consequences of tourism development remain a significant concern. There is, therefore, a need to re-examine the relationship between tourism, its role as an agent of development and its potential environmental consequences within a broader framework than that permitted by the conceptual principles of sustainable tourism development. In other words, the impasse reached in the academic study of sustainable tourism development suggests that it is time to move beyond its restrictive, managerialist ideals and to explore tourism and development within a contemporary global political-economic and environmental framework.

The purpose of this book and, in fact, the series for which this is the inaugural text is to do just that. It sets out to challenge the 'status quo' of sustainable tourism development and to explore the tourism–development– environment nexus from a perspective that recognizes tourism as a valuable and powerful sector of the global capitalist economy and, for many destinations, a potentially vital catalyst of development. This is not to suggest, of course, that sustainable resource use should not be an underlying principle of tourism development; as with all economic activities, there is a need to conserve and enhance the resource base upon which the future health of tourism depends. Nor is it to suggest that the extensive research into sustainable tourism development has been fruitless. On the contrary, there now exists a substantial and detailed body of knowledge with respect to models of tourism planning and development, the environmental and socio-cultural consequences of tourism and the specific conditions under which sustainable forms of tourism might be operationalized. Nevertheless, as this book will suggest, it has proved difficult, if not impossible, to adapt the idealism of sustainable tourism development to the enormous diversity of developmental, environmental and socio-cultural contexts within which tourism occurs; to paraphrase Howie (1990), referred to above, sustainable tourism is an idea whose time has now passed. Therefore, it is now necessary to explore tourism and development from a more pragmatic perspective unencumbered by that idealism, a perspective that, as will be suggested, returns to the 'basics' of tourism as, in essence, a manifestation of capitalistic endeavour that has the potential to bring substantial economic benefits to destinations.

List of Acronyms and Abbreviations

APRC   Alliance for Patriotic Reorientation and Construction [The Gambia]
ASEAN   Association of Southeast Asian Nations
ASSET   Association of Small Scale Enterprises in Tourism [The Gambia]
CAA   Civil Aviation Authority
COMECON   Council for Mutual Economic Assistance
CTO   Cyprus Tourism Organisation
DCTPB   Dubai Commerce and Tourism Promotion Board
DFID   Department for International Development
DSTC   Department of State for Tourism and Culture
EAP   East Asia Pacific (region)
ECOMOST   European Community Model of Sustainable Tourism
ETB   English Tourist Board
GCC   Gulf Cooperation Council
GDP   Gross Domestic Product
GHG   Greenhouse Gas
GNH   Gross National Happiness
GNI   Gross National Income
GTA   Gambia Tourism Authority
HDI   Human Development Index
IATA   the International Air Transport Association
ICAO   International Civil Aviation Organisation
IIED   International Institute for Environment and Development
IFTO   International Federation of Tourist Operators
IMF   International Monetary Fund
INTUR   Instituto Nacional de Turismo
IPCC   Intergovernmental Panel on Climate Change
ISEW   Index of Sustainable Economic Welfare
IUCN   International Union for Conservation of Nature
LDC   Least Developed Country
MDGs   Millennium Development Goals
MSME   Micro, Small and Medium sized Enterprise
NAFTA   North American Free Trade Agreement
NEAP   Nature & Ecotourism Accreditation Program

NGO	Non-Government Organization
ODI	Overseas Development Institute
OECD	Organisation for Economic Co-operation and Development
PPTP	Pro-Poor Tourism Partnership
SALP	Structural Adjustment Lending Programmes
SARS	Severe Acute Respiratory Syndrome
SLA	Sustainable Livelihoods Approach
STCRC	Sustainable Tourism Co-operative Research Centre
ST-EP	Sustainable Tourism-Eliminating Poverty
UAE	United Arab Emirates
UN	United Nations
UNCHE	United Nations Conference on the Human Environment
UNDP	United Nations Development Programme
UNEP	United Nations Environment Programme
UNESCO	United Nations Educational, Scientific and Cultural Organization
UNWTO	United Nations World Tourism Organization
USAID	United States Agency for International Development
VFR	(tourists) Visiting friends and relatives (tourists)
WCED	World Commission on Environment and Development
WSSD	World Summit on Sustainable Development
WTTC	World Travel and Tourism Council

1
Tourism, Development and the Environment: An Introduction

Over the last half century, the growth and development of tourism as both a social and economic activity has, by any stretch of the imagination, been remarkable. In 1950, total worldwide international tourist arrivals amounted to just over 25 million; by the start of the new millennium, that figure had risen to more than 687 million and since then international tourism has continued its inexorable growth. In 2007, over 903 million international arrivals were recorded (UNWTO, 2008b) and, despite the global 'credit crunch' and dramatic increases in the price of oil, most recent figures point to continuing increases in international tourist arrivals. Moreover, if domestic tourism activity (that is, people visiting destinations within their own country) is also taken into account, the total worldwide number of tourist trips is estimated to be some six to ten times higher than the international figures. For example, Americans make an estimated 990 million domestic tourism trips every year (outnumbering by some way the current total of international trips worldwide), whilst the domestic tourism markets in China and India, with an annual 644 million and 320 million domestic tourism trips respectively, are far greater than their international markets (Bigano et al, 2007).

Beneath these 'headline' data, other statistics also point to the growth and significance of tourism. For example, Sheller and Urry (2004) note that every day around 4 million people travel by air whilst, 'at any one time 300,000 passengers are in flight above the United States, equivalent to a substantial city' (2004, p3). Increasing car ownership, too, has played a fundamental role in the growth in tourist activity, the great majority of tourist trips being by car. Over the last 60 years or so, the global population has roughly tripled; in comparison, global car ownership has increased by a factor of 18. Putting it another way, there is now, worldwide, one car per 7.5 people compared with one car per 49 people in 1940 although, of course, national variations exist. Whilst there are 745 cars per 1000 people in the US, for two-thirds of the world's population there are fewer than 50 cars per 1000 people. At the same time, car miles travelled have increased dramatically; again in the US, car ownership grew by 60 per cent between 1970 and 2000, but over the same period miles travelled increased by 146 per cent (Renner, 2003). Given such increases in travel and mobility, it is not surprising, therefore, that the growth and 'democratization' (Urry, 2002) of tourism is considered by some to be one of the major social phenomena of the modern era.

Commensurate with its dramatic and continuing growth in scale, the global economic contribution of tourism has also demonstrated significant growth over the last half century. In 1950, total international tourist receipts alone amounted to just US$2.1 billion. By 2000, this figure had reached US$473 billion and, by 2007, US$856 billion, a 5.6 per cent increase over the previous year (UNWTO, 2008b). If current forecasts prove to be correct, this figure could rise to US$2 trillion by 2020, along with an increase in international arrivals to 1.6 billion (WTO, 1998). However, these figures reflect only direct income from international tourism and, therefore, reveal only part of the story of tourism's economic contribution. In many countries, the value of domestic tourism is far greater than that of incoming international tourism – in the UK, for example, international tourist expenditure in 2007 amounted to £16 billion; in contrast, domestic tourism, including day trips, generated almost £67 billion expenditure (VisitBritain, 2008). At the same time, the development and provision of tourism services (both domestic and international) generates significant levels of secondary or indirect expenditure. If this is added to direct expenditure then, according to the World Travel and Tourism Council, the global 'tourism economy' was worth an astounding US$7 trillion, or 10.47 per cent of global gross domestic product (GDP), in 2007 (WTTC, 2008). Not surprisingly, perhaps, tourism is also a major source of employment, accounting for 231 million jobs, or 8.3 per cent of global employment.

Two competing consequences have arisen from this rapid emergence of tourism as a global socio-economic force. On the one hand, as a valuable and continually growing source of income, foreign exchange earnings and employment, tourism has long been considered an effective means of achieving regional or national socio-economic development. That is, the justification for its promotion, whether locally or nationally and in both less developed and industrialized countries, is its alleged contribution to economic growth, regeneration and development. In 1980, the World Tourism Organization (WTO, now the United Nations World Tourism Organization or UNWTO), reflecting its specific focus on the less developed world, effectively sanctioned the developmental role of tourism by stating that:

> *World tourism can contribute to the establishment of a new international economic order that will help eliminate the widening economic gap between developed and developing countries and ensure the steady acceleration of economic and social development and progress, in particular in developing countries.*
> (WTO, 1980, p1)

Since then, not only have many developing countries embraced tourism as an integral element of their development strategies – few, if any, countries do not promote themselves as tourist destinations and the UNWTO now publishes statistics for 215 states – but also some, such as Thailand, Mexico and Egypt, have successfully utilized tourism as a catalyst for wider economic and social development (Clancy, 1999; Tohamy and Swinscoe, 2000). In others, particularly least developed countries (LDCs) with few, if any, other developmental options, tourism has become the dominant economic sector; it represents almost 70 per cent of service exports in LDCs collectively whilst it is amongst the top three export industries in almost half of them (UNCTAD, 2001, p4).

The potential of tourism to contribute to development in modern, industrialized countries is also widely recognized with tourism playing an increasingly important role in most, if not all, Organisation for Economic Co-operation and Development (OECD) countries. There has, for example, long been evidence of national government support for tourism in many European countries and by the 1980s tourism featured prominently in their economic development strategies (Williams and Shaw, 1998). Notable examples include Spain, Portugal and Greece although, more generally in the developed world, both international and domestic tourism has become a favoured means of addressing the socio-economic challenges facing peripheral rural areas (Hoggart et al, 1995) – often benefiting from structural funding support – and urban areas adapting to a post-industrial era (for example, Law, 2002).

On the other hand, of course, the rapid growth and global spread of tourism has been accompanied by no less a rapid increase in the number of commentators drawing attention to the potentially negative or destructive consequences of tourism development on destination environments and societies. Evidence has always existed of the damaging impacts of tourism or, more precisely, tourists at sites and destinations; for example, carved graffiti dating back centuries have been found on the pyramids at Giza whilst, in 1848, Thomas Cook wrote in a handbook for visitors that 'to the shame of some rude folk from Lincolnshire, there have been just causes of complaint at Belvoir Castle: some large parties have behaved indecorously... Conduct of this sort is abominable, and cannot be too strongly reprobated' (cited in Ousby, 1990, p89). However, as early as the 1960s, when a nascent tourism industry began to introduce packaged summer holidays to the mass markets of northern Europe, concerns over the unbridled growth of tourism, manifested principally in the rapid and seemingly unplanned expansion of resorts on the Spanish 'Costas' (Barke et al, 1996), led to calls for restraint in its development (Mishan, 1969; Young, 1973). Subsequently, attention turned to more specific environmental, political, socio-cultural and economic consequences of tourism development and it is probably true to say that, by the 1990s, no topic concerned tourism academics, pressure groups, journalists and certain sectors of the tourism industry more than the 'impacts of tourism'. To a great extent, criticism was directed, sometimes justifiably, towards the phenomenon of so-called mass tourism; that is, the problems associated with the development of tourism in general were considered by many to reflect the alleged 'crisis' of mass tourism in particular (Poon, 1993). At the same time, the debate and analysis of tourism's consequences ranged from theoretically rigorous research to apocalyptic journalism. For example, according to one critic:

> *A spectre is haunting our planet: the spectre of tourism. It's said that travel broadens the mind. Today, in its modern guise of tourism, it can also ruin landscapes, destroy communities, pollute air and water, trivialise cultures, bring about uniformity, and generally contribute to the continuing degradation of life on our planet.* (Croall, 1995, p1)

In a sense, tourism became a specific lens through which concerns over the environmental and social consequences of economic growth, capitalism and globalization could be focused – in effect, it became a scapegoat for the problems associated with economic growth and development in general. Why this should be so is unclear; tourism was, perhaps, seen as an 'easy target' or, mistakenly, as a frivolous industry catering to the leisure needs of primarily wealthy, western nations. Conversely, as Cater (1995) observes, 'no other economic activity ... transects so many sectors, levels and interests as tourism' and, therefore, it was inevitable that it would become the focus of environmental concern. Either way, it is difficult to identify any other economic sector or activity that, over the last two decades, has attracted more widespread concern and criticism than tourism, and continues to do so. For example, the recent and remarkable transformation of Dubai from oil producer to iconic tourism destination has been criticized on the grounds of both the potentially disastrous long-term environmental consequences of the developments that are taking place there and the local employment practices that have facilitated such developments (Hickman, 2007), whilst, more generally, tourism and specifically air travel figure prominently in contemporary debates over climate change (UNWTO/ UNEP, 2008).

The role of tourism as an agent of development and the environmental consequences of tourism provide the framework for much of this book. The fundamental point here, however, is that there has long existed what might be termed a 'tourism development dilemma' (Telfer and Sharpley, 2008). That is, tourism undoubtedly represents a potentially valuable, effective and, in some cases, the only viable catalyst of economic and social development in destinations, either locally or nationally. However, given the intimate two-way relationship between tourism and the environments in which it occurs (tourism depends upon attractive physical and socio-cultural environments yet possesses the potential to degrade or destroy them), that development might only be achieved at significant social, economic and environmental costs to destinations. Consequently, the dilemma or challenge facing tourism destinations is how to achieve a balance between the potential developmental contribution of tourism and its negative consequences or, more simply, how to manage effectively the development of tourism.

Since the early 1990s the solution to this dilemma has been seen to lie in the concept of sustainable tourism development. Reflecting the emergence and adoption of sustainable development as the dominant global development paradigm in general, sustainable *tourism* development has similarly been widely accepted and adopted as a planning policy and objective for tourism in particular. However, just as its parental paradigm remains highly controversial, so too has sustainable tourism development proved to be a contested and ambiguous concept, attracting both support and criticism in equal measure. Indeed, and as noted in the introduction to this book, despite a plethora of policy documents and planning guidelines promoting sustainable tourism development at the local, national and international levels, there is relatively limited evidence of its implementation in practice. Similarly, since the publication of *The Good Tourist: A Worldwide Guide for the Green Traveller* (Wood and House, 1991), numerous guides, newspaper articles and codes of practice have been produced, exhorting 'responsible' behaviour on the part of tourists. Again, however, and despite an apparent increase in demand for so-called ecotourism products – an equally contentious manifestation of sustainable tourism development (Duffy, 2002) – there is little to suggest that tourists are adopting a more responsible or 'green' approach to the consumption of tourism experiences (Sharpley, 2006a). In short, the idea of sustainable tourism development has, in practice, fallen largely on deaf ears.

At the same time, sustainable tourism development has for almost 20 years remained a dominant theme within the academic study of tourism. However, although significant knowledge and understanding of the interaction between tourism, the environment and wider development has been generated, relatively little progress has been made beyond the basic principles of sustainable tourism development first espoused in the early 1990s. Not only does there remain a lack of consensus over the theoretical validity of the concept, but there has also been a failure to transpose the conceptual principles and objectives of sustainable tourism development into a workable set of policies and practices relevant to global tourism in its totality. To put it more succinctly, sustainable tourism development has, in academic terms, reached an impasse. Arguably, therefore, there is a need to progress the debate beyond the rigid and restrictive framework within which the study of sustainable tourism development has found itself, to re-examine the relationship between tourism as an agent of development and the environments in which it occurs, and upon which it depends, within a more holistic context.

This book aims, perhaps somewhat controversially, to do just that. Based upon the premise that tourism is, fundamentally, a specific yet complex manifestation of capitalist production and consumption that is inextricably linked with the global political economy, this book sets out to identify the limitations of the concept of sustainable tourism development before going on to propose an alternative means by which tourism's developmental potential may be optimized within evident environmental limits. That is, it does not adopt a techno-centric stance, subordinating environmental concerns to technological solutions to tourism resource issues; however, it does seek to explore the tourism–development–environment nexus unencumbered by the environmental managerialism that, it will be suggested, underpins contemporary principles of sustainable tourism development. By way of introduction, therefore, the purpose of this first chapter is to briefly review the evolution and transformations in the demand for and supply of tourism related to the dynamic understanding of the tourism-environment relationship and tourism's role as an agent of development, thereby providing a basis for the subsequent chapters. The first task, however, is to define tourism as a contemporary phenomenon and the activity or process that potentially acts as a catalyst of development.

Defining tourism

An analysis of tourism within a development–environment context cannot, or should not, be undertaken without defining the character and scope of tourism as a social and economic activity. More specifically, although concerns over the impacts of tourism are, as observed earlier, frequently directed, either implicitly or explicitly, at the phenomenon of 'mass tourism', this is a value-laden label attached to a particular type of tourism/tourist, and certainly neither embraces the diversity and breadth of tourism nor reveals the extent to which it is interconnected with other social, economic and political systems. However, despite its ubiquity and, consequently, the likelihood that most people possess an understanding of the term, tourism remains variously defined and interpreted, reflecting both the 'abstract nature of the concept' (Burns and Holden, 1995, p5) and the multi-disciplinary foundations to its study.

Generally but somewhat ambiguously, the Chambers English dictionary defines tourism as 'the activities of tourists and those who cater for them', immediately distinguishing between tourism as a social phenomenon (that is, the movement and activities of people participating in tourism) and the so-called 'tourism industry', or the myriad of businesses and organizations that supplies or facilitates tourist experiences, usually but not always for profit. This distinction reflects two core concepts that tourism describes – the movement of people and tourism as an economic sector – to which a third may be added: tourism as a system of interacting people, places and processes (see Hall, 2005). Each of these warrants some attention in understanding the meaning and scope of contemporary tourism in general, and its relationship to developmental and environmental processes in particular.

The movement of people

Typically, definitions of tourism as the movement or travel of people fall under either 'technical' or 'conceptual' headings. Technical definitions identify different types of tourist and tourism activities (for example, holidaymakers, business travellers or VFR tourists – those visiting friends and relatives) and are utilized for statistical or legislative purposes, primarily the quantitative measurement of tourist traffic. They employ a variety of temporal and spatial parameters, such as minimum (one day) and maximum (one year) lengths of stay or minimum distance travelled from home, though the choice of such parameters is somewhat arbitrary. Distinctions are also made between tourists (those who spend at least one night away from home) and international excursionists (those visiting another country for less than 24 hours and not spending a night there, such as cruise ship visitors) or domestic day-trippers.

Table 1.1 *Technical definitions of tourists*

To be included in tourism statistics		Not to be included in tourism statistics
Category	Purpose	Category
Tourists:	Holidays	Border workers
Non-residents	Business	Transit passengers
Nationals resident abroad	Health	Nomads
	Study	Refugees
Crew members	Meetings/missions	Members of armed forces
Excursionists:	VFR	Diplomats
Cruise passengers	Religion	Temporary immigrants
Day visitors	Sport	Permanent immigrants
Crews	Others	

Source: adapted from WTO, 1994

However, tourism statistics increasingly include both 'staying' visitors and excursionists/day-trippers; whilst this gives due recognition to the importance of the latter category to many destinations (WTO, 1994), it also blurs the distinction between tourism, leisure and recreation, thereby potentially expanding the limits of what might traditionally be thought of as tourism to include a wide variety of other activities. Table 1.1 summarizes the technical definitions of tourism/tourists.

In contrast, conceptual definitions of tourism attempt to convey the meaning or function of tourism, in particular from the perspective of tourists themselves: as Nash (1981) observes 'at the heart of any definition of tourism is the person we conceive to be a tourist'. Typically, such definitions emphasize the nature of tourism as a voluntary, leisure-focused activity that enables people to experience a change or separation from their non-discretionary or instrumental day-to-day lives and activities. However, such definitions exclude a number of recognized categories of tourism, such as business travel, educational tourism, pilgrimages, or so-called frontier journeys (for example, trekking through extreme environments). At the same time, such is the diversity of tourism types and experiences in general that to propose a single, all-embracing conceptual definition of tourism is an unrealistic task. In addition, three further points deserve emphasis.

Firstly, tourism, by definition, involves travel; indeed, in some countries the term 'travel' is synonymous with tourism whilst, more often than not, newspapers, magazines and television programmes offer 'travel', rather than 'tourism', features. Consequently, the distinction between travel and the activity of tourism, as an ill-defined subset of travel, is becoming increasingly unclear, particularly as newer forms of tourism-related travel emerge. For example, the evolution of low-cost airlines in Europe has encouraged regular travel amongst UK residents to second homes on the continent (essentially regular leisure travel as opposed to more traditional concepts of tourism), whilst research exploring the relationship between tourism and other forms of migration, such as international labour migration or retirement migration, expands the boundaries of what might be considered tourism (Williams and Hall, 2000; O'Reilly, 2003).

Secondly, many definitions, particularly from a conceptual perspective, reflect the somewhat outdated notion that tourism is an activity both temporarily and spatially separated from normal, day-to-day life, and that it is motivated primarily by the desire to escape, for change or a search for the 'other'. Certainly, many forms of 'mass' tourism, from the 'ritualised pleasure' (Shields, 1991) of the 19th century seaside resort through to contemporary packaged sun–sea–sand holidays were, and remain, a separate, identifiable activity differentiated by time, location and behaviour from normal social activities and institutions. However, it has been suggested that, over the last 30 years or so, this differentiation has become less apparent: 'tourism is no longer a differentiated set of social practices with its distinct rules, times and spaces' (Urry, 1994). Rather, it has merged into other social activities, such as shopping, eating out, sport, watching television and leisure time more generally, whilst the internet in particular, offering products such as Google Earth or real-time/regularly updated travel blogs, has blurred the distinction between actual and virtual travel, between how, when and where travel (or tourism) may be experienced. As Molz (2004, p169) explains:

> *websites not only constitute a new kind of tourist destination...,*
> *but they also have implications for how we think about the meaning*
> *of corporeal travel. As new mobile communications technologies*
> *such as the internet rework the distinction between home and*
> *away, work and leisure, and real and virtual, the definition of*
> *travel as an escape from the routines and social obligations of the*
> *everyday is called into question.*

In short, tourism has in many ways diffused into the everyday. Whilst certain tourist practices remain spatially and temporarily distinct, many people are, according to Urry (1994), tourists most of the time.

Thirdly, and following on from these preceding points, tourism is no longer being considered in isolation from other social practices and transformations; rather, it is 'increasingly being interpreted as but one, albeit highly significant, dimension of temporary mobility' (Hall, 2005, p21). To put it another way, the concept of mobility or multiple mobilities – that is, the increasing and widespread movement of people, capital, information and material goods around the world, as well as more localized movements of people and things – is not only becoming a defining characteristic of contemporary societies, but is also adopting the mantle of a new social scientific paradigm. That is, social and economic life is increasingly patterned and influenced by networks of mobilities – and, indeed, immobilities – and, therefore, the study of mobilities provides a theoretical framework for the study of societies more generally. Evidently, tourism is one manifestation of mobility; the dramatic growth in the scope and scale of tourism reflects, or has contributed to, the increasing mobility of both people and the services (finance, information, communication and so on) that facilitate tourism. At the same time, however, touristic mobility is related to or influenced by wider debates surrounding the mobilities concept:

> From SARS and avian influenza to train crashes, from airport expansion controversies to controlling global warming, from urban congestion charging to networked global terrorism, from emergency management in the onslaught of tsunamis and hurricanes to oil wars in the Middle East, issues of 'mobility' are centre-stage. Many public, private and not-for-profit organizations are seeking to understand, monitor, manage and transform aspects of these multiple mobilities. (Hannam et al, 2006)

Not surprisingly, therefore, the study of tourism is increasingly being located within a mobilities framework (Hall, 2005), it now being accepted that a fuller explanation of contemporary tourism requires knowledge and understanding of the meanings and implications of the multiple mobilities of people, capital, culture, information, goods and services more generally (Coles et al, 2004). This suggests, perhaps, that tourism, in terms of the movement of people, is in fact indefinable – it is, simply, one dimension of mobility. More specifically, the merging of tourism (or travel) into everyday social and economic life as but one of numerous contemporary mobilities also suggests that the study of tourism in a (sustainable) developmental and environmental context should recognize its inter-connectedness with these mobilities.

Tourism as an economic sector

Although tourism and travel is a social activity, that activity is to a great extent dependent upon the provision of goods and services that facilitate people's travel and their activities at the destination. In fact, as long as people have been able to travel they have required a variety of services, such as lodging, food and refreshments, whilst the growth of international organized mass tourism, particularly from the 1960s onwards, was largely underpinned by the development of an innovative and increasingly sophisticated travel industry. Collectively, these goods and services represent, quite simply, big business. Reference has already been made above to the global economic value of tourism, with international tourism alone, as measured by tourism receipts, totalling US$856 billion in 2007 and thus representing one of the world's most valuable export sectors; in 2002, international tourism, including receipts from international travel fares, was the world's fourth largest export category after chemical, automotive products and fuels. More significantly, the total global tourism economy, embracing direct and indirect expenditure arising from both international and domestic travel and tourism, amounts to an estimated US$7 trillion. It is not surprising, therefore, that tourism is often referred to as the world's largest industry or economic sector.

Whilst these total figures are undoubtedly impressive, however, it is important to note that they are at best estimates. Given the scale and diversity of tourism, the paucity of accurate data in many countries and, as will be discussed shortly, the difficulty in defining the composition and extent of the tourism economy, it is unlikely that the true value of tourism could ever be revealed. At the same time, they hide the varying significance of tourism to national and local economies. In the world's top international tourism destinations, for example, tourism makes a relatively small contribution to GDP – in the UK, the figure is around 3.5 per cent – whereas in the Maldives, which attract under half a million visitors a year, tourism accounts for around 70 per cent of the total economy. Similarly, local or sub-national variations also exist. Tenerife, one of the Canary Islands which collectively comprise one of Spain's 17 politically autonomous regions, is highly dependent upon tourism; the local tourism economy contributes some 65 per cent of the island's GDP (Sharpley, 2007a, p117) compared with a figure of around 10 per cent for Spain as a whole. Equally, in the Lake District in northwest England, the tourism economy accounts for well over half of the region's GDP. Thus, any consideration of tourism's developmental role and environmental consequences must, necessarily, be undertaken within the context of the relevant local or national economy.

It is also important to appreciate the nature or structure of tourism as an economic sector. Many texts refer to the existence of the 'tourism industry'; however, whilst the notion of a tourism industry may be synonymous with certain sub-sectors of the tourism economy, such as the now highly-integrated European tour-operating sector, tourism as a whole cannot be considered an industry. The term 'industry' usually refers to a single, clearly identifiable economic activity with particular production methods, recognizable chains of supply and specific products or outputs; the automobile industry is in the business of designing, manufacturing and selling cars and basically comprises car manufacturers, the multitude of smaller businesses that supply products or parts to them, and networks of dealerships that sell and perhaps service, cars.

In the case of tourism, the inputs, products, methods of production and chains of supply are much less clear (Mill and Morrison, 1998). Firstly, there is no single, definable tourism 'product'. Tourists consume experiences, the nature of which are as much dependent on the activities of tourists themselves as they are on the supply of specific tourism products and services. Secondly, tourist services are supplied by an enormous variety of businesses and organizations, many of which, such as airlines or accommodation, are industries in their own right. Thirdly, although some businesses, such as tour operating or travel retailing, are quite evidently directly involved in tourism, the relationship between tourism and other businesses or organizations is less clear. For example, financial institutions provide foreign currency services and insurance companies provide travel insurance, yet neither could be described as tourism businesses. Similarly, publishing companies may produce travel guides or television companies may produce travel or holiday programmes, but of course neither would normally be considered to be part of the tourism sector. In short, numerous businesses operate in industries that are only partly or indirectly linked to tourism. Fourthly, a number of other organizations in the public sector, from locally run information centres to national tourism bodies, also play a role in the production of tourism, though often on a non-commercial basis. Finally, no single management structure operates within tourism; there is no distinct chain of command in tourism and, frequently, the power lies not with 'producers', such as airlines or hotels, but with intermediaries, such as tour operators. Consequently, the sector is defined by complex networks and power relations and is, perhaps, best thought of as a capitalist production system comprising innumerable primarily small, profit-driven businesses, the structure and nature of which may vary in different contexts according to the differing relationship between its different elements.

Moreover, this tourism production system is itself a constituent part of a broader system. That is, the tourism production system is but one element of a wider set of inter-related structures and processes that collectively have been referred to as the tourism system, a concept which, as the following section now discusses, provides a useful framework for the study of tourism as a whole.

Tourism as a system

It is already evident that tourism is a complex, multi-dimensional phenomenon that is difficult, if not impossible, to define. That is, it is a social phenomenon, manifested in the increasing mobility of people locally, nationally and internationally for a variety of purposes that are frequently, but not always, leisure-driven. However, that movement of people would not, for the most part, occur without the goods and services provided by the tourism production system and purchased by tourists. Thus, at one level tourism can be seen simplistically as a functioning economic system of demand and supply within which the needs of tourists are met by a wide diversity of businesses selling goods and services for profit. However, that economic system itself can be located within a wider system in which both the demand for and supply of tourism influence, and are influenced by, a variety of 'external' factors and forces. These may be political, economic, technological, socio-cultural, legislative and environmental or, in other words, these factors usually comprise an organization's external or environmental strategic analysis.

This wider tourism system is commonly conceptualized as a geographically based model comprising four key components (Leiper, 1979; Mill and Morrison, 1998; Farrell and Twining-Ward, 2004):

- The tourism generating region: the region that is the source of tourists and where significant sectors of the tourism production system (for example, airlines, tour operators, travel retailers, international accommodation providers) may be located or based.
- The tourism destination region: the region that attracts tourists, which experiences the consequences of tourism development and where the primary elements of the production system (hotels, attractions, facilities) are located.
- The transit region: the region or route a tourist travels through to reach the destination.
- The environment within which the tourism generating, transit and destination regions are located and with which tourists interact.

This tourism system is represented in a simple form in Figure 1.1 below.

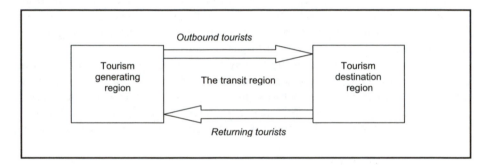

Figure 1.1 *The tourism system*

There are clear relationships throughout this system. Firstly, the generating and destination regions depend upon each other for the efficient functioning of the economic (tourism) system; for example, the businesses and organizations in each region are mutually dependent, whilst the attractions, facilities and amenities in the destination region must satisfy the needs of tourists, needs which are created or influenced by the own, home environment. Secondly, the regions collectively interact with elements of the wider environment in which they are located. For example, tourists and the tourism sector consume or impact upon the local environment and communities in both regions, whilst external factors influence tourists, their consumption patterns and tourism businesses. In late 2008, for example, the global economic slowdown became manifested in decreased demands for air travel. Specifically, it was reported that globally half a million fewer flights would operate in the last three months of the year compared with the same period in 2007, with 265,000 fewer domestic flights (or 21 million fewer seats) operating in the US alone (Millward and Starmer-Smith, 2008). As a consequence, over 200 airports worldwide would cease offering scheduled air services, with inevitable local direct and indirect income and employment consequences, and many destinations would suffer decreased levels of incoming tourism activity, again with local economic consequences. At the same time, however, the decrease in the number of flights would have some (albeit limited) environmental benefit in terms of reduced emissions from aircraft.

Thirdly, it is possible to conceptualize a global tourism system, comprising the totality of specific, generating and destination region-defined tourism sub-systems. Within this global system, an inter-relationship exists between these sub-systems. For example, transformations in a single tourism generating region (cultural, economic, political) may result in shifts in tourist flows between different destination regions, benefiting some and disadvantaging others. Equally, changing external influences may have a similar impact. Thus, a number of commentators suggest that a potential improvement in Cuban–US relations in a post-Castro era would enable the island to regain its position as the dominant tourist destination in the Caribbean to the cost of other destinations in the region (Khrushchev et al, 2007; Padilla and McElroy, 2007) although, as argued elsewhere (Sharpley and Knight, 2009), a closer examination of Cuba's political economy reveals that this may not be the case. Conversely, events in a particular destination region, such as the 2003 Severe Acute Respiratory Syndrome (SARS) outbreak in southeast Asia, not only resulted in cases being reported in 30 countries around the world but also led to a severe, though temporary, decline in arrivals in major destinations such as Hong Kong.

Numerous other examples could be provided that demonstrate the inter-connectedness of all the constituent elements of the global tourism system. The important point is, though, as Hall (2005, p61) suggests, that:

> *much research in tourism only examines specific elements in the tourism system rather than the interplay between these elements. This issue becomes especially important in considering the impacts of tourism, with most studies only looking at the impact of tourism at the destination rather than over space and time in all stages of tourism mobility.*

The same argument may be applied to the concept of sustainable tourism development in particular. That is, although some researchers adopt a broader perspective on the subject, recognizing tourism as one manifestation of a broader social mobility (for example, Høyer, 2000), both the developmental and the sustainability concerns of sustainable tourism development typically focus upon the specific destination region to the exclusion of both the generating and transit regions as well as other destination regions. Hence, as observed in the introduction to this book, almost from the outset sustainable tourism development has been seen by some as a micro solution to a macro problem (Wheeller, 1991). However, such is the complexity, multi-dimensionality and inter-connectedness of the global tourism system in general, and the degree of embeddedness of tourism in both social mobility and global economic structures especially, that a uni-dimensional focus on the destination is, quite simply, wrong. This, in turn, suggests that the application of the principles of sustainable development to the specific activity of tourism (however narrowly or broadly defined) is, as experience has shown, doomed to failure, and that an alternative approach to resolving the development–environment dilemma is required.

This is, of course, the principal focus of this book, and subsequent chapters, expanding on some of the points raised here, will critique more comprehensively the concept of sustainable tourism development before going on to explore an alternative approach to balancing tourism's developmental potential with environmental considerations. Following an introduction to the role of tourism as an agent of development, however, the rest of this chapter reviews the evolution of the demand for and supply of tourism and consequential transformations in the tourism-environment relationship.

Tourism as development

As previously noted, the rapid growth and spread of tourism around the world has resulted in its virtually universal integration into local and national development policies and plans. In some cases, of course, tourism may play only a limited role in development; in other cases, particularly in less developed countries, it may represent the only realistic choice (Brown, 1998). Either way, the *raison d'être* of tourism, from a destinational perspective, is its perceived role as a catalyst of development or, more precisely, economic growth (a distinction that is explored later in this book). That is, the most compelling reason for adopting tourism as a development strategy is its potential contribution to the local or national economy as a source of income, foreign exchange, employment and government revenues.

The question to be asked, however, is: why is tourism in particular favoured as a development option? Beyond the basic economic drivers, a number of factors can be identified.

Tourism is a growth industry
International tourism has demonstrated remarkable growth over the last half century. Moreover, between 1975 and 2000, the average annual growth in tourism was 4.6 per cent, outpacing the annual growth in global GDP of 3.5 per cent over that period. However, the rate of growth has been steadily declining; during the 1990s, for example, the average annual growth in tourist arrivals worldwide was 4.2 per cent, the lowest rate since the 1950s (see Table 1.2).

Nevertheless, tourism remains one of the world's fastest growing industries and, globally, that growth is forecast to continue. Thus, tourism is seen essentially as a safe development option.

Tourism redistributes wealth
Tourism is, in principle, an effective means of transferring wealth, either through direct tourist expenditure or international investment in tourism infrastructure

Table 1.2 *Tourism arrivals and receipts growth rates 1950–2000*

Decade	Arrivals (average annual increase %)	Receipts (average annual increase %)
1950–1960	10.6	12.6
1960–1970	9.1	10.1
1970–1980	5.6	19.4
1980–1990	4.8	9.8
1990–2000	4.2	6.5

Source: adapted from UNWTO, 2008a

and facilities, from richer, developed countries to poorer regions. Through the promotion of domestic tourism, it also potentially redistributes wealth on a national scale. However, the gross value and net retention of tourist spending varies considerably from one destination to another – many destinations suffer 'leakages', whereby tourist expenditure finances the import of goods to meet tourists' needs.

Backward linkages

Given the variety of goods and services demanded by tourists in the destination, from accommodation to local transport and souvenirs, tourism potentially offers more opportunities than other industries for backward linkages through-out the local economy, whether directly meeting tourists' needs, such as the provision of food to hotels (Telfer, 1996), or through indirect links with, for example, the construction industry. Again, the extent to which such linkages can be developed depends upon a variety of factors, such as the availability of finance, the diversity and maturity of the local economy or the quality of locally produced goods.

Tourism utilizes natural, 'free' infrastructure

The development of tourism is frequently based on existing natural or man-made attractions, such as beaches, wilderness areas or heritage sites. Thus, tourism may be considered to have low 'start-up' costs when compared with other industries; as such resources are, in a simplistic sense, 'free'. Increasingly, however, attempts are being made to place an economic value on the use of these basic resources whilst, inevitably, costs are incurred in the protection, upkeep and management of all tourism resources.

No tourism trade barriers

With some notable exceptions, countries rarely place limitations on the right of their citizens to travel overseas, on where they visit and how much they spend (although travel advisories are one form of limitation on travel). Con-sequently, in principle, destination countries have free and equal access to the international tourism market. However, the extent to which destinations can take advantage of this 'barrier-free' market is, of course, determined by a variety of factors, not least international competition in general and by the structure and control of the international tourism system in particular. Indeed, as the following overview of tourism demand demonstrates, on a global scale tourist flows follow distinctive patterns with consequential implications for tourism's developmental contribution.

Tourism demand

Though often described as a phenomenon of the modern temporal (as opposed to cultural) era, its roots lying in the socio-economic changes of the 19th and 20th centuries, tourism has existed in one form or another for as long as the means to travel have existed. In other words, people have travelled for educational, trade, exploration, spiritual and other purposes for as long as they have been able physically to move from one place to another. For most of its history, however, tourism (or more precisely travel, as the term 'tourism' did not enter common usage until about 1800), remained a benign activity. Few people had the ability or means to travel and, until the development of railway networks from the mid-1800s, it remained largely the preserve of the wealthy. Thus, tourism imposed few and limited social, environmental and economic impacts on transit and destination regions although the experiences of some travellers, such as the Grand Tourists of the 18th century, were reflected in new architectural styles, art collections and other cultural activities on their return home (Towner, 1996).

By the early 20th century, domestic tourism was firmly established in Europe and North America. At the same time, international tourism was also on the increase. Thomas Cook had organized his first round-the-world tour in 1872 and, along with a growing band of travel companies, was offering tours to Europe and other international destinations. By 1900, over a million people were crossing the English channel annually whilst, prior to the outbreak of the First World War, up to 150,000 American tourists were visiting Europe each year. Nevertheless, it is the decades since the 1950s that have undoubtedly been the most significant in the history of tourism. Not only has this period witnessed the dramatic and sustained growth of international tourism in terms of both scale and scope (and, of course, the consequences of that growth) but, socially, tourism has been transformed from a luxury enjoyed by a privileged minority into a democratized activity available to ever increasing numbers of people. Moreover, since the 1950s tourism has come to be viewed as a potential vehicle of development, not coincidently reflecting the emergence of 'development' as an international political-economic process and goal in the years following the end of the Second World War. Conveniently, regular international tourism data have also been published from 1950 onwards and so it is from that date that international tourism flows and trends are usually described in the literature.

Similar data for domestic tourism, however, are not available, despite the greater volume and economic value of domestic tourism in its global totality. Not all countries collate domestic tourism statistics whilst those that do employ different collection methods and varying definitions of domestic tourist trips. Moreover, domestic tourism is, by definition, of greater concern from a national as opposed to international perspective, particularly in a developmental context. It is also, frequently, culturally defined; Scandinavian countries, for example, have a strong tradition of domestic holidays in second homes, whereas in India much domestic travel is related to religious festivals. Thus, international comparisons of domestic tourism volumes and trends are neither possible nor valid. Nevertheless, academic attention has more recently turned to domestic tourism (Ghimire, 2001) and, given the volume of domestic tourism trips – for example, it is estimated that, in 1997, there were 3.5 billion domestic tourism trips worldwide compared with around 600 million international trips, suggesting that around 85 per cent of global tourism is domestic (Bigano et al, 2007) – there can be no doubting its potential environmental and developmental consequences. Therefore, although an overview of domestic tourism cannot be realistically provided here, it is explicitly embraced throughout the rest of the book with respect to its developmental and environmental consequences.

There are two perspectives from which the demand for international tourism may be reviewed, namely: historical and contemporary data revealing patterns and trends in international tourism flows; and transformations in the nature and style of tourism demand.

International tourism demand: Flows and trends

As has already been observed, international tourism is notable in particular for its rapid and sustained growth in both volume and value since 1950. Not only has it sustained an overall average annual growth rate of 6.2 per cent in terms of international arrivals and over 10 per cent annual growth in receipts, but it has proved to be remarkably resilient to external events, such as international conflicts, global economic recession, oil crises, health scares, natural disasters and so on. Consequently, although certain regions have experienced temporary declines in international arrivals, such as those destinations affected by the 2004 Indian Ocean tsunami, global tourist arrivals have only rarely experienced a decline, such as in 2001 following the events of '9/11' (Table 1.3).

A number of factors have underpinned this growth in tourism and, as will be discussed shortly, these go some way to explaining contemporary patterns of tourist flows. Typically, three key influences are referred to in the literature: technological developments, particularly in air travel; increases in personal wealth; and greater amounts of socially-sanctioned free time, such as holidays with pay, all of which have enabled more people to travel internationally and more frequently, or, more succinctly, contributed to greater international mobility. At the same time, however, tourism has, in many countries, adopted an enhanced position as a specific form of consumption, an issue which is central to debates surrounding sustainability and sustainable development (see Chapter 3). Moreover, the role of what has been described earlier as the tourism production system cannot be underestimated. In other words, innovation in business models (for example, charter and low-cost airline operations, and

Table 1.3 *International tourist arrivals and receipts 1950–2007*

Year	Arrivals (million)	Receipts (US$bn)	Year	Arrivals (million)	Receipts (US$bn)
1950	25.3	2.1	1996	575.0	446.0
1960	69.3	6.9	1997	598.6	450.4
1965	112.9	11.6	1998	616.7	451.4
1970	165.8	17.9	1999	639.6	464.5
1975	222.3	40.7	2000	687.0	481.6
1980	278.1	104.4	2001	686.7	469.9
1985	320.1	119.1	2002	707.0	488.2
1990	439.5	270.2	2003	694.6	534.6
1991	442.5	283.4	2004	765.1	634.7
1992	479.8	326.6	2005	806.6	682.7
1993	495.7	332.6	2006	847.0	742.0
1994	519.8	362.1	2007	903.0	856.0
1995	540.6	410.7			

Source: adapted from UNWTO 2008c; 2009

'all-inclusives' or time-share within the accommodation sector), the emergence of sophisticated and integrated tour operating and travel retail businesses offering significant economies of scale, developments in support services (finance, insurance, health and information) and public sector intervention through, for example, positive policies to develop tourism and consumer protection regulations, have all contributed to the growth and geographical spread of international tourist flows.

Importantly, however, the global growth of international tourism has been and remains inequitable. In other words, not all parts of the world have experienced similar growth rates in tourism and, by implication, the perceived benefits of tourism development have not been equitably enjoyed. Indeed, if tourism is seen primarily as an agent of development then, arguably, those countries and regions that have the greatest need of tourism have collectively benefited least. Major international tourist flows remain highly polarized and regionalized, particularly between the more developed, industrialized nations and, to a lesser extent, between developed and less developed countries. Despite the emergence of new and increasingly popular international destinations, such as China, Mexico and Thailand, flows of tourists and the financial benefits of tourism continue to be primarily 'North-North between a combination of industrialised and newly industrialised countries' (Vellas and Bécherel, 1995, p1). As Table 1.4 demonstrates, over 42 per cent of international arrivals are accounted for by just ten countries – a share that has, however, been declining in recent years – the great majority within Europe (including Turkey and Ukraine) and the US, although China is rapidly becoming one of the most popular destinations.

Not surprisingly, a similar pattern is evident in terms of international tourism receipts (Table 1.5). The US has long been the greatest beneficiary, in financial terms, of international tourism, reflecting the fact that it attracts a greater share of higher-spend long-haul visitors compared with European

Table 1.4 *The world's top ten international tourism destinations 2007*

		Arrivals (million)	Share of total (%)
1	France	81.9	9.1
2	Spain	59.2	6.6
3	United States	56.0	6.2
4	China	54.7	6.1
5	Italy	43.7	4.8
6	UK	30.7	3.4
7	Germany	24.4	2.7
8	Ukraine	23.1	2.6
9	Turkey	22.2	2.5
10	Mexico	21.4	2.4

Source: adapted from UNWTO, 2008c

Table 1.5 *The world's top ten international tourism earners 2007*

		Receipts ($billion)	Share of total (%)
1	United States	96.7	11.3
2	Spain	57.8	6.8
3	France	54.2	6.3
4	Italy	42.7	5.0
5	China	41.9	4.9
6	UK	37.6	4.4
7	Germany	36.0	4.2
8	Australia	22.2	2.6
9	Austria	18.9	2.2
10	Greece	18.5	2.2

Source: adapted from UNWTO, 2008c

destinations whilst in 2007 almost 50 per cent of worldwide international tourism receipts were earned by the top ten destinations.

These patterns of tourist flows are reflected in the fact that industrialized countries as a whole continue to attract the greatest share of international tourism, accounting for approximately two-thirds of arrival and receipts. More specifically, Europe has long received the greatest proportion of international arrivals – indeed, intra-European travel has always dominated international tourist flows, reflecting not only the high levels of income and holiday allowances across the region, but also the relatively short distances and highly developed transport infrastructure between European nations – although its share of the global tourism market has been declining steadily, despite continuing to enjoy annual increases in the number of tourist arrivals (Table 1.6).

Conversely, the East Asia Pacific (EAP) region (now combined with South Asia to comprise the Asia and Pacific region) has, in particular, enjoyed spectacular growth in tourist arrivals, overtaking the Americas in 2002 to

Table 1.6 *Percentage share of international tourist arrivals by region 1960–2007*

	Africa	Americas	EAP	S. Asia	Europe	M. East
1960	1.1	24.1	1.1	0.3	72.6	0.9
1970	1.5	25.5	3.2	0.6	68.2	1.1
1980	2.6	21.6	7.4	0.8	65.6	2.1
1990	3.3	20.4	12.0	0.7	61.6	2.2
1995	3.6	19.8	14.8	0.8	58.6	2.5
2000	4.0	18.6	15.9	0.9	57.1	3.5
2005	4.6	16.6	18.2	1.0	54.8	4.7
2006	4.9	16.0	18.6	1.1	54.6	4.8
2007	4.9	15.8	19.3	1.1	53.6	5.3

Source: adapted from UNWTO, 2008c

become the world's second most visited region that year. Certainly, during the 1990s annual arrivals in the region doubled whilst receipts grew by 121 per cent, both figures being twice the global rate. Much of this growth reflects China's emergence as a major global destination although other countries in the region, including Thailand, Vietnam, Cambodia, Myanmar, Laos and Polynesia, have successfully developed their tourism sectors. Other regions of the world have also increased their share of the global tourism market. Annual international arrivals in the Middle East more than doubled during the 1990s, with Egypt, Bahrain, Jordan and, in particular, Saudi Arabia and the United Arab Emirates (UAE) enjoying rapid growth. Thus, overall, the traditional destinations of Europe and North America have been losing their share of global tourist arrivals to other regions of the world, a trend that reflects increases in both long-haul travel from major generating countries and in intra-regional travel in Asia and the Middle East.

International tourism demand: Trends in style
Tourism has not only grown dramatically in terms of scale over recent decades; it has also increased in terms of scope. That is, the nature of tourism demand has undergone a fundamental transformation, with new types of holidays, new tourism experiences, new patterns of tourism behaviour and, indeed, new forms of tourism purchasing emerging. The 'traditional' two-week summer sun package holiday, produced by tour operators and sold through travel retailers, still remains popular, but there has been a rapid growth in demand for more individualistic, active/participatory and meaningful forms of tourism that provide a broader or more fulfilling experience. These include innumerable specific types of holiday or tourism experience that fall under broader headings, such as so-called cultural tourism, embracing educational, historical, art, music and other such experiences (in fact, it is not unreasonable to suggest that all forms of tourism are, to some extent, cultural!), adventure tourism, new-age tourism (including 'wellness tourism' and spiritual tourism activities) and, perhaps most significantly in the context of this book, ecotourism. The

latter is often (and incorrectly) considered synonymous with wildlife, nature or 'green' tourism – for example, some view ecotourism as a 'trendy, catch-all word applied to almost any activity that links tourism and nature' (Russell and Wallace, 2004) – and is thought to be one of the fastest growing sectors of contemporary tourism.

At the same time, patterns of tourism consumption are changing. Advances in information and communication technology and, in particular, the rapid growth in internet-based shopping have resulted in a trend towards independently-organized travel and tourism, or 'dynamic-packaging', whereby tourists can construct their own holidays by booking transport, accommodation, car hire and other services from different suppliers rather than purchasing them 'pre-packaged' by a tour operator. Equally, the evolution of low-cost flights has, in part, fuelled the growth in short-break tourism: in the major tourism generating regions, the continuing growth in outbound international tourism generally reflects not an increase in the number of people participating in tourism, but an increase in the number of holidays/trips that people take each year.

These transformations in the nature of tourism demand can be explained from a number of perspectives. Generally, for example, changes in the way in which tourism is consumed are thought to reflect broader transformations in the relationship between production and consumption, in particular, the alleged shift from modernist, 'Fordist' methods of production, typified by mass production and economies of scale, to 'post-Fordist' production focusing on so-called 'economies of scope' in response to changing consumer tastes and needs. Certainly, many newer, specialist tourism products are, in fact, simply refinements of the traditional package holiday (transport, accommodation, activities), adapted and, in some cases, 'greenwashed' to meet contemporary consumer demands. More specifically, there is no doubt that tourists have 'come of age'. That is, the initial popularity of package tourism in the 1960s and 1970s arose, in part, from the fact that it provided apparently safe, predictable holidays for those with little or no experience of international travel. However, as tourists have become more experienced, having climbed what has been described as the 'travel career ladder' (Pearce, 2005), not only have they become more confident and experienced as tourists, but they have also become more discerning, quality-conscious and adventurous. Indeed, it has been claimed that transformations in the demand for tourism have been characterized by the emergence of the 'new tourist' (Poon, 1993). Tourists are now considered to be more flexible, more environmentally sensitive, more adventurous and more responsible in their consumption of tourism; they are inclined to seek out more meaningful experiences that are less environmentally harmful or that make a positive contribution to destination environments and communities. In fact, the assumed (but unsubstantiated) increase in environmental awareness on the part of tourists and the alleged growth in demand for responsible holidays have long been key justifications for the promotion of sustainable tourism development, although there is little evidence to suggest that the 'new tourist' exists in reality.

The important point is that the complex, multi-dimensional character of tourism in general is mirrored in the complexity of tourism demand in particular. Therefore, when tourism is seen, as suggested above, as a functioning economic system of demand and supply within which the needs of tourists are met by a wide diversity of businesses selling goods and services, the role of tourists as consumers of tourism products and experiences must be taken into account when considering the development of tourism. In other words, the concept of sustainable tourism development assumes, or requires, a particular (responsible) approach to consumption on the part of tourists that, as will be argued later in this book, reflects neither the basic principles of doing business nor the contemporary realities of tourism consumption.

The tourism environment

Tourism is an environmentally dependent activity (Mowl, 2002, p219). That is, the environment is a fundamental element of the tourism experience: tourists seek out attractive, different or distinctive environments which may support specific touristic activities. At the same time, however, tourism is resource-hungry; the development and practice of tourism consumes resources, creates waste and requires significant infrastructural development (McKercher, 1993), all of which may frequently, but not always or inevitably, contribute to the potential reduction, degradation or destruction of the tourism environment. Therefore, the maintenance of a healthy, attractive environment is essential to the longer-term success of tourism both in its own right and, of greater significance, as a potential vehicle of social and economic development throughout the tourism system. In short, environmental sustainability is a prerequisite to optimizing tourism's developmental potential.

The relationship between tourism and the environment has, of course, long been recognized. As pointed out earlier, the emergence of domestic and international tourism on a mass scale from the 1960s onwards was soon to be accompanied by increasing concern about the negative consequences of tourism development although, initially, criticism was rare. Indeed, the early development of tourism was, in many quarters, welcomed, 'the image of tourism being predominantly one of an environmentally friendly activity, the "smokeless industry"' (Holden 2000, p65) and tourism was seen as having few, if any, deleterious impacts on the environment (Dowling, 1992). Such impacts that did occur were, to a great extent, ignored; within the prevailing techno-centrist environmental ideology, tourism and environmental protection were considered separate issues and tourism development was viewed from an 'advocacy' platform (Jafari, 1989) which highlighted its perceived economic benefits.

However, as international mass tourism grew rapidly from the late 1960s and into the 1970s, the environmental, socio-cultural, economic and political consequences of tourism development (or, more specifically, its costs, the early optimism surrounding tourism's potential benefits being replaced by widespread negativism) became more widely recognized. Such concern undoubtedly reflected, or was reinforced by, the broader environmental movement that was growing in support and gaining international political prominence at that time (Lowe and Rüdig, 1986). More specifically, at a time when the 'dependency' development paradigm was gaining increasing currency (see Chapter 2), there was also concern that tourism was evolving 'in a way that closely matches historical patterns of colonialism and economic dependency' (Lea, 1988, p10). Thus, establishing an academic and journalistic trend that continues to this day, numerous commentators began to focus their attention on the negative impacts of tourism development; at the same time, an OECD report based upon a three-year study concluded that the further uncontrolled expansion of tourism would seriously damage the global environment (OECD, 1981).

As a result, the 1980s witnessed the first attempts to mange the relationship between tourism and the environment more effectively. Initially and somewhat idealistically, it was believed that, with appropriate planning and management, not only could tourism be developed in harmony with the environment but also that it could be a mutually supportive, 'symbiotic' process (Budowski, 1976). Alternatives (to mass tourism) and community-based tourism development (Murphy, 1985) emerged as dominant approaches to tourism development, yet these largely overlooked the exogenous factors – as defined by the tourism system perspective – that influence both the production and consumption of tourism. Hence, the acceptance that some degree of tourism-related environmental impact is inevitable led to a more realistic approach that sought to balance environmental sustainability with optimizing the benefits to local communities, the tourism sector and tourists themselves (Dowling, 1992). In short, attention turned to sustainable tourism development as a means of maintaining a balanced relationship between tourism and the environment upon which it depends.

The environmental consequences of tourism development are referred to explicitly throughout this book. For the purposes of this introductory chapter, however, three issues are of relevance. Firstly, it is important to understand what the 'tourism environment' comprises. At one level, of course, it can be thought of simply in terms of the physical attributes of the destination – 'environment' becomes synonymous with the natural or built environment and it is no coincidence that many texts refer explicitly to the physical impacts of tourism (Wall and Mathieson, 2006). However, most, if not all, destinations are defined not only by their natural or built environment but also by their social, cultural, economic and political attributes, any of which may predominate. For example, reference was made earlier to Cuba, an island to which tourists are drawn by a variety of natural and built attractions, such as the heritage of Havana or the beaches of Varadero. However, contemporary Cuba is, first and foremost, a product of its recent political history, a history which is undoubtedly a principal draw for many tourists. Therefore, the tourism environment 'can be viewed as possessing social, cultural, economic and political dimensions, beside a physical one' (Holden, 2000, p24) and, in this sense, may be defined as:

*That vast array of factors which represent external (dis)-economies
of a tourism resort: natural ... anthropological, economic, social,
cultural, historical, architectural and infrastrauctural factors which
represent a habitat onto which tourism activities are grafted and
which is thereby exploited and changed by the exercise of tourism
business.* (EC, 1993, p4)

At the same time, it is important to appreciate the spatial dimensions of the
tourism environment. Typically, concerns for the consequences or impacts of
tourism development (and solutions) focus on the destination. Within that
context, impacts may be of local concern (that is, primarily affecting local
communities) or they may be of wider significance. Thus, for example, the
scale or architectural style of resort development is, fundamentally, a local
issue; conversely, the destruction of coral reefs through touristic exploitation
has much broader implications. However, from the tourism system perspective,
the tourism environment embraces not only destinations regions but also
generating regions and, of course, transit regions. The generating region may
be affected both adversely (for example, additional local noise and emissions
through airport expansion) or positively (jobs created by new tour operating
businesses) by tourism development, whilst transit region impacts include the
environmental issue which is, arguably, of greatest contemporary concern,
namely, climate change resulting from, amongst other things, motor car
and aircraft emissions. Inevitably, different types and degree of impact are
experienced in different regions; the point is, however, that the environmental
consequences of tourism can, or logically should, only be considered from a
wider, tourism system perspective – that is, in relation to other elements of the
tourism system and wider social, economic and political processes.

Secondly, it is important to consider not only the *parameters* of the tourism environment but also varying *perceptions* of it. In other words, the ways
in which tourism environments, as defined above, are perceived or valued
by different groups may vary considerably, an issue which comes to the fore
in the argument that sustainable (tourism) development is a manifestation
of western environmental hegemony. This debate is explored more fully in
Chapter 3 but, generally, there is likely to be a distinction between the ways
in which local communities, tourists and other stakeholders perceive or value
the environment, particularly (in this context) the destination environment.
On the one hand, for example, whilst tourists may value highly a pristine
or undeveloped traditional environment, local communities may view it as a
legitimate resource for development; on the other hand, particular elements of
the environment may be valued by local communities to such an extent that
they seek to protect them, despite their attraction to tourists. As an example
of the latter situation, tourism development policy in Bhutan has long focused
on low volume, high-yield tourism as a means of protecting Bhutanese cultural
heritage (Brunet et al, 2001; Dorji, 2001).

At the same time, tourists do not represent an homogeneous group of
consumers (Holden, 2000); they are likely to perceive and interact with the

destination environment in a multitude of different ways, depending upon their attitudes, motivations and behaviours. Consequently, any one tourism environment may be perceived and consumed in different ways through differing modes of behaviour on the part of the tourist and, hence, the impacts of tourism development may vary according to the behaviour of different tourist groups (see Figure 1.2). Therefore, any tourism development policy should take into account the varying needs and perceptions of potential tourists but, in particular, should arguably give primacy to the perceptions, knowledge and developmental needs of local communities.

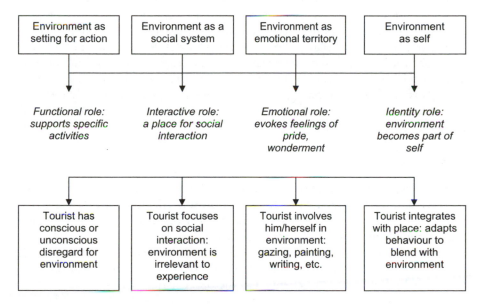

Figure 1.2 *Tourist experiences of destination environments*

Thirdly, and as hinted at in the preceding paragraphs, the tourism environment or, more precisely, the constituent elements of the tourism environment (physical, social, cultural, political) all have a value. In some instances, such value may be economic in the traditional sense that they may be exploited or commodified for tourist consumption. Thus, land may be sold for building hotels or adapted for tourist activities, such as the development of ski slopes; similarly, cultural activities, such as festivals, may be adapted and commodified for the enjoyment of tourists. The economic value of these elements of the tourism environment lies in the revenue that is eventually generated from their exploitation. Conversely, other elements of the environment may not have direct economic value (for example, pristine natural environments) but nevertheless contribute to the generation of tourist revenues – hence the perceived attraction of tourism as a developmental option as it utilizes 'free' resources. Collectively, however, these elements of the tourism environment may be thought of as forms of capital; that is, whether directly or indirectly, they collectively represent the tourism environment that attracts and supports tourism and that, as a consequence, underpins tourism's potential contribution to development.

Of course, the idea that the tourism environment comprises a number of capitals is significantly more complex than suggested here. A single resource or environment may possess different, competing values, for example, economic return compared with less tangible values, such as open space or landscape beauty. This, in turn, is further complicated by issues of ownership and distinctions between private and public goods, or between the market and public/state intervention. These issues are returned to in Chapter 5 but, in short, the point here is that the tourism environment comprises various capitals that have the potential to generate benefits (that is, 'development'). Therefore, it is logical that policies for tourism development should at least recognize the tourism environment as possessing capital value of one form or another. However, although environmental economics has long contributed to the sustainable development debate in general (Pearce et al, 1989; 1990), its application to tourism development in particular has been more limited (Mihalič, 2002).

Summary

The remarkable and continuing growth in the scale and scope of tourism over the last century has been something of a double-edged sword. On the one hand, it has proved to be a valuable and, in many cases, vital source of income and employment, potentially acting as a catalyst for wider socio-economic development or regeneration. At the same time, it has enabled ever increasing numbers of people, both individually and collectively as societies, to participate in tourism and to enjoy its benefits. On the other hand, of course, the growth and expansion of tourism has not been without cost; the degradation, misallocation or destruction of natural resources has been accompanied by or contributed to a variety of economic social, cultural and political consequences that are widely discussed in the tourism literature. In other words, it has long been recognized that, in the absence of appropriate policies, planning and management, tourism has the ability to destroy the very resources upon which it depends.

Since the 1990s, the solution to this tourism development dilemma has been seen to lie in sustainable tourism development. As this introductory chapter has observed, however, the academic study of the concept has reached an impasse whilst there is limited evidence of its successful application in practice. Thus, there is a need to progress the tourism–development–environment debate beyond the arguably restrictive, tightly-focused principles of sustainable tourism development and to explore alternative perspectives on tourism and development. In order to do so, however, a number of issues revealed by this chapter must be addressed, including:

- the scope of tourism as a widespread social activity and a manifestation of,

or contributor to, contemporary mobilities;
- the nature of tourism as, essentially, a functioning economic system of supply and demand;
- the inter-relationship between tourism (or innumerable tourism systems) and the broader 'external' environment which occurs locally, nationally and globally;
- the nature and significance of the tourism environment which represents the capital upon which tourism's developmental potential is built.

These issues are explored in more detail in subsequent chapters. Nonetheless, given the prevalence of tourism in local and national development policies, reflecting the long-held assumption that it represents an effective catalyst of development, and the fact that sustainable tourism development explicitly embraces 'development' as an objective, it is first of all necessary to review the meaning and processes of development and the relationship of tourism in particular to those processes. This is the focus of the next chapter.

2
Tourism and Development: From Economic Growth to Sustainability

As explained in the preceding chapter, the principal reason for promoting tourism is its perceived role as a catalyst of development. More precisely, tourism has long been considered a valuable source of income, foreign exchange and employment and, especially, an effective means of transferring wealth from richer to poorer countries or regions, the social mobility of tourists driving the mobility of financial capital through, for example, tourist expenditure on goods and services and foreign or external investment in tourism facilities. Therefore, the promotion of tourism, whether locally, regionally or nationally, is based essentially upon its potential to generate direct and indirect economic benefits in destination areas, although it should be noted, of course, that economic benefits also accrue directly to tourism generating regions through the development of businesses and services facilitating outbound travel.

This potential role of tourism in stimulating economic growth underpinned the initial enthusiasm surrounding its emergence on a mass scale in the 1960s (Davies, 1968; Archer, 1977), not altogether unsurprising given that, at that time, economic growth was considered not only a prerequisite for, but synonymous with, development more generally (Mabogunje, 1980; Willis, 2005). Thus, tourism was initially seen as an effective vehicle of development in as much as it represented an increasingly significant stimulant of economic growth, particularly internationally though also in a national or sub-national/regional context. However, as understanding of development processes in general evolved, transformations occurred not only in the objectives or meaning of development but also in the theories or 'paradigms' of development, or the means by which development, however defined, might be achieved. As a consequence, the desired objective of tourism-related development in particular has also implicitly expanded from economic growth to a broader concept embracing socio-cultural, political and environmental, as well as economic, dimensions – a concept widely referred to as sustainable tourism development.

The purpose of this chapter is to review the evolution of the relationship between tourism and development as a background to the critique of sustainable tourism development in Chapter 3. In so doing, it traces the path from tourism as economic growth to tourism as sustainable development within the framework of the evolution of development theory more generally. Firstly, however, it explores contemporary meanings of development as the goal or justification for developing tourism, for although the initial conceptualization – of development as economic growth – has expanded to embrace a variety of non-economic parameters or measures, the extent to which tourism is able to contribute to this broader set of objectives remains unclear. Indeed, one of the fundamental arguments in this book is that tourism can be viewed *only* as a vehicle of economic growth, the potential for the translation of its economic contribution into wider development being dependent upon or restricted by factors external to the tourism system.

Thinking about development

Development is a term that is widely used and recognized yet 'seems to defy definition, although not for want of definitions on offer' (Cowen and Shenton, 1996, p3). On the one hand, it is used descriptively to refer to 'an historical process of social change in which societies are transformed over long periods' (Thomas, 2000a, p29), or a process through which societies change from one condition to, implicitly, a better condition. On the other hand, it is used normatively to refer to the goal of that process or, as Thomas (2000a, p29) puts it, to refer to 'a vision, description or measure of the state of being of a desirable society'. At the same time, development may also be viewed more pragmatically as the plans, policies and activities of those organizations – governments, Non-government Organizations (NGOs), voluntary/third sector agencies, and so on – that 'do' development or work to support or encourage social change. Thus, in short, the term 'development' can be used in three senses, namely: a process, the outcome of that process, and the activities that support the process, each of which embrace or may be considered from competing social, economic, political and environmental ideological perspectives (Goldsworthy, 1988).

Here, we are concerned primarily with development in the sense of a vision or desired future condition of society, the achievement of which, it is claimed, tourism may contribute to. In other words, what is the goal of tourism-related development? Generally, though somewhat simplistically, development is considered to be synonymous with progress or positive transformation, or what Thomas (2000a, p23) refers to as 'good change'. This suggests that there is no finality about development; that is, it is a continually evolving goal of betterment (however defined) towards which all societies strive. In other words, although development is most commonly considered in the context of less developed countries, it is a concept that 'relates to all parts of the world at every level, from the individual to global transformations' (Elliot, 1999, p10). Therefore, a 'developed' country or society does not cease to change, progress or even, perhaps, regress – indeed, some developed nations may be thought of as experiencing, against certain indicators, what could be described as 'negative' development, or a reduction in some aspects of well-being.

This specific issue is returned to shortly but if the objective of development can be generalized as 'good change', then a number of questions immediately arise. For example, what are the parameters of 'good' change? Who decides what good change is? How can such change be achieved? For whom is change good? And, in particular, if change is for the good of society, do all members of that society benefit or are there winners and losers? Certainly, the narrow conception of development as economic growth in the early post-Second World War years was soon rejected for not only failing to solve but also for exacerbating social and economic problems in many societies (Todaro, 2000). More specifically, it became evident that the prevailing modernization development paradigm, espousing interventionist Keynesian economic policies to promote economic growth and consequential western-style modernization (Harrison, 1988), was having little or no impact upon the developmental challenges then, and still, faced by both rich and poor countries. Such challenges include persistent poverty (relative and absolute), unmet basic needs (food, sanitation, health care and so on), unemployment, low levels of education and literacy, restrictions on political and cultural freedom, gender inequalities (particularly neglect of the interests of women) and environmental problems. In fact, the continuing incidence of these problems and, more particularly, evidence of increasing poverty, inequality, lack of opportunity and environmental damage in many parts of the world is generally seen by some (the 'post-development' school) as the failure of development as a global project and more specifically by others as the inevitable outcome of development policy based upon western economic ideology, so that many have become 'victims of development':

> *Development was exclusively defined as economic development, reducing the degree of progress and maturity in a society to be measured by the level of its production... The result? The economic benefits of such development have not even trickled down to the vast majority of the people in most countries honourably referred to as 'developing'... They have suffered not only economic impoverishment, but also a loss of identity and ability to develop endogenously, authentically, within their own culture and capabilities.* (Seabrook, 1993, pp8–9)

Given this apparent failure of economic growth policies to meet the wider developmental challenges referred to above, development came to be conceptualized more broadly, incorporating social, ethical and political factors, though not rejecting economic growth out of hand, for such growth 'may matter a great deal ... because of some associated benefits that are realised in the process of economic growth' (Sen, 1994, p220). Economic growth remained, and remains, a prerequisite to development, a fact recognized, somewhat controversially, by the Brundtland Commission which suggested that global sustainable development requires growth in the world economy by a factor of five to ten (WCED, 1987, p50). Nevertheless, Dudley Seers, writing in 1969, asserted that:

> *The questions to ask about a country's development are therefore: what has been happening to poverty? What has been happening to unemployment? What has been happening to inequality? If all three of these have declined from high levels, then beyond a doubt this has been a period of development for the country concerned. If one or two of these central problems has been growing worse, especially if all three have, it would be strange to call the result 'development', even if per capita income had doubled.* (Seers, 1969)

Despite remarkable increases in global wealth, 40 years later these questions remain just as relevant in most, if not all, the world's countries.

To these three conditions Seers later added a fourth, self-reliance, or the need to 'reduce cultural dependence on one or more of the great powers' (Seers, 1977). In other words, social or distributive justice and self-determination became fundamental objectives of development, shifting the emphasis from a process lying in the 'trusteeship' (Cowen and Shenton, 1996, px) of western nations to one emanating from those peoples and societies experiencing or desiring change. Thus, development became conceptualized as embracing three core values, summarized by Goulet (1968) as the 'good life':

- The sustenance of life: access to and satisfaction of basic needs, such as food, shelter and health care.
- Esteem: a sense of identity, self-respect or dignity, dependent upon increased wealth and education, but also upon spiritual and cultural well-being.
- Freedom: the expansion of social and economic choice, as well as freedom from servitude to ignorance, nature, other societies, beliefs and institutions. Indeed, for Sen (1999), freedom in its broadest sense lies as the heart of development.

Since the 1980s, of course, an additional component or dimension has been added to the concept of development: environmental sustainability. More precisely, the term 'development' has evolved into 'sustainable development', a concept that, according to Dresner (2002), attempts to 'square the circle of competing demands for environmental protection and economic development'. First referred to almost 30 years ago in the *World Conservation Strategy* (IUCN, 1980) and subsequently popularized and politicized in the World Commission on Environment and Development (or Brundtland) Report (WCED, 1987), sustainable development remains a highly contested and widely defined concept. Rogers et al (2008, p42), for example, refer to the vast literature and numerous definitions of the term, suggesting that 'reviewing these and other relevant references constitutes a major task in trying to understand the meaning and significance of the term'. Nevertheless, it is generally accepted, albeit somewhat simplistically, that sustainable development has three dimensions, namely, economic, social and environmental (the so-called 'triple bottom line'). The first two embrace the economic and human objectives of development as defined in the core values described above; the third emphasizes the objective of sustaining the global ecosystem within which the human-economic sub-system operates.

The concept of sustainable development, its controversies, inherent con-tradictions and, in particular, its relationship and relevance to tourism are looked at in more detail in the latter part of this chapter and in Chapter 3. The important point here, though, is that the meaning of development, as the explicit objective and desired outcome of tourism, has evolved from a focus on economic growth and modernization to the structural transformation of societies embracing economic, social, cultural and political change. Collectively, these are broadly reflected in the United Nations (UN) Millennium Project's goals and targets, usually referred to as the Millennium Development Goals (MDGs) – see Table 2.1. This multi-dimensionality of development, in turn, suggests that there can be no single definition of development; as a process

Table 2.1 *The Millennium Project: Goals and targets*

Goal 1: Eradicate extreme poverty and hunger
Target 1: reduce by half the proportion of people whose income is less than $1 a day
Target 2: reduce by half the proportion of people who suffer from hunger

Goal 2: Achieve universal primary education
Target 3: ensure that children everywhere are able to complete full primary schooling

Goal 3: Promote gender equality and empower women
Target 4: eliminate gender disparity in all levels of education

Goal 4: Reduce child mortality
Target 5: reduce the under-5 mortality rate by two-thirds

Goal 5: Improve maternal health
Target 6: reduce the maternal mortality rate by three-quarters

Goal 6: Combat HIV/AIDS, malaria and other diseases
Target 7: halt/reverse the spread of HIV/AIDS
Target 8: halt/reverse the incidence of malaria and other serious diseases

Goal 7: Ensure environmental sustainability
Target 9: integrate the principles of sustainable development into national development policies
Target 10: halve the proportion of people without access to basic sanitation and drinking water
Target 11: achieve a significant improvement in the lives of 100 million slum dwellers

Goal 8: Develop a global partnership for development
Target 12: develop an open, non-discriminatory trading and financial system
Target 13: address the special needs of least developed countries
Target 14: address the special needs of landlocked developing countries and small island developing states
Target 15: deal comprehensively with the developing countries' debt problems

---

Source: adapted from www.millenniumproject.org

and goal, it will vary according to particular contexts with, as we shall see, significant implications for tourism development.

Measuring development

If development, however defined, is thought of as a vision or desirable state then, by implication, some form of measurement is necessary in order to ascertain the extent of progress made towards achieving that state. More pragmatically, of course, governments, NGOs and other agencies need information for policy formation or may wish to assess the effectiveness of particular initiatives or policies (including the promotion of tourism) and, hence, also require measurements of development.

Not surprisingly, measures of development have evolved as the meaning or objectives of development itself have expanded. At the same time, they also reveal some of the difficulties and inconsistencies in defining development. For example, development was traditionally measured in terms of gross domestic product (GDP) or per capita GDP (and interestingly, tourism's developmental contribution is also measured most commonly in contribution to GDP, although a high contribution indicates a significant degree of (potentially unsustainable) dependency on the tourism sector).

The World Bank continues to categorize the developmental status of countries according to wealth measures, specifically per capita GNI (Gross National Income) – see Table 2.2.

Table 2.2 *Per capita GNI country classifications*

	Low income economies	Lower-middle income economies	Upper-middle income economies	High income economies
Per capita GNI	$735 or less	$736–$2935	$2936–$9075	$9076 or above
Number of countries in group	64	54	34	56

Source: World Bank, 2005

However, average income data mask the distribution of wealth between the rich and poor, an issue that is of equal relevance to both developed and less developed countries. As Willis (2005, p8) observes, 'high levels of economic development do not necessarily mean great equality'. The US, for example, has the highest income inequality amongst developed countries and, over the last 30 years, has experienced the greatest increase in income inequality in the developed world (Smeeding, 2005). Moreover, quantitative measures of wealth do not necessarily reflect culturally defined, non-economic interpretations in some countries:

> There may be as many poor and as many perceptions of poverty as there are human beings. The fantastic variety of cases entitling

a person to be called poor in different cultures and languages is such that, all in all, everything and everyone under the sun could be labelled as poor, in one way or another... For long, and in many cultures of the world, poor was not always the opposite of rich. Other considerations, such as falling from one's station in life, being deprived of one's instruments of labour, the loss of one's status or the marks of one's profession ... defined the poor.
(Rahnema, 1992, p158)

Therefore, new measures have been sought. Perhaps the best known alternative measure of economic development is the Index of Sustainable Economic Welfare (ISEW) which, in addition to correcting for income inequalities hidden in standard GDP figures, attempts to make adjustments for environmental costs, the depreciation of natural capital, unpaid work, 'defensive' health care and other indicators of overall welfare (Daly and Cobb, 1989). Whilst both controversial and applied to relatively few, mostly developed, countries, the results of the ISEW are interesting in that they consistently demonstrate a perceived increase in welfare below the rate of increase in GDP and in some countries, notably the US and the UK, a decline in welfare over the last 20 years. In other words, some developed countries are experiencing 'negative' development according to broader welfare indicators, a trend supported by specific examples, such as a report in late 2008 indicating that male life expectancy in east Glasgow, one of the most socially deprived areas of Scotland, is 54 years, compared with 63 years in India. It is also likely that if an ISEW could be applied to some popular tourist regions, such as the English Lake District, a similar story would emerge. Whilst tourism contributes a growing proportion of income and employment in the region (Sharpley, 2004), low levels of pay (income inequality), high levels of second home ownership/high house prices (limited access to affordable housing for local communities), seasonality (job insecurity) and localized environmental damage would undoubtedly contribute to a decline in welfare for local communities.

Since 1990, the United Nations Development Programme (UNDP) has published its annual Human Development Index (HDI) which, in addition to an economic component (per capita GDP as a measure of prosperity), is based upon additional dimensions of longevity and knowledge, each assessed by a variety of indicators. Although the position of many countries on the index reflects national and per capita wealth, some achieve a higher position on the HDI than on a simple ranking of per capita GDP, thus partially severing the link between wealth and development. Nevertheless, like all quantitative measures, such indices are unable to account for individual perceptions of poverty, lack of opportunity, underdevelopment and so on. In other words, development, as a vision or goal, can really only be thought about at the level of the individual. At the same time, such 'league tables' of development status cannot, of course, reveal the underlying economic, political, social and cultural processes, structures and institutions that facilitate or hinder development. It is interesting to note, for example, that Iceland has occupied the top position in the HDI for a number of years, making it the world's most 'developed' country. However, Iceland effectively became bankrupt in the financial crisis of 2008, demonstrating the fragile foundations or the lack of sustainability of its national well-being (and, as explored in Chapter 3, the potential contribution of tourism to the national economy).

Thus, overall, not only does development continue to defy definition but also significant doubts remain over its validity as a global process and goal; indeed, the belief in development as progress has, for some, been replaced by a concern that development represents regression. In effect, it remains a term described by Welch (1984) as 'bereft of precise meaning ... used to mean anything from broad, undefined change to quite specific events'. Consequently, though it is easy to talk about tourism in particular as an agent of development, it is much more difficult to define what tourism-related development might be, what contribution (if any) tourism makes to development, and the processes by which that contribution might be operationalized or optimized. It is to this last point that this chapter now turns.

Tourism and development theory: The path to sustainability

Just as notions of development have expanded from basic economic growth to a broader concept that not only embraces both economic and human dimensions but also explicitly links development with environmental sustainability, so too has development theory evolved into a more holistic perspective on social change (Hettne, 1995). As Telfer (2002a) observes, development theory (or paradigms) combine development ideology, or the *ends* of development, with development strategy, or the *means* of achieving those ends. Consequently, development strategy, or the process by which development may be achieved, is inevitably influenced or guided by the ideological or desired outcomes of that process: that is, by the development vision referred to above. This, in turn, suggests that development is an inherently political process, that the goals and processes of development reflect prevailing political ideologies and structures (Goldsworthy, 1988).

According to Thomas (2000a), the political dimension of development may be conceptualized along a continuum of development's relationship with capitalism. At one end of this continuum, capitalism and development may be considered to be synonymous, with development or progress occurring immanently as the 'natural' outcome of capitalism. At the other end, the idea of development is rejected and, hence, has no relationship with capitalism. Within these two extremes, development may, on the one hand, occur alongside capitalism, whereby capitalism is seen as the most appropriate vehicle for human progress and modernization, although some degree of intervention may be necessary to either regulate markets or to achieve particular social objectives. On the other hand, development may occur against capitalism. That is, although the modernization/industrialization of society remains the objective, capitalism is rejected in favour of more radical state intervention or a more grassroots, people-focused approach to development (see Table 2.3).

Table 2.3 *The relationship between development and capitalism*

	Capitalism as development	*Development with capitalism*	*Development against capitalism*	*Alternative (grassroots) development*	*Rejection of development*
Ideology	Neoliberalism	Interventionism	Structuralism		Post-development
Vision	Liberal, modern, capitalist society		Modern, non-capitalist society	Potential of all people realized	Development not desirable
Strategy	Immanent process of capitalism	Legislation, controls, policies to meet intended social goals	Central planning/class struggle	Individual / group empower-ment	

Source: adapted from Thomas, 2000a

Since the 1950s, when development first emerged as a global project (the need to rebuild Europe in the post-war years combined with a US-inspired desire to encourage western-style development in the 'south' underpinned the emergence of development policies and institutions, most notably the World Bank and the International Monetary Fund (IMF)), both 'development with capitalism' and 'development against capitalism' have been in evidence, most clearly delineated, at least until the late 1980s, by the east–west divide. Moreover, tourism itself reflected this divide, with tourism development in the west displaying the characteristics of capitalist endeavour whilst, in the Eastern Bloc, much tourism development was state sponsored as a social good. Following the collapse of the Soviet Bloc, of course, the last 20 years have witnessed the spread of market economies and liberal democracy or, in some cases, pseudo-democracy, although exceptions remain (see, for example the case study of Cuba at the end of the chapter). However, development paradigms have, for the most part, fallen under the 'development with capitalism' umbrella; even dependency theory (see below) is, essentially, a critique of rather than an alternative to global capitalism, albeit a Marxist-inspired critique. Where politically-influenced strategies did emerge, it was in response to perceived dependency; for some, the answer lay in the reform of capitalist trade systems (for example, import substitution policies) whereas for others, such as André Gunder Frank, the only solution was the overthrow of capitalism (Frank, 1967). Nevertheless, sustainable development appears to draw upon both the 'with' and 'against capitalism' positions; though requiring capitalism-generated economic growth, it favours at the same time a grassroots, bottom-up approach, thereby contributing, perhaps, to the inherent contradiction of the concept.

It is not relevant here to review development theories in depth (see, for example, Preston, 1996; Willis, 2005). However, as a framework for exploring the trajectory of tourism and development policy from economic growth to sustainable tourism development, it is useful to summarize the evolution of development theory and the relationship (accidental or otherwise) of tourism to this process. We are concerned primarily with the emergence of sustainable development in general as a basis for comparing the factors that led to the adoption of sustainable tourism development in particular as the dominant approach to tourism development from the 1990s onwards.

Typically, development theory is described in chronological, though not necessarily consequential, sequence. In other words, distinctive approaches to development have emerged at certain times, displaying a shift from traditional, top-down economic growth-based models through to more broad-based approaches focusing on bottom-up, people-centred planning within environmental limits and, most recently, evidence of the rejection of 'meta-narratives' of development in favour of a variety of micro-conceptualizations of development. However, it is important to note that earlier theories have not been completely rejected; despite criticisms elements of each remain relevant. Moreover, the timelines are intended only as guides as to when particular theories or approaches gained prominence. The main approaches to development are summarized in Table 2.4.

Table 2.4 *Development theory from the 1950s*

Timeline	Development process	Key concepts and strategies
1950s–1960s	Modernization theory	*Dominance of western economic growth based models:* – Stages of growth – Structural theories – Diffusion: growth poles and trickle down – State intervention: regulation/protectionism
1960s–1970s	Modernization theory/ dependency theory	*Underdevelopment the result of domination/ exploitation by developed countries* – Economic restructuring: import substitution, protectionism; development of domestic markets – Limits to growth: neo-Malthusian theories in response to environmental concerns
1970s–1980s	Neo-liberalism	*Promotion of the free market* – Limits on government intervention in economic activity – Deregulation/privatization – Structural adjustment programmes – New economic order; one world
1980s	Neo-liberalism/ alternative development	*Awareness of effects of development on different cultures/societies* – Grassroots/people-centred development – Basic needs: food, housing, education, health – Local context/indigenous knowledge – Environmental sustainability
1990s	Alternative/ sustainable development	*Dominance of sustainable development paradigm, but emergence of post-development school* – Grassroots/people-centred development – Environmental management – Engagement with globalization – The development 'impasse'
2000s	Beyond the impasse: a new paradigm?	*Post-development: rejection of overarching development concepts* – Global environmental policies/protocols – Transnational movements – Micro-level strategies – Poverty reduction – State security and development

Source: adapted from Willis, 2005, p2; Telfer and Sharpley, 2008, p12

As is evident from Table 2.4, four identifiable development paradigms have, at one time or another, dominated development thinking. It is also evident that, since the 1990s, a development 'impasse' (Schuurman, 1993) has been reached or, more accurately perhaps, the point beyond which overarching development theories or approaches are no longer relevant to the characteristics and developmental challenges of the contemporary global political-economy has been passed. Thus, it is likely that the impasse in the study and application of sustainable tourism development in particular, as suggested in Chapter 1, reflects this apparent end of development meta-narrative and the beginnings of a more fractured, context-specific perspective on development. Chapter 4 explores this in more detail.

Modernization

As already noted, development processes initially focused on economic growth, the objective being the modernization (in effect, westernization) of societies. Based upon the notion that all societies follow an inevitable evolutionary path from traditional to modern structures, institutions and values, development/ modernization is considered to be possible once the 'take-off stage' (Rostow, 1967) – manifested in the emergence of one or more significant industries which induce wider growth and investment – has been reached. A key element in the process is the introduction of one or more 'growth poles', such as particular industries or sectors, often requiring foreign investment. From these, 'growth impulses' diffuse throughout the region, in principle stimulating wider modernization, although as Mydral (1963) argued 'backwash effects' may occur. That is, a 'growth pole' may act as a magnet to people and resources, thereby reducing the diffusion of economic growth, leaving other areas depleted and, thus, potentially enhancing socio-economic inequalities.

The relationship between economic growth-based modernization and tourism is clearly evident. In many countries, tourism has in effect been introduced as a growth pole, the purpose being to stimulate national economic growth and development. This is certainly the case for numerous island micro-states, for example, as well as for many smaller less developed countries. Equally, tourism is widely considered to be an effective regional development tool (Telfer, 2002b). In many industrialized countries, tourism is promoted for the economic regeneration of both peripheral rural regions and declining, post-industrial urban areas, whilst Cancún in Mexico is a notable example of the state-driven development of a tourist resort as a regional growth pole (Clancy, 1999). At the same time, concepts associated with modernization theory in general are mirrored in tourism development in particular. The notion of backward linkages and tourism multipliers are directly related to growth impulses and 'trickle down' effects – in fact, with reference again to Cancún, research has demonstrated the extent to which such expected benefits fail to occur (Torres, 2003) – whilst 'backwash effects' are a recognized effect of tourism resort development, with rural hinterlands experiencing significant population imbalance as younger people move to find employment in resort areas. The stages-of-growth concept also remains relevant to tourism development. The ability of any destination to take advantage of the development opportunities offered by tourism is dependent upon, amongst other things, the diversity and maturity of the local economy or, in short, whether or not it has reached the 'take-off' stage. Thus, although a number of so-called least developed countries (an officially recognized grouping comprising around 50 of the world's poorest countries) boast relatively successful tourism sectors, this has not always been translated into broader economic growth and development (UNCTAD, 2001; Sharpley, forthcoming).

The relevance of modernization theory to tourism development is explored in depth elsewhere (Opperman and Chon, 1997; Telfer, 2002a). For now, however, it suffices to state that the concept of economic growth-based modernization arguably remains the most appropriate framework for exploring tourism's developmental potential and, therefore, we shall return to it later in the book.

Dependency

Whilst modernization theory attempts to explain how development may occur as the result of capitalist economic growth, albeit with state intervention, dependency theory suggests why such development or modernization *fails* to occur. Alternatively referred to as underdevelopment theory, it proposes that the failure of (less developed) countries to develop/modernize reflects their economic and political position relative to developed nations. In other words, global political-economic relations are such that wealthy, industrialized nations (the metropolitan 'centre') are able to exploit weaker, peripheral nations, hence restricting developmental opportunities in the latter. A variety of theories is embraced by the broader concept of dependency, whilst world-systems theory (Wallerstein, 1979) expands upon the centre–periphery dualism of the dependency model by introducing the concept of the semi-periphery to take into account the emergence of the newly-industrialized economies, such as Singapore, Taiwan and Brazil.

The relevance of dependency or world-systems models to the contemporary global political-economy is debatable. In particular, the globalization of trade, investment and communication, as well as environmental challenges such as climate change, have served to reduce the role of the nation-state and, hence, the relevance of relationships between nation-states. Nevertheless, dependency theory has long provided a basis for considering the negative consequences of tourism development, particularly in terms of the relationship between destinations and the organization/ownership of the production of tourism (Britton, 1991). International tourism has long been described as a form of imperialism or neo-colonialism (Nash, 1989), whilst the centre–periphery model of dependency has provided a framework for exploring tourism development both generally (Høivik and Heiberg, 1980) and in specific contexts, such as island micro-states (Wilkinson, 1989). At the same time, it has also been argued that international tourism may result in cultural dependency, whereby tourism planning and policy reflects external (western) ideals (Erisman, 1989). Of course, reducing levels of dependency (or, as a corollary, enhancing self-reliance) is, as we shall see, one of the objectives of sustainable tourism development. Ironically, however, the very process of encouraging destinations to adopt sustainable community-focused tourism development (a role often undertaken by western-based agencies) may itself be seen as a form of cultural imperialism. In 2000, for example, and following the advice of London-based pressure group Tourism Concern, the tourism authorities in The Gambia banned all-inclusive holidays in order to enhance out-of-pocket tourist expenditure in the local economy. This policy decision contributed to an immediate decline in tourist arrivals and, hence, was reversed the following year.

Neo-liberalism

During the1970s, some economists suggested that economic growth and development was being restricted by excessive state intervention in economic affairs. Drawing on the classic theories of Adam Smith, they argued that the market would operate more effectively if left to its own devices (Willis, 2005). Consequently a shift occurred in development thinking, rejecting the Keynesian fiscal approach underpinning modernization and economic growth policies and moving towards a liberal, free market approach. Referred to as a 'counter revolution' to Keynesian policies (Toye, 1993), economic liberalism became more entrenched in the Reagan–Thatcher era of the 1980s and was manifested in development policy through World Bank/IMF administered structural adjustment lending programmes (SALPs), which provided development loans conditional on economic liberalization in recipient countries. These SALPs were later widely discredited for increasing poverty and unemployment in many recipient countries (Harrigan and Mosley, 1991) whilst the more recent Poverty Reduction Strategy Papers have also been similarly criticized.

Tourism development has long benefited from international structural funding, either from the World Bank (Inskeep and Kallenberger, 1992) or regional bodies such as the European Union. However, no explicit link was established between SALPs in particular and tourism, although the structure and operations of the tourism sector in those countries receiving such loans were undoubtedly influenced by local economic liberalization policies. Indeed, despite increasing concerns over the consequences of tourism development, tourism development policy remained firmly focused on economic growth until the advent of alternative development in the late 1970s and early 1980s.

Alternative development ...

The alternative development paradigm emerged in response to the apparent failure of mainstream, economic-growth based models to deliver development. In other words, alternative development represents, literally, an alternative to top-down, western-centric, economic growth models of development, adopting instead a bottom-up or grassroots approach to development that focuses primarily on human and environmental concerns. The fundamental tenet of alternative development is, therefore, that development should be endogenous. That is, the developmental process should emanate from and be guided by the needs of each society, rather than being imposed or implemented exogenously. Thus, alternative development is a people-centred, or 'popular' (Brohman, 1996a) approach to development that focuses not only on basic needs (physical and social well-being) but also upon the encouragement of self-reliance, drawing upon indigenous systems and knowledge to strengthen the developmental process. As a consequence, the alternative development process advocates decentralization or localization (compared with the state-led, economic growth-based modernization), with an emphasis on community participation and decision-making. This, in turn, is seen to contribute to the empowerment of local communities and the potential enhancement of the role of women. At the same time, the greater involvement of NGOs has been seen as an essential ingredient of alternative, grassroots approaches to development (Willis, 2005), although the multiple accountabilities of NGOs (Edwards and Hulme, 1995) and their reliance on international aid support may limit the true extent of their focus on local communities' needs.

With development being increasingly linked with environmental sustainability, from the late 1980s alternative development effectively became, as will be discussed shortly, synonymous with sustainable development. However, it is important to note here that the concept of alternative development was reflected in the emergence during the 1980s of what became referred to as 'alternative tourism development' (Smith and Eadington, 1992). This, too, emphasized a community-participatory approach to tourism (Murphy, 1983; 1985), laying the foundation for the continuing importance assigned to inclusive partnerships in general (Bramwell and Lane, 2000) and community-based tourism in particular within sustainable tourism development and, more specifically, ecotourism development. Equally, issues of gender equality (Kinnaird and Hall, 1994), empowerment (Scheyvens, 2002) and, of course, environmental sustainability have also entered alternative/sustainable tourism development discourse and, to many, alternative tourism is now synonymous with sustainable tourism development.

The principal objective of alternative tourism was, or is, to develop tourism that is appropriate to local environmental, social and cultural values (that is, tourism that minimizes the negative consequences for local communities) and to optimize the benefits in terms of local control, enhancing the local economy and promoting proactive, meaningful encounters between tourists and local people. However, alternative tourism is also an 'oppositional' approach to tourism development, falling within the 'development against capitalism' category described earlier in this chapter. Thus, although it reflects the broader aims of alternative development, it is proposed explicitly as an alternative to mass tourism development. That is, it is characterized, in terms of both production and consumption, as a more appropriate or 'better' form of tourism (see Table 2.5) than conventional mass tourism.

In other words, alternative tourism generally, or in more specific guises such as 'responsible', 'appropriate', 'green' or 'ecotourism', is seen to be 'good'. Certainly, the projects or resorts that deservedly win accolades in schemes such as the World Travel and Tourism Council's (WTTC's) Tourism for Tomorrow Awards or the more recently launched Virgin Responsible Tourism Awards tend to meet the requirements suggested in Table 2.5, as do the holidays or tourism experiences that feature in alternative or responsible tourism guides, such as

Table 2.5 *Characteristics of mass versus alternative tourism*

Conventional mass tourism	Alternative forms of tourism
General features	
Rapid development	Slow development
Maximizes	Optimizes
Socially/environmentally inconsiderate	Socially/environmentally considerate
Uncontrolled	Controlled
Short-term	Long-term
Sectoral	Holistic
Remote control	Local control
Development strategies	
Development without planning	First plan, then develop
Project-led schemes	Concept-led schemes
Tourism development everywhere	Development in suitable places
Concentration on 'honeypots'	Pressures and benefits diffused
New building	Re-use of existing building
Development by outsiders	Local developers
Employees imported	Local employment utilized
Urban architecture	Vernacular architecture
Tourist behaviour	
Large groups	Singles, families, friends
Fixed programme	Spontaneous decisions
Little time	Much time
'Sights'	'Experiences'
Imported lifestyle	Local lifestyle
Comfortable/passive	Demanding/active
Loud	Quiet
Shopping	Bring presents

Source: adapted from Butler, 1990; Lane, 1990

The Community Tourism Guide (Mann, 2000). Similarly, Responsible Travel, allegedly the largest online supplier of responsible holidays, promotes holidays that meet social, economic and environmental criteria for 'responsible travel' as defined by that organization (see www.responsibletravel.com). However, the website states that:

> *Responsible travel is a new way of travelling for those who've had enough of mass tourism. It's about respecting and benefiting local people and the environment – but it's about far more than that. If you travel for relaxation, fulfillment, discovery, adventure and to learn – rather than simply to tick off 'places and things' – then responsible travel is for you.* (Responsible Travel, 2008)

Thus, first and foremost, responsible travel is, simply, travel that cannot be labelled as 'mass tourism'; it is also sold on the basis of the tourist experience, appealing to those who seek (whether for altruistic or more egotistical reasons) distinctive or non-mass produced holidays. Again from the website:

The responsible traveller values authenticity – experiences integral to local people's traditions, cultures and rituals – rather than those created for tourism, or those whose existing meanings and uses have become lost as they have been packaged up for tourism. No more 'Greek nights' in resorts with the only Greek people there to serve food please! (Responsible Travel, 2008)

What is not revealed is how or to what extent responsible travel benefits local communities and environments, although more recently increasing academic attention has been paid to the concept of responsible tourism. For example, a special issue of the *Journal of Sustainable Tourism* (2008, 16(3)), is dedicated to the topic whilst, more specifically, Spenceley's (2008) edited collection of case studies explores the costs, benefits and policy implementation successes and failures of a variety of responsible tourism initiatives in South Africa. However, most, if not all, of the cases focus on local, community-based projects and thus mass tourism, again in terms of both production and consumption, is implicitly seen to be 'bad', a consistent theme in the academic and journalistic literature that explores the negative consequences of tourism development. Moreover, this dichotomy between 'good' alternative tourism and 'bad' mass tourism underpins many of the typical principles of sustainable tourism development, although, as we shall see, more recent definitions of the concept attempt to embrace all forms of tourism, including mass tourism, within a sustainability framework.

... and sustainable development

It may seem somewhat artificial to distinguish between alternative development and sustainable development (and, indeed, between their tourism derivatives). Fundamental to both is a focus on human development and well-being, whilst the environment is also a factor that both take into account. However, sustainable development, as generally conceived, differs in a number of ways from the alternative development paradigm, particularly in terms of its spatial and temporal parameters. Alternative development suggests a focus upon specific societal contexts at specific times; sustainable development, however, adopts a much broader focus. In fact, the three key principles underpinning sustainable development are that (a) an holistic perspective is required – both development and environmental sustainability are global challenges; (b) the emphasis should be on the long-term future; and (c), although the focus of development should be people-centred, the challenge is to achieve both intra- and inter-generational equity; development should be fair and equitable for all people both within and between generations.

These principles reflect what Rogers et al (2008, p47) neatly summarize as the 'factors governing sustainable development' or, more succinctly, global developmental challenges:

- Poverty: latest figures suggest that globally some 1.1 billion people, roughly one-fifth of the world's population, live on less than US$1 a day. Conversely, worldwide there are almost 500 billionaires whose collective wealth is greater than the total wealth of the poorest half of the world's population. The challenge, therefore, is to reduce levels of both economic poverty and other indicators of poverty, such as limited access to clean water, sanitation, basic health care and so on. For example, 1.2 billion people live without access to safe water and 2.6 billion without access to sanitation (UNDP, 2006).

- Population: in 1920, the world's population stood at 2 billion; this is expected to increase fourfold by 2020 and to just over 9 billion by 2050. Such growth inevitably increases demands on resources, although it is economic growth, such as that seen in China and India in recent years, rather than absolute population levels, that has greater environmental impact.
- Participation: reflecting the broader concept of development outlined earlier, a fundamental requirement for sustainable development is an increased degree of participation (that is, influencing development and resource use planning) amongst all stakeholders from the international and national to the local levels.
- Policy and governance: effective and sustainable development requires appropriate policy decisions and governance with respect to resource exploitation and allocation, as well as development more generally. As is discussed in more detail in Chapter 4, the lack of development in many of the world's poorest countries, both generally and related to tourism development in particular, or 'failing states' can be attributed directly to poor governance (Ghani and Lockhart, 2008).
- Prevention and management of disasters: sustainable development is concerned with global human well-being. Therefore, an essential require-ment is the prevention of disasters caused by human activity and the management of natural disasters (though some 'natural' disasters can be linked to climate change and, hence, human activity). Specifically, terrorism-related threats to global security, and their potential political and socio-economic consequences, are of increasing concern. Consequently, national and international security has become the focus of development policy.

A common thread throughout these factors of sustainable development is the environment or, more precisely, the sustainable use and allocation of resources. Indeed, the defining feature of sustainable development that sets it apart from preceding development paradigms is the explicit location of 'development' within an environmental framework. Sustainable development does not simply embrace environmental factors; its very foundation is environmental sustainability.

This is not to say, of course, that development was not previously related to environmental issues. Societies have always suffered (and caused) a variety of environmental problems, including over-population, pollution and resource depletion, sometimes with long-lasting impacts. For example, the final evacuation in 1930 of the small remote archipelago of St Kilda, lying in the Atlantic

Ocean to the northwest of Scotland, partly resulted from the contamination of the fields by use of bird carcasses, peat ash and human waste as fertilizer. Moreover, increasing industrialization and urbanization in the 19th century led to the establishment of organized conservation movements (McCormick, 1995). However, it was not until the 1960s that environmentalism, as opposed to conservation, became a popular ideology with a set of preoccupations that went far beyond the specific concerns of protecting natural areas and species threatened by modernization and development. Rather than focusing simply on resource depletion, the actual scientific, technological and economic processes upon which human progress was previously seen to depend were also questioned. At the same time, it was acknowledged that the by-products of industrialization, the so-called 'effluence of affluence', did not respect national boundaries; environmental problems, such as air and water pollution, frequently originated in one country but adversely affected another. Influenced by Boulding's (1992) notion of 'spaceship earth', environmentalism took on an international dimension. The earth became viewed as a closed system with finite resources and a limited capacity to absorb waste and, as a result, the threat to the world's environment came to be seen as a global crisis. Thus, it was no coincidence that the motto of the United Nations Conference on the Human Environment (UNCHE) in 1972 was 'Only One Earth'.

Nevertheless, it was only with the advent of sustainable development in the 1980s that development and environmentalism became explicitly articulated; as Dresner (2002, p64) notes, sustainable development represents a 'meeting point for environmentalists and developers'. However, sustainable development has long been, and remains, a variously defined, ambiguous, contested and contradictory concept (Redclift, 1987), particularly as the twin objectives of development (requiring resource exploitation) and sustainability (requiring resource protection) are considered by many to be oxymoronic. According to Porritt (2007), one factor underpinning the continuing debate surrounding the concept is that, mistakenly, 'sustainable development' and 'sustainability' are used interchangeably, or taken to mean the same thing. This is not the case. Sustainability, on the one hand, is the 'capacity for continuance into the long-term future' (Porritt, 2007, p33); it is, in effect, the vision or goal for the human species. Sustainable development, on the other hand, is 'the process by which we move towards sustainability' (2007, p33). It is the process by which human well-being, on a global scale, is optimized at the same time as the earth's resources upon which human existence depends are maintained and enhanced. For Porritt the vision, sustainability, is a given, a non-negotiable goal; where the confusion and debate arises is in the context of the *process* towards achieving that goal. Not only is development, as discussed earlier in this chapter, subject to varying definitions, but the process of environmentally sustainable development can be viewed from differing ideological perspectives (for example, capitalist/Marxist, technocentric/ecocentric, eco-feminist and so on).

An analysis of sustainable development as a process is well beyond the scope of this chapter. The important point, however, is that all human existence and activity depends upon three sets of services provided by the natural world (Porritt, 2007, p36): the supply of resources to support human life and activity (a source function); the absorption and recycling of the waste produced by those activities (a sink function); and additional ecological services, such as climate regulation or pollination (a service function). A threat to the provision of any of these is, ultimately, a threat to human sustainability. Therefore, sustainability is underpinned by the following principles (Goodland, 1992):

- The stock of natural (non-renewable) resources should be exploited no faster than the rate at which substitute, renewable resources are developed;
- The rate at which waste is deposited back into the ecosystem should be relative to the assimilative capacity of the environment;
- Technological advance should focus on increasing efficiency rather than throughput;
- Global population levels and *per capita* levels of consumption should remain within the earth's capacity.

In practical terms, this suggests in turn that sustainable development, however defined, is dependent upon, on a global scale, sustainable production, sustainable consumption (or sustainable lifestyles) and equitable distribution of resources. The controversies and challenges facing sustainability and tourism are discussed in more detail in Chapter 3. However, the next section of this chapter will review the most recent stage of tourism's transformation from a catalyst of economic growth to a potential factor in sustainable development.

Sustainable tourism development

As discussed earlier, the roots of the concept of sustainable tourism development lay in the strategies for developing alternative forms of tourism that emerged in the 1980s, strategies which reflected the alternative development paradigm more generally. However, it is probably true to say that, whereas alternative development emerged as a result of the perceived failure of preceding paradigms to address widespread developmental challenges in general, such as poverty, unemployment and inequality, alternative tourism was advocated as the antithesis to mass tourism in particular. In other words, alternative tourism emerged primarily as a reaction to increasing concerns over the negative consequences of the production and consumption of a particular form of tourism (labelled mass tourism) rather than to concerns about tourism's relationship to development more generally. Indeed, even when the word 'sustainable' was first linked to tourism, it was suggested that for tourism development to be sustainable it should be based upon 'options or strategies considered preferable to mass tourism' (Pigram, 1990).

As a consequence, early conceptualizations of sustainable tourism development focused on what might be termed the sustainable development of tourism (or sustainable tourism) – that is, a 'tourism-centric' approach (Hunter, 1995) that has, as its prime objective, the preservation of the natural, built and socio-cultural upon which tourism depends, rather than on tourism's potential contribution to the sustainable development of a destination or region. As Butler (1993) noted, sustainable tourism 'may be thought of as tourism which is in a form which can maintain its viability in an area for an indefinite period of time', an interpretation that was reflected in early definitions. For example, in the first issue of the *Journal of Sustainable Tourism*, Bramwell and Lane (1993) defined sustainable tourism as 'a positive approach intended to reduce tensions and friction created by the complex interactions between the tourism industry, visitors, the environment and the communities which are host to holiday makers' whilst, more ambiguously and paraphrasing Brundtland's widely cited definition of sustainable development, the World Tourism Organization (WTO, now the United Nations World Tourism Organization or UNWTO) defined it as 'development ... [which] ... meets the needs of present tourists and host regions while protecting and enhancing opportunity for the future' (WTO/WTTC, 1996, p30).

Interestingly, a broader perspective was adopted at the Globe '90 Conference in Canada, an international conference held in Vancouver in March 1990 from which, as noted in the introduction to this book, emerged, amongst other things, a 'strategy for sustainable tourism development' (Cronin, 1990). Pre-empting Hunter's (1995) assertion that 'those who insert the word "tourism" between "sustainable" and "development" ... [should] ... ensure that, under all circumstances, the resultant principles of sustainable tourism development are also principles of sustainable development', the conference proposed three fundamental principles for sustainable tourism development (Cronin, 1990):

- *Tourism must be a recognized sustainable economic development option, considered equally with other economic activities when jurisdictions are making development decisions.*
- *There must be a relevant tourism information base to permit recognition, analysis and monitoring of the tourism industry in relation to other sectors of the economy.*
- *Tourism development must be carried out in a way that is compatible with the principles of sustainable development.*

This approach explicitly aligns tourism with sustainable development and, to an extent, overrides the mass tourism–alternative tourism dichotomy referred to above. At the same time, however, it exposes tourism to the ambiguity and contradictions of the concept of sustainable development itself.

This issue is discussed in more detail in the next chapter, as is the tendency for tourism development in practice to reflect the 'tourism–centric' approach. Nevertheless, throughout the 1990s, innumerable policy documents, planning guidelines, statements of good practice, codes of conduct and other publications were produced, many reflecting the broader principles and objectives of sustainable development. Frequently, such documents focused on specific destinations, tourism developmental contexts (for example, national parks and protected areas) or sectors of the industry; equally, numerous labels were attached to what Mowforth and Munt (2003) refer to as new forms of tourism, such as agri-tourism, soft tourism, nature tourism, cottage tourism, alternative tourism, green tourism and, of course, ecotourism, each embracing a variety of principles and planning guidelines. As a consequence, sustainable tourism development in the 1990s was characterized by a lack of both definitional consensus and a common set of principles. However, there is no doubt that, typically, most tourism planning and policy documents attempted to embrace the principles of sustainable development, in particular the sustainable use of natural resources and the appropriate development of tourism within physical and socio-cultural capacities, as well as the principles of participation, self-reliance and endogenous development (see Table 2.6).

Perhaps in recognition of the diversity of approaches to sustainable tourism development and, more specifically, the inherent divisiveness of segregating new, alternative and, implicitly, sustainable forms of tourism from

Table 2.6 Sustainable tourism development: A summary of principles

The conservation and sustainable use of natural, social and cultural resources is crucial. Therefore, tourism should be planned and managed within environmental limits and with due regard for the long-term appropriate use of natural and human resources.

Tourism planning, development and operation should be integrated into national and local sustainable development strategies. In particular, consideration should be given to different types of tourism development and the ways in which they link with existing land and resource uses and socio-cultural factors.

Tourism should support a wide range of local economic activities, taking environmental costs and benefits into account, but it should not be permitted to become an activity which dominates the economic base of an area.

Local communities should be encouraged and expected to participate in the planning, development and control of tourism with the support of government and the industry. Particular attention should be paid to involving indigenous people, women and minority groups to ensure the equitable distribution of the benefits of tourism.

All organizations and individuals should respect the culture, the economy, the way of life, the environment and political structures in the destination area.

All stakeholders within tourism should be educated about the need to develop more sustainable forms of tourism. This includes staff training and raising awareness, through education and marketing tourism responsibly, of sustainability issues amongst host communities and tourists themselves.

Research should be undertaken throughout all stages of tourism development and operation to monitor impacts, to solve problems and to allow local people and others to respond to changes and to take advantages of opportunities.

All agencies, organizations, businesses and individuals should cooperate and work together to avoid potential conflict and to optimize the benefits to all involved in the development and management of tourism.

Source: adapted from: ETB, 1991; Eber, 1992; EC, 1993; WTO, 1993; WTO/WTTC, 1996

traditional, mass (inherently unsustainable) tourism, there has more recently been a shift in favour of more all-embracing definitions of sustainable tourism development that also reflect the distinction between sustainability (the vision) and sustainable development (the process or means of achieving sustainability) within the contemporary development literature. In other words, the focus of tourism development has become sustainability, although it remains unclear whether it is the sustainability *of* tourism or the sustainability *through* tourism that is the objective. For example, the UNWTO's most recent conceptualization of sustainable tourism development states that:

> *Sustainable tourism development guidelines and management practices are applicable to all forms of tourism in all types of destinations, including mass tourism and the various niche tourism segments. Sustainability principles refer to the environmental, economic and socio-cultural aspects of tourism development, and a suitable balance must be established between these three dimensions to guarantee its long-term sustainability.* (UNWTO, 2008d)

Thus, the 'triple bottom line' of economic, environmental and socio-cultural sustainability is explicit within the definition of sustainable tourism development, as detailed in the UNWTO's statement that sustainable tourism should:

- *Make optimal use of environmental resources that constitute a key element in tourism development, maintaining essential ecological processes and helping to conserve natural heritage and biodiversity.*
- *Respect the socio-cultural authenticity of host communities, conserve their built and living cultural heritage and traditional values, and contribute to inter-cultural understanding and tolerance.*
- *Ensure viable, long-term economic operations, providing socio-economic benefits to all stakeholders that are fairly distributed, including stable employment and income-earning opportunities and social services to host communities, and contributing to poverty alleviation.* (UNWTO, 2008)

The UNWTO also suggests that stakeholder participation and continual monitoring of progress are fundamental requirements, whilst meaningful tourist experiences should also remain an objective. However, the only reference to wider (sustainable) development is the objective of contributing to poverty alleviation. In contrast, *Making Tourism More Sustainable: A Guide for Policy Makers* (UNEP/WTO, 2005, p9) claims that 'tourism is in a special position in the contribution it can make to sustainable development', thus explicitly locating tourism in a broader developmental context. The report goes on to state that:

it must be clear that the term 'sustainable tourism' – meaning tourism that is based on the principles of sustainable development – refers to a fundamental objective: to make all tourism more sustainable. The term should be used to refer to a condition of tourism, not a type of tourism.

Again, however, it is unclear to what extent tourism's contribution to sustainable development can be achieved in practice; for example, whilst the *Making Tourism More Sustainable* report provides a range of strategies and guidelines, there is little evidence in the supporting case studies of progress towards broader sustainability as opposed to the development of specific sustainable tourism projects.

A critique of the concept of sustainable tourism development is the subject of the next chapter. Nonetheless, as this chapter has demonstrated, although tourism has long been seen as a potential catalyst of or contributor to development, development itself remains a dynamic, elusive concept that is difficult to define. As a goal or objective, it has long been accepted that economic growth on its own is not synonymous with development; although, for many societies, economic growth and development remains a prerequisite, other indicators of human development, including basic needs, equality, opportunity, political and cultural freedom, and the environment have come to be embraced as goals of development. The objectives of tourism development, however, remain focused on economic indicators, whether as a source of income and employment or for financially supporting conservation work. Indeed, it remains unclear how tourism itself might contribute to wider human development goals.

As a process, too, development has been viewed within an evolving para-digmatic framework, from growth-based modernization theory through to contemporary approaches to sustainability. Tourism development in part-icular has run in parallel with these transformations in development theory, from tourism as economic growth to sustainable tourism development. How-ever, whilst an evident relationship exists between tourism development and modernization theory, direct links between tourism and subsequent develop-ment paradigms are more coincidental than purposeful, although most recent conceptualizations of sustainable tourism explicitly align tourism with sustainable development. In fact, although there is now recognition that all forms of tourism should be embraced within the sustainability objective, tourism development in practice continues to reflect economic growth models of development – that is, the reason for developing or promoting a tourism sector has always been, and remains, its potential to generate income and employment. Certainly, as the following case study of tourism in Cuba demonstrates, not only is it the economic imperative that drives the development of the tourism sector on the island but also the nature of that development is shaped by the domestic and international political-economy within which the Cuban tourism sector operates.

Case study: Tourism development in Cuba

(Note: this case study draws on a more detailed analysis by Sharpley and Knight, 2009.)

It has long been recognized that the planning and development of tourism is inextricably linked with the state. More specifically, some degree of government intervention, appropriate to the social, political and economic characteristics or developmental needs of the destination region, is necessary throughout the tourism planning and development process. The nature of that intervention is a function of both economic and political factors: in less developed countries, the state typically adopts a more managerial and entrepreneurial role, whilst tourism planning and development also tends to reflect both the structures and political ideologies of the state and its international political-economic relations.

This is certainly the case with Cuba, a country that, despite the collapse of communism elsewhere and the increasing pervasiveness of market-led economies, is one of world's few remaining centrally-planned economies and the only one to boast a significant international tourism sector. Since finally achieving independence from Spanish colonial rule in May 1902, the island has experienced three distinct political-economic phases during which the relationship between tourism development, the state's political structures and policies, its economy and its international relations is clearly evident.

In the first phase, particularly between 1945 and 1959, tourism became a major economic sector on the island, providing a vital source of both employment and hard currency – by the late 1950s, some 350,000 (mostly American) tourists arrived annually; tourism was second only to sugar in terms of foreign currency earnings and Cuba had become the hub of international tourism in the Caribbean. At the same time, the characteristics of tourism during this phase, in terms of both demand and supply, reflected the island's dependence on the US; not only did the US account for almost 90 per cent of international tourist arrivals but also the control and nature of tourism development reflected American dominance of the tourism sector on the island.

Following the 1959 revolution, however, the island entered a second political-economic phase that was to last until the collapse of the Soviet Union in 1989. Tourism was seen as a hedonistic vice incompatible with the aims of the new socialist regime and, as a consequence, all major international hotels were nationalized and the attention of the new revolutionary government focused primarily on socio-economic equality and the promotion of domestic tourism. By 1961, the year of the abortive Bay of Pigs invasion, international arrivals had fallen to just 4180 and, following President Kennedy's imposition of the embargo on all US trade with Cuba in 1962, Americans were no longer able to visit Cuba legally. With increasing economic dependence on the Soviet Union, international tourism was no longer considered a key economic activity.

Since the late 1980s, Cuba's third political-economic phase has been dominated by the remarkable revitalization of its tourism sector, driven primarily by the need to exploit new sources of foreign exchange in the post-Soviet era. Over a period of some 15 years, tourist arrivals in Cuba grew by an annual average of 17.5 per cent, reaching 1.9 million in 2003. By 2005, annual arrivals had increased to 2.3 million and the tourism sector was directly contributing some US$1.9 billion to the national economy. However, although the push to redevelop the tourism sector in the late 1980s is generally associated with the collapse of the Soviet Union, the subsequent dissolution of the Council for Mutual Economic Assistance (COMECON) and, hence, the loss of trade and aid arrangements that Cuba had enjoyed with the Eastern European Bloc, the roots of tourism's redevelopment in Cuba lay in the economic challenges facing the island in the early 1980s. Domestic economic growth had slowed dramatically as a result of poor harvests and low productivity whilst, from 1984, the country suffered a serious negative trade balance, largely as a result of a long-term decline in the volume of sugar exports combined with a collapse in the world sugar price during the first half of the decade. At the same time, the price of oil fell by some 40 per cent in 1986, significantly reducing hard currency earnings from oil re-exports. Under a sugar-for-oil barter agreement, Cuba imported almost all its oil from the Soviet Union. Surplus oil was then re-exported to earn hard currency and, by 1985, over 40 per cent of the island's hard currency income was generated from oil re-exports. Thus, domestic economic problems were compounded by worsening trade relations with market economies and, like many other developing nations at that time, Cuba faced significant problems in servicing its external (hard currency) debt.

As a consequence, the government was obliged to pursue western economic investment, primarily through joint ventures with western companies though under the control of so-called *sociedades anónimas*, or semi-autonomous state agencies, set up to attract western investment. International tourism was already being promoted – the Instituto Nacional de Turismo (INTUR) had been established in 1976 and by 1979 some 130,000 international arrivals were recorded, but from the mid-1980s tourism became a principal focus for economic development. Consequently, the state-controlled tourism development agency Cubanacán was established in 1987 followed by Gaviota in 1988 and, by 1989, the state earned around US$200 million from tourism. In other words, by the late 1980s, both the administrative and physical infrastructure, the great majority under state control and ownership, was in place for the further development of tourism. The subsequent collapse of the Soviet Bloc and its impact on the Cuban economy merely served to enhance the economic importance of tourism to the island.

Over a 15-year period from 1990, tourist arrivals increased sixfold and tourism-related income eightfold, whilst room capacity trebled (mostly in Havana and on the Varadero peninsula) and employment in tourism doubled. Nevertheless, the contribution of the travel and tourism industry to the economy remains, in a regional context, relatively limited, accounting for 3.5 per cent of total employment and 4 per cent of GDP. The wider travel and tourism economy contributes an estimated 11.2 per cent of employment and 13.1 per cent of GDP (WTTC, 2007a). However, travel and tourism represents over 40 per cent of all exports and 65 per cent of the export of services, demonstrating its importance as a source of foreign exchange earnings, although with an estimated 'leakage' rate of between 40 and 50 per cent, net earnings may be significantly lower. The key indicators of tourism in Cuba since 1990 are shown in Table 2.7.

Table 2.7 *Cuba: Key tourism indicators 1990–2005*

Year	Arrivals ('000)	% growth on year	Receipts ($US '000)	% growth on year	Average per person receipts (US$)	Hotel rooms
1990	340	–	243	–	714	12,900
1991	424	24.7	387	59.2	913	16,600
1992	461	8.7	443	14.5	962	18,700
1993	546	18.4	636	43.6	1169	22,100
1994	619	12.4	763	20.0	1236	23,300
1995	746	20.5	977	28.1	1311	24,200
1996	1004	34.6	1185	21.3	1180	26,900
1997	1170	16.5	1345	13.5	1149	27,400
1998	1416	21.0	1571	16.8	1110	30,900
1999	1603	13.2	1714	9.1	1069	32,300
2000	1774	10.7	1737	1.3	979	35,300
2001	1765	−0.5	1692	−2.6	959	37,200
2002	1686	−4.5	1633	−3.5	968	39,500
2003	1906	13.0	1846	13.0	968	40,800
2004	2048	7.5	1915	3.7	935	41,100
2005	2315	13.0	1920	0.3	829	42,600

Source: adapted from Espino, 2000; González, 2007; Grihault, 2007; UNWTO data

These figures demonstrate a declining rate of increase in arrivals (in 2006, arrivals fell by 4 per cent) and more significantly in receipts, with a significant reduction in per person average receipts. The key market is Canada (26 per cent), with the UK, Spain and Italy each accounting for around 7 per cent of arrivals.

Overall, then, since 1990 Cuba has emerged as, principally, a relatively cheap sun-beach, package/all-inclusive destination, albeit augmented by opportunities for cultural and sporting activities based upon the islands' historic and natural heritage. Dependent upon a number of key markets, the island attracts a relatively low level of repeat business and is, therefore, susceptible to changes in demand from those key markets. A recent decline in tourist arrivals may be largely attributable to a combination of higher prices and poor quality whilst, given the dependency of the Cuban economy on tourism as a source of foreign exchange, declining levels of tourism receipts, underpinned by a continuing fall in average tourist receipts, threaten the sustainability of the tourism sector and the economy as a whole. These problems may be exacerbated by a number of factors, including the following:

- Although the redevelopment of tourism was initially based upon international joint ventures with up to 49 per cent foreign ownership, the majority of hotels are now state owned with international involvement restricted to management contracts; just 14 hotels (5530 rooms) or 13 per cent of the total in Cuba are under joint ownership and international management. A further 44 per cent are state owned but under international management and the remaining 43 per cent are state owned and managed.
- State control of the tourism sector is manifested in five *sociedades anónimas* which, collectively, control the tourism sector, including hotels, restaurants, tourist cafés, tourist attractions, travel agencies and associated services, such as car rental and taxi services. Thus, all tourism industry employees, with the exception of expatriate workers, are state employees. Internationally operated hotels are obliged to hire employees through an employment agency and to pay established salaries (in US dollars) to the agency; employees are, however, paid at local rates in pesos.
- There are limited opportunities for self-employment within the tourism sector; self-employment is also tightly regulated, with monthly licence fees charged irrespective of earnings; it has also, however, been restricted in recent years as part of the state's recentralization efforts.
- State tourism enterprises are largely controlled by the communist party and the Revolutionary Armed Forces. Consequently, employment is also controlled by these organizations. For example, Cuban employees working for internationally-managed hotels are selected not by the international partner but by the Cuban state, usually on the basis of patronage or relationships with the communist party. Individuals without links to the communist party/state machinery are unlikely to have access to the tourism sector other than through informal or illegal occupations.

Tourism's role in economic growth and development in Cuba is, therefore, restricted by limited opportunities for international investment (and a lack of investment by the state), limited opportunities for self-employment and entrepreneurship and a system of employment and remuneration that provides subsistence level wages. Employees receive no incentive or productivity payments and, as a consequence, motivation and productivity are low. Collectively, these contribute to low levels of quality and service within the tourism sector, further compromising the economic sustainability of tourism in Cuba.

3
Sustainable Tourism Development: A Critique

Since it first emerged some 20 years ago, the concept of sustainable tourism development has achieved and maintained, at least in policy circles, 'virtual global endorsement as the new [tourism] industry paradigm' (Godfrey, 1996, p60). Although academic interest in the subject as a general perspective on tourism development has in more recent times begun to wane, with the attention of researchers turning to more specific and, arguably, more practical themes, such as poverty reduction through so-called pro-poor tourism (Harrison, 2008) or the relationship between tourism and climate change, sustainable tourism development has remained a guiding principle of tourism policy and planning at global and national levels. In fact, in contrast to typically idealistic, politically attractive yet vague policy statements during the 1990s, global tourism development policy has not only become more explicitly aligned with the principles of sustainable development, but it has also embraced a more pragmatic perspective in addressing contemporary developmental challenges. For example, the United Nations World Tourism Organization's (UNWTO's) Sustainable Tourism-Eliminating Poverty (ST-EP) programme highlights tourism's potential contribution to achieving the Millennium Development Goal (MDG) of halving the incidence of global poverty by 2015, whilst the Davos Declaration on climate change and tourism (UNWTO-UNEP-WMO, 2007, p2) states that:

> Given tourism's importance in the global challenges of climate change and poverty reduction, there is a need to urgently adopt a range of policies which encourages truly sustainable tourism that reflects a 'quadruple bottom line' of environmental, social, economic and climate responsiveness.

Whilst there is no indication of what 'truly' sustainable tourism might comprise, the addition of climate to the traditional 'triple bottom line' of sustainability objectives represents a significant globally-focused departure from previous, destination-oriented sustainable tourism development policies. It is also interesting to note that the World Summit on Sustainable Development (WSSD), held in Johannesburg in 2002 (also known as 'Rio +10', following on from the Earth Summit in Rio de Janeiro in 1992), explicitly refers to sustainable tourism development in its Plan of Implementation:

> *Promote sustainable tourism development, including non-consumptive and eco-tourism ... in order to increase the benefits from tourism resources for the population in host communities while maintaining the cultural and environmental integrity of the host communities and enhancing the protection of ecologically sensitive areas and natural heritages. Promote sustainable tourism development and capacity-building in order to contribute to the strengthening of rural and local communities.* (WSSD, 2002, IV, Para 43)

The issues of poverty reduction and climate change are returned to later in this chapter. The point here, however, is that from the outset sustainable tourism development has also been subjected to constant and, in some quarters, vociferous criticism. In the introduction to this book, for example, reference is made to what was probably the first conference (held in Edinburgh in 1990) dedicated specifically to sustainable tourism development. Here, sustainable tourism was described as 'an idea whose time has come' (Howie, 1990, p3) yet, at the same conference, a dissenting voice attempted to 'introduce a measure of realism into the ... proceedings', raising the now familiar issue of scale: 'we have, on the one hand, a problem of mass tourism growing globally, out of control, at an alarming rate. And what is our answer? Small scale, slow, steady controlled development' (Wheeller, 1990, pp61–2). Since then, the criticisms levelled against the concept of sustainable tourism development have become more theoretically informed, sophisticated and compelling, yet many of the initial concerns remain both valid and unresolved.

The purpose of this chapter is to critique sustainable tourism development, both reviewing the principal arguments against the concept and exploring its relevance within the broader understanding of tourism as a socio-economic phenomenon as outlined in Chapter 1. In so doing, it suggests that the time has come to 'close the book' on sustainable tourism development in favour of an alternative perspective on tourism, development and the environment. This is not to say, of course, that the notion of (environmental) sustainability should be rejected; as discussed in the last chapter, the sustainability of all human activity, including tourism, requires the support and maintenance of the services provided by the natural world – in short, the global ecosystem's source, sink and service functions. Thus, sustainability remains a prerequisite of tourism development. However, beyond this principle of sustainability, the relationship between tourism, development and the environment may be enhanced by an alternative perspective on the development of tourism that, unhindered by the prescriptive principles of sustainable tourism development, seeks to optimize tourism's socio-economic contribution within environmental parameters.

But what is sustainable tourism development?

Just as its parental paradigm, sustainable development, is widely and variously defined (Rogers et al, 2008), so too has sustainable tourism development been subject to diverse interpretation and multiple definitions. Indeed, despite the degree of academic attention paid to the subject over the last 20 years, the failure to achieve definitional consensus, or even an agreement over terminology, is seen by some as evidence of the inherent fallibility of the concept (Twining-Ward and Butler, 2002; Liu, 2003). Nevertheless, it is both possible and necessary to consider what is meant (or should be meant) by the term as a basis for critically appraising its viability as a practical and widely applicable approach to the development of tourism.

As with development more generally (see Chapter 2), there are three senses in which sustainable tourism development can be thought about: as a goal or vision; as a process of achieving or moving towards that vision; and as the policies, plans and activities of those organizations, whether private, public or third sector, that are involved in sustainable tourism development. In principle, distinguishing between these three senses should be a relatively simple task; in practice, however, this is not the case, the distinctions between them frequently being unclear or confused. In particular, the objective or purpose of sustainable tourism development (the vision) is often blurred with the principles, policies and processes for its achievement, to the extent that the concept of sustainable tourism development is most commonly associated with a prescriptive set of principles and practices rather than a broader objective. Moreover, those principles and practices inevitably focus upon the development of tourism itself, particularly in destinational contexts, with two related consequences. Firstly, rather than the vision defining the plans, policies and processes necessary for its achievement, the vision is defined by those plans, policies and processes. Secondly, that vision or objective is, typically, *sustainable tourism*, or sustaining the resources upon which tourism as a specific socio-economic activity depends, rather than *sustainable tourism development*, or broader sustainable development through tourism. In other words, and as noted in the previous chapter, sustainable tourism development is most frequently conceptualized from a parochial, 'tourism-centric' (Hunter, 1995) perspective that emphasizes the sustainability of tourism itself rather than tourism's potential contribution to sustainable development more generally.

The extent to which this implicitly reflects, or is an inherent weakness of, the concept of sustainable tourism development is considered shortly. However, although its roots lie in the concerns over the environmental consequences of rapid and unplanned mass tourism development and the subsequent emergence of alternative (to mass) tourism, early conceptualizations of sustainable tourism development explicitly linked tourism to sustainable development. Reference has already been made to the Globe '90 Conference which proposed that tourism should be viewed as a 'sustainable economic development option' and that tourism development should be 'compatible with the principles of sustainable development' (Cronin, 1990). Though not referring to sustainable development specifically, Müller (1994) similarly suggested that:

...the objective of environmentally and socially compatible tourism has a lot to do with the frequently quoted ... strategy of 'qualitative growth'. 'Qualitative growth' can be described as any increase in quality of life (i.e. economic growth and subjective well-being) which can be achieved with less use of non-renewable resources and less stress on the environment and people.

In effect, Müller linked tourism development with what has come to be referred to as sustainability, firmly establishing sustainable tourism development, in principle, as a vehicle of or contributor to sustainable development more generally. That is, sustaining tourism is a prerequisite for, but is subordinate to, sustainable development within the overall objective of sustainable tourism development. He also proposed that sustainable tourism development could be conceptualized as a 'magic pentagon' (Figure 3.1) within which a balance is achieved between the five objectives so that no single one predominates.

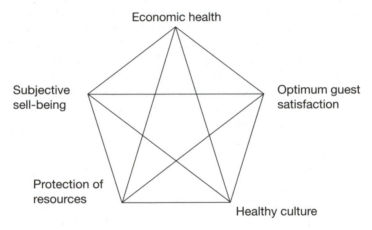

Figure 3.1 *Müller's 'magic pentagon'*

Since these early attempts to establish the meaning, scope and purpose of sustainable tourism development, numerous definitions have been proposed. These, according to Lim and Cooper (2009), have been criticized for being 'ambiguous, vague, sectoral, too conceptual and confused with environmental issues'. However, such a volume and diversity of definitions is not surprising given the vagueness and adaptability of multiple contexts of the concept. As a recent United States Agency for International Development (USAID) report notes, the term 'sustainable tourism' means different things to different stakeholders:

The private tourism industry views it largely in economic and marketing terms. How can the tourism market be sustained and grow in the long term? The local community may see it in terms of socio-economic benefits and cultural preservation...

> *An environmental NGO would present more of an ecological perspective. How can tourism help to sustain, rather than mar, natural systems?* (USAID, 2005, p5)

Thus, it may simply be the case that sustainable tourism development (and, indeed, sustainable development) defies precise definition, though this is not necessarily a problem – a precise definition might disenfranchise those stakeholders whose views are not expressed in or embraced by that definition, whilst definitional vagueness serves to enhance the political acceptability of the concept (Robinson, 2004).

Nevertheless, both initial and contemporary definitions of sustainable tourism development align it closely with the broader principles of sustainable development or sustainability. For example, *Making Tourism More Sustainable: A Guide for Policy Makers* (UNEP/WTO, 2005), referred to in the previous chapter, explains that sustainable tourism is a 'condition' relevant to all forms of tourism and simply means tourism that is developed in accordance with the principles of sustainable development. In other words, sustainable tourism development can be thought of as one of numerous sectors or processes that contribute to sustainable development, itself a process leading towards sustainability or harmony between humankind and the natural world. Thus, a working definition proposed by Butler in 1993 remains relevant, with slight adaptation, to contemporary conceptualizations of sustainable tourism development:

> *Tourism which is developed and maintained ... in such a manner and at such a scale that it remains viable over an indefinite period and does not degrade or alter the environment (human and physical) in which it exists to such a degree that it prohibits the successful development and wellbeing of other activities and processes.* (Butler, 1993, p29)

Such an approach is reflected in numerous policy documents. For example, the South Australian Tourism Commission's report *Design Guidelines for Sustainable Tourism Development* (SATC, 2007) explicitly links sustainable tourism to the three sustainability pillars (economic, social and environmental) of sustainable development, and proposes 12 principles for sustainable tourism (Table 3.1).

However, despite the recognition of the need to align tourism development with the principles of sustainable development, the extent to which this can be done in practice remains questionable. Many contemporary definitions of sustainable tourism continue to display a local destination, tourism-centric perspective (see, for example, definitions listed on the *Sustainable Tourism Gateway*: www.gdrc.org/uem/eco-tour/eco-tour.html), reflecting just one of a number of criticisms that have long been levelled at the concept. Therefore, the following section explores the relationship between sustainable development/sustainability principles and tourism as a specific socio-economic activity as a basis for identifying and reviewing the inherent weaknesses and limitations of sustainable tourism development.

Table 3.1 *Principles of sustainable tourism*

Minimizing environmental impacts:
Tourism should consider both local and global environmental impacts.

Achieving conservation outcomes:
Tourism should seek to support the conservation of natural areas, habitats and wildlife and minimize damage to them.

Being different:
One of the keys to successful and sustainable tourism is achieving a clear sense of difference from other competing destinations.

Achieving authenticity:
The attractions most likely to be successful and of enduring appeal are those which are genuinely relevant to local history, industry, culture, lifestyle and natural resources.

Reflecting community values:
This means representing the past, present and future aspirations of the local community in a living and dynamic way.

Understanding and targeting the market:
Understanding broad market trends and the needs and expectations of specific segments is critical.

Enhancing the experience:
The 'bundling' of attributes enhances the appeal of a place and the likelihood of visitation.

Adding value:
Adding value to existing attributes achieves a richer tourism experience and helps to diversify the local economy.

Having good content:
Telling the story provides a more rewarding experience and ultimately helps conserve the destination.

Enhancing sense of place through design:
Good design respects the resource, achieves conservation, reflects community values and is instrumental in telling the story.

Providing mutual benefits to visitors and hosts:
Tourism is an economic and community development tool and must take into account the benefits that both the host community and the visitor seek.

Building local capacity:
Good tourism businesses get involved with the community and collaborate with other businesses and stakeholders and help to build local capacity.

Source: adapted from SATC, 2007

Aligning tourism with sustainable development

As discussed in Chapter 2, sustainable development's emergence and evolution into the dominant development paradigm of the 1980s and 1990s was founded upon two principal influences, summarized by Kemp at al (2005) as:

> *increasingly worrisome evidence of ecological degradation and other biophysical damage, both despite and because of the greater wherewithal provided by greater economic growth, and the largely disappointing record of post-WWII 'development' efforts, particularly the persistence, and in some places worsening, of poverty and desperation in a period of huge overall increases in material wealth.*

The first attempt to reconcile these two challenges within a common approach was manifested in the World Commission on Environment and Development's report *Our Common Future* (WCED, 1987) – widely referred to as the Brundtland Report – which not only sought to link poverty alleviation, environmental improvement and social equity with sustainable economic growth but also established a controversial foundation for the contemporary debate on sustainability and sustainable development (Mebratu, 1998). In particular, Brundtland argued that a five- to tenfold increase in global economic activity was necessary to meet the needs of the world's poor but, recognizing the environmental costs of overdevelopment, that such an increase should be within the world's technological and environmental limits. The proposed solution, of course, was sustainable development, famously but vaguely defined as development that 'meets the needs of the present without compromising the ability of future generations to meet their own needs' (WCED, 1987, p48). Therein, however, lies one of the principal and most enduring criticisms of sustainable development: namely, that it is an oxymoron. In other words, it is argued by many that development based upon economic growth, particularly on a scale proposed by Brundtland, cannot be reconciled with environmental sustainability.

Since the publication of *Our Common Future*, sustainable development has attracted a variety of criticisms with respect to both its philosophical underpinnings and practical implementation issues. Though significant to the sustainable development debate in general, they are also of relevance to a critique of sustainable tourism development in particular for the simple reason that if tourism is to be developed according to the principles of sustainable development, then by association it is open to the same criticisms as sustainable development. Therefore, in the context of this chapter, it is useful to consider briefly these criticisms.

It is important to note that the constituent elements of sustainable development – that is, development and environmental sustainability (Lélé 1991) – are themselves variously definable according to philosophical perspectives. The different meanings of development have already been explored in Chapter 2 but, with respect to the environment, competing positions on environmental protection and management existed well before the emergence of sustainable development. Thus, as Robinson (2004) explains, there has long been a distinction between 'preservationists', or those who, reflecting a Romantic or spiritual philosophy, sought to preserve natural areas in a pristine, undeveloped state, and 'conservationists', who favoured the protection of natural areas and resources for subsequent utilitarian exploitation. A similar debate focused on alternative means of managing environmental resources; a 'preservationist' stance favours a transformation in values and lifestyles (for example, the adoption of sustainable consumer behaviour), whilst the 'conservationist' stance promotes efficiency gains and technological solutions. Similar to the techno-centric and eco-centric perspectives on the environment (O'Riordan, 1981), these opposing positions were inherited by sustainable development and remain a contested area within the relevant literature. In short, the concept of sustainable development is built on what might be described as unstable foundations.

To further complicate matters, the meaning and objectives of sustainable development have been interpreted according to a variety of different 'schools'. On the one hand, there exists 'mainstream' sustainable development (Adams, 2001), or what Mebratu (1998) refers to as the 'institutional' version of sustainability. Advocating reform rather than rejection of economic-growth based development, mainstream sustainable development is based upon capitalistic free markets, economic growth, technological advance and environmental self-regulation, and closely reflects the institutional agenda for sustainable development. On the other hand, the 'ideological' version of sustainability (Mebratu, 1998) offers a variety of more radical countermeasures which seek to replace the dominant mainstream approach to the environment and sustainable development. These include eco-feminism, eco-socialism, eco-anarchism and eco-theology and are explored in some depth by Adams (2001). Mebratu (1998) also proposes a third school, the 'academic' version of sustainability, which introduces environmental economics, deep ecology and social ecology into the sustainable development 'mix'. A full consideration of these is beyond the scope of this chapter. The main point is, however, that definitions, meanings and interpretations of sustainable development inevitably reflect a diversity of philosophical, ideological, socio-cultural and political-economic positions and, also inevitably, mainstream sustainable development will continue to be criticized by alternative schools. At the same time, there are those who reject the concept of sustainable development outright. Lomborg, for example, is a well-known sceptic who claims that the state of the natural environment is much healthier than suggested by environmentalists, that human activity has little environmental impact and that the solution lies in a combination of economic growth and technological advance (Lomborg, 2001).

Specifically, sustainable development is criticized on a number of grounds. Reference has already been made to its inherently contradictory nature (Redclift, 1987): semantically, 'sustainability requires a long term perspective and something that is sustained should be enduring and, ideally, exists in perpetuity. In contrast, development implies change' (Wall and Mathieson, 2006, p290) whilst, at a more practical level, it is certainly logical to ask how development, necessitating resource exploitation, can be achieved at the same time as environmental sustainability. It is also contradictory within a global developmental context, in the sense that it is criticized for being just another manifestation of western hegemony. As Adams (2001, p108) observes, 'mainstream sustainable development is firmly anchored within the existing economic paradigms of the industrialized North', yet it is the dominance of western economic models that contemporary perspectives on human development seek to challenge.

Sustainable tourism development can, in particular, be viewed as a manifestation of western hegemony or, as Cater describes in a powerful critique of ecotourism, as a specific nature-based form of sustainable tourism, a western construct: 'There is a lot to suggest that, because the origins of ecotourism lie in Western ideology and values, and its practice is frequently dominated by Western interests, the advocacy of ecotourism as a universal template arises from Western hegemony' (Cater, 2006). Though she focuses specifically on ecotourism, the points Cater raises are of direct relevance to sustainable tourism development more generally. In particular, she cites the role and influence of the UNWTO and World Travel and Tourism Council (WTTC), their 'blueprints' for sustainable or 'new' tourism and the funding of local ecotourism projects by organizations such as the World Bank's Global Environmental Facility or Conservation International based upon an explicitly western development agenda. At the same time, the design of ecotourism (and, implicitly, sustainable tourism) projects based upon the mainstream conservation-for-development perspective and western notions of nature fails to account for alternative natures or, more broadly, alternative environments and interpretations of conservation and guardianship. In other words, different natures and environments are, in essence, the product of socio-cultural, political and economic processes and, thus, sustainable tourism/ecotourism development constructed on western-centric interpretations of nature may not match local constructs of nature, with the result that tourism may be seen as a form of eco-colonialism. This also points to the more general criticism of sustainable tourism development that its principles and objectives are typically manifested in overarching sets of prescriptive guidelines, usually based upon managing the limits (according to western criteria) of acceptable environmental and social change, that fail to account for the almost infinite diversity of tourism development contexts and, importantly, the meaning, knowledge and understanding of those environments amongst local communities.

Other criticisms of sustainable development are usefully summarized by Robinson (2004) under three broad headings:

1   Vagueness/ambiguity: sustainable development is not only vague in terms of meaning and definition; it is also semantically ambiguous. Does it mean development that can be sustained, thereby giving precedence to development (as in the tourism-centric perspective on sustainable tourism

development), or development restricted by environmental sustainability limits? Either way, as already noted, such vagueness is not necessarily a problem, although it does give rise to a number of fundamental questions, including: what should be developed sustainably (personal wealth, national wealth, human society, ecological diversity)? Against what baseline can sustainable development be measured? Who is responsible for sustainable development? And, under what political-economic conditions is sustainable development viable?

2   Hypocrisy: sustainable development language or eco-speak may be used to disguise unsustainable activities through what is now referred to as 'greenwashing'. Products, services and other activities may have green or eco-labels attached to them (ecotourism being an obvious example in the context of this book), yet their environmental credentials may be difficult to identify or measure. On the one hand, such greenwashing may serve to assuage the environmental 'guilt' of consumers; tourists may feel more 're-sponsible' by going on ecotours, for example, whether or not such holidays are genuinely 'green' (Robbins, 2008). On the other hand, as Robinson (2004) suggests, the challenge of hypocrisy has stimulated the development of sustainability indicators (interestingly, the World Tourism Organization (now UNWTO) investigated the development of international indicators for sustainable tourism in the early 1990s – see WTO (1993)) and accreditation schemes, a number of which exist for tourism at the national (for example, Australia's Nature & Ecotourism Accreditation Program, or NEAP) and international levels, such as Green Globe, administered by EC3, a wholly-owned subsidiary of Australia's Sustainable Tourism Co-operative Research Centre (STCRC).

3   Delusions: According to Robinson (2004), the most significant criticism of sustainable development is that it fosters delusions, in two particular ways. The first relates to the oxymoronic character of the concept discussed above, in as much as it provides a framework for continued development under the possibly misguided belief that such development can occur within biophysical limits, either through efficiencies or technological advance. Thus, a continuing focus on 'sustainable' growth and development may simply hasten ecological collapse, an argument which is of direct relevance to tourism. Secondly, he suggests that sustainable development, as currently conceptualized, may 'distract us from the real problems and potential solutions by focussing our attention on the wrong issues' (Robinson, 2004). Sustainable development remains rooted in the 'conservationist' perspective mentioned earlier; it is anthropocentric in that it seeks ways of sustaining the environment for human use, whereas a biocentric approach would suggest the need to find a more appropriate relationship between humanity and nature. Equally, issues of power, exploitation and privilege are not adequately addressed although, from a more radical viewpoint, these may be the real challenges facing human well-being. Again, sustainable tourism development may, in this sense, be delusional. That is, the 'problem' of tourism may not lie in the mis-management or excessive

exploitation of resources; in fact, tourism may not be a problem at all, but a symptom of a more deep-rooted issue, namely: the state of contemporary modern societies that encourages people to travel in greater numbers and ever more frequently. Thus, the solution, as the late Krippendorf argued some years ago, may be to improve people's day-to-day social well-being, thereby reducing their need to 'escape' periodically from modern society (Krippendorf, 1987). However, this would, of course, represent a threat to the potential, economic lifeline provided by tourism to societies and nations with few alternative developmental opportunities.

Beyond these general criticisms of sustainable development and their relevance to tourism, sustainable tourism development itself may be critiqued from two perspectives. Firstly, if tourism should be developed according to the principles of sustainable development, as proposed by contemporary policy documents and guidelines suggest, then it is logical to explore the extent to which the production and consumption of tourism can reflect or match the principles, objectives and determinants of sustainable development. Secondly, the principles and objectives of sustainable tourism development may be compared with the contemporary nature and character of tourism itself.

Tourism as sustainable development

In the very first issue of the *Journal of Sustainable Tourism*, Mckercher argued that the actual process of developing tourism 'provides the catalyst for a wide range of potential impacts' (McKercher, 1993). This reflects the existence of what he referred to as 'fundamental truths' that are relevant to all forms of tourism development. Though widely cited in the literature, it is worthwhile summarizing these 'truths' here as they not only remain relevant today but also identify potential disarticulation points in the relationship between tourism and sustainable development. They are also key issues to be considered when exploring alternative approaches to tourism, development and the environment. McKercher proposed eight 'truths', as follows:

1 *As a major global activity, tourism consumes resources, creates waste and requires significant infrastructural development*: Tourism inevitably exploits resources (natural, man-made, cultural and human) both through its development and through the activities of tourists. It also creates waste, both at the destinational level and more generally in terms of pollution and greenhouse gas (GHG) emissions.
2 *The development of tourism may, potentially, result in the over-exploitation of resources*: the widely recognized 'impacts' of tourism (Wall and Mathieson, 2006) occur when resources are exploited beyond a sustainable threshold.
3 *In order to survive and grow, the industry has to compete for scarce resources*: tourism most commonly competes with the needs of local communities, such as public spaces or specific resources (water, power, etc.).

4 *The tourism industry is predominantly made up of smaller, private-sector businesses striving for short-term profit maximization*: tourism business decisions will typically prioritize profit generating activities as opposed to 'cost' activities, such as environmental protection.

5 *As a global, multi-sectoral industry, tourism is impossible to control*: the tourism industry or production system comprises an enormous number of primarily small to medium size enterprises within diverse sectors. Public sector administration is also fragmented and, as a result, overall policy for and control of tourism is unachievable.

6 *'Tourists are consumers, not anthropologists'; they do not wish to 'work' at being tourists*: tourists are consumers of tourism products and experiences, frequently displaying excessive and hedonistic behaviour (expenditure, alcohol consumption, sexual activity, etc) that are in opposition to 'responsible' behaviour.

7 *Most tourists seek relaxation, fun, escape and entertainment*: the main function of tourist destinations and attractions is to entertain tourists and to meet their expectations/needs. Thus, existing attractions may need to be modified to meet these needs

8 *Although an export, tourism experiences are produced and consumed 'on site'*: interaction (and consequential impacts) between tourists and the local environment and communities is inevitable.

Three primary issues which relate to the three requirements of sustainable development identified in Chapter 2 (sustainable production, sustainable consumption and equitable distribution) emerge from these 'truths'. Firstly, and contrary to earlier misconceptions, tourism is not a 'smokeless' industry. As has long been recognized, the development or 'production' of tourism may result in significant environmental and social impacts for destinations. To an extent, such impacts are inevitable and, more contentiously, should be both expected and accepted by destination communities – it could be argued that for destinations to seek the economic benefits of tourism whilst expecting tourists to behave 'responsibly' (in the broader sense of responsible tourism) is a case of having one's cake and eating it. Nevertheless, effective management of the development of tourism may be necessary to contain its negative consequences within acceptable limits.

Secondly, just as sustainable development more generally is dependent upon sustainable consumption, the consumption of tourism in particular is of direct relevance to its (sustainable) developmental contribution – the scale, scope and nature of the demand for tourism represent significant challenges to sustainable development. However, despite surveys which suggest that tourists are increasingly aware of the impacts of their activities and, hence, claim they adapt their behaviour accordingly (for example, selecting tourism products/holidays on environmental criteria), there is little empirical evidence of the adoption of such behaviour in practice. Thirdly, the structure, scale and inherent power relations of the tourism industry raise important questions about the equitable ownership and distribution of, and access to, tourism resources, as well as the likelihood of a collective, uniform commitment to the principles of sustainable development on the part of the industry.

The significance of these issues becomes evident when the characteristics of tourism are 'mapped' against the fundamental elements of sustainable development. It has, of course, long been argued that 'sustainable tourism should be consistent with the tenets of sustainable development' (Stabler and Goodall, 1996, p170); Table 3.2 summarizing the key principles and require-ments of (mainstream) sustainable development as currently defined within the literature and the extent to which tourism development may meet these, provides a useful, if somewhat simplistic, basis for doing so. As is evident from the table, the compatibility between tourism and sustainable development is weak in a number of areas, reflecting some of the now well-rehearsed arguments against sustainable tourism development (see Sharpley, 2000a). These are widely discussed in the literature but, nevertheless, a brief overview not only reveals the inevitability of the tourism-centric perspective on sustainable tourism development discussed earlier, but it also hints at alternative ways of looking at tourism and its potential developmental contribution.

Scale: An holistic perspective

A fundamental principle of sustainable development is the need for an holistic perspective; that is, development can only be sustainable if it is considered within a global political, economic, socio-cultural and ecological framework. With regards to tourism, this requirement can be looked at from two perspectives. Firstly, it suggests that the development of tourism should be viewed in its totality within the context of global economic, social and environmental systems. Moreover, all forms of tourism (domestic/international, mass/niche, day trips/overnight stays, and so on) should be considered, in terms of their benefits and costs, within that global framework. As Butler (1998, p30) argues, 'to apply the principles ... [of sustainable development] ... to any single sector is unrealistic and ... sustainability in that sense is unachievable. Since the global environment represents the only complete discrete system, it is only at that scale, if any, that true sustainability can be achieved'.

However, although more recent conceptualizations now refer to sustain-able tourism development as a condition applicable to all types of tourism as opposed to specific, niche tourism products such as ecotourism, it is quite evident that, given the scale, complexity and diversity of tourism and its inter-connectedness with other sectors and activities, such a global perspective is difficult, if not impossible, to achieve. Nevertheless, certain aspects of tourism, in particular the issue of tourism-related GHG emissions and the consequential potential effects of climate change, demand a global approach. This issue is returned to in more detail in Chapter 4 but, generally, a fundamental challenge to sustainable tourism development is the inherent unsustainability of most modes of transport (Høyer, 2000); even if a particular local tourism project meets sustainability criteria, the travel component may render it unsustainable in a broader environmental context. By definition, tourism involves travel by

Table 3.2 *Sustainable development and tourism: Principles and objectives*

	Sustainable development	Tourism compatibility
Fundamental principles:	• *Holistic approach*: development and environmental issues integrated within a global social, economic and ecological context • *Futurity*: focus on long-term capacity for continuance of the global ecosystem, including the human sub-system • *Equity*: development that is fair and equitable and which provides opportunities for access to and use of resources for all members of all societies, both in the present and future	Tourism is a diverse, multi-sectoral and fragmented sector, comprising innumerable small business and organizations. Hence, limited possibilities for an holistic approach Tourism businesses typically focus on short-term profit objectives Access to tourism as a social activity and an economic sector remains inequitable
Development objectives:	• Millennium Development Goals • Improvement of the quality of life for all people: education, life expectancy, opportunities to fulfil potential • Satisfaction of basic needs; concentration on the nature of what is provided rather than income • Self-reliance: political freedom and local decision-making for local needs • Endogenous development	Tourism brings potential economic benefits; broader developmental benefits are not an inevitable outcome of tourism, and are dependent on local socio-cultural and political-economic conditions Ecotourism projects may contribute to basic needs and cultural sustainability Low compatibility between tourism and development gaols
Sustainability objectives:	• Poverty reduction • Sustainable population levels • Minimal depletion of non-renewable natural resources • Sustainable use of renewable resources • Pollution emissions within the assimilative capacity of the environment	Specific programmes (pro-poor tourism) may be targeted at specific groups Local projects may minimize resource depletion and enhance environmental conservation Tourism (i.e. travel) will inevitably be a major contributor of greenhouse gases
Requirements for sustainable development:	• *Sustainable consumption*: adoption of a new social paradigm relevant to sustainable living • *Sustainable production*: biodiversity conservation; technological systems that can search continuously for new solutions to environmental problems • *Sustainable distribution*: international and national political and economic systems dedicated to equitable development and resource use • Global alliance facilitating integrated development policies at local, national and international levels	Limited evidence of 'responsible' tourism consumption in practice. 'Tourists are consumers, not anthropologists' Some evidence of 'corporate social responsibility' and environmental programmes within some organizations: also benchmarking schemes Limited opportunities for global alliances or global systems equitable access to and distribution of tourism resources

Source: adapted from Telfer and Sharpley, 2008, p36

land, sea or air, and the environmental impact of air travel in particular (both aircraft emissions and infrastructural developments related to air transport) has not only emerged as a major contemporary concern, but is also a highly controversial topic (Becken and Simmons, 2005; Becken and Hay, 2007). For example, in the UK, government proposals to build a third runway at Heathrow airport are supported by the business community on economic grounds, but are opposed by environmental groups for directly contradicting the government's commitment to reducing carbon emissions. Certainly, carbon offset schemes such as those provided by ClimateCare (www.climatecare.org) or Virgin Atlantic's in-flight scheme run in partnership with Myclimate (www. myclimate.org) offer air passengers the opportunity to offset (voluntarily) their journey's carbon footprint, yet the benefits of such schemes are insignificant in relation to total tourism-related carbon emissions.

Secondly, sustainable tourism development should, as recommended at the Globe '90 Conference, be 'considered equally with other economic activities when jurisdictions are making development decisions' (Cronin, 1990). In practice, however, sustainable tourism development strategies tend to focus almost exclusively on tourism itself at the destinational level and attention is rarely paid to the relationship between tourism and other economic sectors and the relative merits of alternative developmental strategies – should opportunities for such alternative strategies exist. Thus, although an over-dependence on tourism has long been recognized as a potential cost of tourism development – and is, by definition, unsustainable – tourism is frequently 'permitted' to become the dominant economic activity, even when developed within a sustainable planning framework (Wall, 1993). This again points to the difficulty in achieving a common, holistic approach, even within a local or regional tourism system within which political-economic tensions and influences come into play.

Futurity: A question of timescales

According to Butler (1998, p31), it is 'in the case of the timescale involved that sustainable development offers the greatest difficulties in the context of tourism'. Generally, the long-term sustainability of any form of developmental activity, including tourism, can only be judged at some time in the future when 'it can be ascertained if the demands of the activity have not prejudiced the needs of what were future generations when the development began' (Butler, 1998, p31). Of course, we have no way of telling in the present what the needs of future generations will be, to what extent those needs will be met and how the inevitable social, economic, political and technological transformations in the intervening period will influence the perception and satisfaction of needs. Thus, a particular 'sustainable' tourism project in the present may provide shorter-term social and economic benefits and be environmentally benign, but longer-term sustainability cannot, or should not, be claimed. This is one of the reasons that some critics of sustainable development, such as Beckerman (2002), argue that the greatest developmental challenge in the present is not environmental degradation but poverty and a lack of respect of human rights. Therefore, he advocates not 'sustainable development' but economic growth and a focus on global peace, harmony and freedom as the basic requirements for development in the present and as a legacy for future generations.

More specifically with regards to the futurity of tourism development, two further points should be emphasized. Firstly, the tourism production system or 'industry' comprises innumerable, principally small, private sector, profit-motivated businesses. Consequently, although longer-term business success (or, in a narrow sense, sustainability) is an objective for most businesses, and whilst there is undoubtedly evidence of some tour companies and other organizations adopting a longer-term 'responsible' perspective (Mann, 2000), it is likely that short-term profit or even survival remains the dominant concern for most tourism-related businesses. Certainly, the global financial crisis in 2008 and the consequential decrease in the growth rate of international tourism (at the time of writing, the UNWTO forecasts growth of between 0 and 2 per cent for 2009) has not only served to focus the attention of all travel and tourism businesses on the financial 'bottom line', but is an acute example of the influence of factors external to the tourism system.

Secondly, and related, future tourism demand and flows, upon which the developmental contribution of tourism depends, cannot be accurately predicted. Despite forecasts of 1.6 billion international arrivals by 2020 (WTO, 1998) and the recent inception of a WTO project to predict global tourism activity through to 2030, such global estimates are likely to be, at best, estimates, albeit based on historical data that would logically suggest continuing growth. However, such growth cannot be taken for granted, dependent as it would be on greater (and more equitable) prosperity and access to travel opportunities around the world. Moreover, global forecasts do not account for changes in demand at the destinational level which may be influenced by a variety of factors, including competition from other destinations, changes in taste and travel behaviour, political and economic conditions and so on. In particular, the high price elasticity of tourism creates significant volatility in demand. For example, in late 2008 the Icelandic Krona's exchange rate decreased significantly and, as a consequence, tourism from the UK (one of Iceland's major markets) grew by some 20 per cent as visitors sought to take advantage of cheaper accommodation and other services. More generally, Liu (2003) notes that, although global tourist arrivals increased by 2.4 per cent in 1997, one-fifth of WTO member countries experienced a decline in international arrivals that year. In short, futurity as defined by sustainable (tourism) development requires a predictability of demand growth and flows that cannot be taken for granted.

Equity: A fair share of the benefits of tourism

Sustainable development calls for both intra- and inter-generational equity – that is, fair and equitable opportunities for the development of all people, both in the present and the future. The challenge of futurity as addressed in the preceding section is also relevant in this context, in as much as inter-generational equity, particularly through tourism, can be neither predicted nor guaranteed. Moreover, despite the emphasis on community-based, participatory or collaborative planning and management within contemporary sustainable tourism development policies, the objective being a more equitable access to and share of the benefits accruing from tourism development (as discussed shortly, one of the principal objectives of contemporary pro-poor tourism projects), in reality both the flows and structure of international tourism suggest that equitable development through tourism is unachievable.

As summarized in Chapter 1, major international tourism flows and the corresponding economic benefits remain highly polarized and regionalized, the main beneficiaries being Europe and North America. Indeed, the disparity between the developed and less developed world in terms of their relative share of tourist arrivals and receipts is thrown into stark relief by comparing the numbers of tourists to population levels and, hence, benefit per head of population from tourism. According to Hall (2007a), the tourist-population ratio for Africa is 1:26.6 compared with 1:1.6 for Europe, although US$1 of tourist spend is, of course, of far greater significance to someone with an annual income of, say, US$310 (average per capita income in The Gambia) than to a European with an annual income of some US$33,000. Despite an increase in arrivals in many less developed countries, again tourism has been monopolized by a few such countries to the exclusion of the rest (Brohman, 1996b). Further, in many less developed countries which are popular destinations (and, of course, in developed countries, although this issue is, perhaps of less relevance to them), tourism is frequently distributed unevenly, diminishing the opport-unities for equitable development even on a national scale (Opperman, 1993), though infrastructural development, transport links and other factors must also be taken into account. Often, tourism development is influenced by local power relationships which favour the political or economic elite, or is concentrated within all-inclusive enclave resorts, thereby potentially contributing to socio-economic inequities. However, it should be pointed out that, although such resorts may not meet broader sustainability criteria, they may provide significant employment opportunities that would not otherwise exist.

The structure of the international tourism production system may also exacerbate inequalities. To a great extent, the 'three most lucrative components of ... [international] ... tourism (i.e. marketing and the procurement of customers, international transportation, and food and lodging) are normally handled by vertically integrated global networks' (Brohman, 1996b). Consequentially, a significant proportion of tourism earnings may be lost through overseas 'leakages', whilst frequently there is a lack of local community control over re-source use. In fact, local communities may be denied access to tourism resources altogether. One extreme example of this has been the recent alleged selling off of prime coastal sites in Cambodia to international investors and developers (Levy and Scott-Clark, 2008). Following the defeat of the Khmer Rouge regime in 1979, thousands of displaced Cambodians moved to previously unoccupied coastal areas and islands, setting up small communities and businesses. By

2006, these communities were firmly established and enjoyed the right under Cambodian law to remain there permanently. Additionally, according to Levy and Scott-Clark, the entire coast and all islands had been designated as public land and, hence, protected from sale or development. Nevertheless, since 2006, much of this land has been sold to foreign investors and property developers, ostensibly for the development of tourist resorts but in practice as speculative land investments. As a consequence, many communities have been displaced and no longer enjoy access to the land on which they had lived and prospered for over 20 years.

More generally, the patterns and structures of international tourism, particularly between the metropolitan centres and peripheral developing nations, reinforce rather than diminish global socio-economic inequities. There are, of course, numerous examples of localized, small-scale developments that attempt to reverse this trend – annual schemes, such as the Responsible Tourism Awards or Tourism for Tomorrow Awards, usually include projects that have promoted wildlife conservation or local community development, or that have reduced poverty, strengthened the role of women and so on – yet much tourism continues to reflect the problems of dependency and the dominance of multinational corporations.

Development and sustainability objectives

If tourism is to be consistent with the principles of sustainable development then, logically, both the developmental and sustainability objectives of tourism should reflect those of sustainable development, as summarized in Table 3.2. However, the extent to which these objectives may be realized in practice remains uncertain. Many of the challenges to tourism's potential contribution to development, as currently conceived, have already been identified in this chapter, whilst doubts have long been expressed about the developmental benefits, however defined, of tourism more generally (de Kadt, 1979). The challenges include the scale and structure of the tourism production system and its inherent power relations, the patterns, ownership and control of tourism development at the destination, and the typically western-centric character or western dominance of tourism development planning and policy. Collectively, these raise fundamental questions about the extent to which, if at all, tourism may contribute to the satisfaction of basic needs, self-reliance and human well-being in general, or developmental targets as proposed by the MDGs in particular. In other words, although tourism is typically associated with certain economic benefits, including income, employment and, in the case of international tourism, foreign exchange earnings, which may then stimulate wider economic growth (economic growth generally being considered within mainstream development theory as prerequisite to broader development), it is unclear how these benefits may be translated into development more generally. Within any national, regional or local developmental context, the extent to which development occurs, or may be stimulated by tourism in particular, is determined by a variety of both endogenous and exogenous political, economic, socio-cultural and environmental factors. Thus, some countries have been able to exploit tourism successfully as an engine of socio-economic development, one notable example being the island of Cyprus; others, however, lacking appropriate economic, human, political, technological or infrastructural resources, have been unable to do so. Consequently, not only should tourism be considered primarily (in developmental terms) as an economic activity, but general assumptions about its contribution to development, however defined, cannot be made, it being necessary to assess tourism's potential within the political-economic contexts of individual countries. In short, if a variety of factors has generally prevented a certain country from developing, there is no reason to assume that tourism specifically is immune to those factors.

It is, perhaps, for this reason that increasing attention is now being paid to tourism's potential contribution to poverty alleviation especially. Implicitly, tourism has always been viewed as a means of reducing poverty through its contribution to income and employment generation. Since the late 1990s, however, a more explicit and, according to Harrison (2008), 'appealing moral focus' on tourism's potential contribution to poverty alleviation has emerged in the form of so-called pro-poor tourism. The roots of pro-poor tourism are described in some detail in the literature (for example, Scheyvens, 2007) but, essentially, in 1998 the Department for International Development (DFID) in the UK commissioned collaborative research into the extent to which outbound tourism from the UK could contribute to reducing poverty in destination areas. The ensuing report identified a number of strategies for addressing the needs of the poor through tourism and, subsequently, two contributors to the original research, the Overseas Development Institute (ODI) and International Institute for Environment and Development (IIED) joined forces with the International Centre for Responsible Tourism – now based at Leeds Metropolitan University in the UK – to form the Pro-Poor Tourism Partnership (PPTP). The Partnership went on to produce a number of case studies of pro-poor tourism in practice in a number of countries, such as The Gambia, Namibia, Nepal, Uganda and Ecuador, as well as numerous working papers on topics relevant to pro-poor tourism (these can all be accessed on the PPTP's website: www.propoortourism. org.uk).

The concept of pro-poor tourism was subsequently adopted by the UNWTO in 2002 within its ST-EP scheme, which both focuses on poverty reduction within the UNWTO's technical assistance programme and funds research, collaboration and technical assistance through the ST-EP Foundation and Trust Fund. The UNWTO highlights seven mechanisms for alleviating poverty through tourism (UNWTO, 2008e):

1 employment of the poor in tourism enterprises;
2 supply of goods and services to tourism enterprises by the poor or by enterprises employing the poor;
3 direct sales of goods and services to visitors by the poor (informal economy);
4 establishment and running of tourism enterprises by the poor – e.g. micro, small and medium sized enterprises (MSMEs), or community-based enterprises (formal economy);

5 tax or levy on tourism income or profits with proceeds benefiting the poor;
6 voluntary giving/support by tourism enterprises and tourists;
7 investment in infrastructure stimulated by tourism also benefiting the poor in the locality, directly or through support to other sectors.

The ST-EP scheme is interesting on two counts. Firstly, the juxtaposition of 'eliminating poverty' with 'sustainable tourism' is, perhaps, curious. The seven mechanisms propose a targeted (on the poor), as opposed to holistic, and highly interventionist approach and, although poverty elimination is seen as a prerequisite to environmental sustainability, the specific strategies of ST-EP, and indeed those of pro-poor tourism, do not address environmental challenges. Thus, not only does ST-EP contrast with the broader aims of sustainable tourism development but it also appears to be a return to top-down, neo-liberal development policy. Secondly, the adoption of poverty reduction by the UNWTO as a specific development aim of tourism may be seen as a tacit admission that, certainly within the context of least developed countries, sustainable tourism development is unachievable.

More recently, academic attention has turned to pro-poor tourism and it has been criticized on both conceptual and practical grounds (see, for example, the special issue of *Current Issues in Tourism*, Vol 10, 2007). These are succinctly reviewed by Harrison (2008) who concludes that conceptual criticisms are misplaced, whilst advocates of pro-poor tourism also accept its practical limitations. Pro-poor tourism is, in simple terms, a practical initiative that seeks to enhance the net benefits of tourism to the poor, to transform the distribution of the economic benefits of all tourism (including mass tourism) to the advantage of poor people who fall outside, or are unable to gain access to, the formal tourism sector. Therefore, whilst it may be easy to criticize pro-poor tourism from a variety of theoretical perspectives, it undoubtedly represents a positive, practical attempt to optimize the benefits of tourism to a specifically targeted group and, as Harrison (2008) suggests, what is needed is 'a balanced approach to, and research *over time* on, the development of tourism in its various forms, how it is articulated, and whom it benefits' [emphasis in original].

To return to the sustainability objectives of tourism as summarized in Table 3.2, again many of the limitations of tourism have already been identified in this chapter. Tourism is, undoubtedly, a 'resource hungry' activity, although most, if not all, sectors of the industry or production system have a vested interest in protecting and enhancing the resources upon which their businesses depend. This may result from either a genuine commitment to sound environmental practice, from the adoption of ethical business principles (Hultsman, 1995) or for more pragmatic business reasons: enhancing profit levels. Nevertheless, the scale and diversity of the tourism system itself may militate against environmental sustainability, whilst 'irrespective of the scale of analysis, [tourism] cannot exist in isolation from regional, national and global resource utilisation concerns' (Hunter, 1995). Thus, whilst there is no doubt that some organizations and industry sectors have, to a lesser or greater extent, attempted to implement sound environmental business practices, and whilst technology has been harnessed to some degree to reduce tourism's impacts, such as quieter and more fuel-efficient jet engines (though, ironically, more efficient aircraft technology has served not only to increase tourist numbers but also to provide access to more distant, fragile environments), it will only be when the entire tourism sector – and, indeed, when tourists themselves – adopt more sustainable practices that it will be able to contribute to global sustainability.

Sustainable development and contemporary tourism

From the preceding discussion, it is clearly evident that to develop tourism according to the principles of sustainable development (as currently advocated by the UNWTO and other bodies concerned with development, the environment and tourism at the global level) is a morally desirable but fundamentally idealistic and impractical objective. Certainly, as this chapter has demonstrated, the concept of sustainable tourism development has long been subject to a variety of criticisms that remain relevant today whilst, more particularly, there is a lack of 'fit' between tourism as a specific socio-economic activity and the principles and objectives of sustainable development.

To summarize the key points, as a concept sustainable tourism development is ambiguous, subject to multiple definitions and based upon fragile theoretical foundations. At the practical level, it suffers a number of limitations. Generally, as an overarching, prescriptive approach to tourism development that largely reflects rigid, western-centric perspectives on nature, conservation and economic-based modernization, and manifested primarily in managerialist 'blueprint' sets of principles and guidelines, it is simply unable to account for the global diversity and dynamism of tourism development contexts. To put it another way, each and every tourism destination is unique in terms of its environmental, political, economic and socio-cultural characteristics, as well as in terms of the scale, scope, nature and stage of development of its tourism sector. By implication, each destination has a unique set of developmental needs that tourism may or may not be able to address. As the following case study demonstrates, as a consequence of the global financial crisis in 2008, tourism in Iceland has been transformed from a relatively niche activity (in terms of national economic development policy) into a potential lifeline for the island's economy. It is, therefore, unrealistic to propose a set of developmental guidelines, or even a universal perspective or 'condition' of tourism applicable to all tourism development contexts.

More specifically, although there are undoubtedly numerous examples of contemporary, localized tourism projects that display some characteristics of sustainability, when tourism is considered from an holistic, global perspective, it is evident that the three determinants of sustainable development (namely sustainable production, sustainable consumption and equitable distribution) simply cannot be collectively achieved. Not only does tourism impose significant strains on the global ecosystem's source and sink functions, but the structure, ownership and control of tourism production, along with patterns and trends in tourist flows, suggest that equitable access to the benefits of tourism is unlikely to occur. Indeed, some would argue that contemporary 'sustainable' tourism policies merely serve to enhance such inequity. At the same time, and reflecting what many advocates of sustainable development recognize to be the greatest challenge to its achievement (Porritt, 2007), sustainable tourism development requires a transformation in social values and lifestyles in general and the adoption of 'responsible' consumption in particular. However, despite surveys which suggest greater environmental awareness on the part of tourists, there is little evidence to suggest that, in reality, more appropriate or responsible forms of tourism consumption are being adopted. In fact, recent reports suggest that the global financial crisis has had a negative influence on people's attitudes: although climate change still attracts widespread concern, fewer are now prepared to change their lifestyles or to spend more to protect the environment.

This last issue points to another criticism of sustainable tourism development identified by Liu (2003). He argues that as it draws heavily on the sustainable development literature, which assumes constantly increasing demand for resources, sustainable tourism development essentially adopts a supply-side perspective. That is, in addition to assuming (incorrectly) the increasingly widespread adoption of responsible tourism consumption, the dynamics of global tourism demand are overlooked. His specific point is that demand management is necessary at the destinational level in order to take into account trends and transformations in demand and the threat of competition in order to enhance the potential sustainability of tourism. Nonetheless, it also hints at a broader and, for this chapter, final challenge to the concept of sustainable tourism development. By definition, the concept is concerned with tourism but, from a demand perspective, we must return to the question: what is tourism?

In Chapter 1, it was suggested that contemporary tourism can no longer be considered a distinctive, definable social activity. Whereas tourism was once an activity defined by particular temporal and spatial characteristics and, largely, by specific modes of behaviour, it has now merged into other activities and practices to the extent that, according to some, it is no longer distinguishable as a separate social institution. Places where people travelled from are now places tourists travel to, whilst day-to-day 'normal' activities, such as shopping, surfing the internet, engaging in sport, eating out or watching television, frequently include a 'touristic' element. Moreover, for some, such as those who move or retire to a 'place in the sun', it is unclear when or if they cease to be tourists and become residents (or 'permanent tourists'). In short, nowadays people are tourists most of the time (Urry, 1994), perhaps reflecting the alleged post-modern condition of contemporary modern societies. Certainly, although many 'traditional' forms of tourism – the skiing holiday, the two-week summer holiday and so on – are still highly popular (and undoubtedly represent social conceptualizations of tourism), in practice the distinctions between tourism, recreation and leisure activities are less clear whilst 'non-leisure' travel, including business, education and spiritual travel, are considered to be a sector of the tourism market. Thus, as suggested in Chapter 1, what is referred to as tourism may be better thought of as a manifestation of contemporary mobilities.

The question then to be asked is: is it possible or logical to separate tourism from other mobilities (or indeed, to separate specific forms of tourism from others) as a focus or target for sustainable development? In fact, is it possible to separate sustainable mobilities from sustainable development more generally? For example, worldwide, cities are, collectively, one of the most visited tourist destinations and, for many, tourism is an essential element of the local economy. At the same time, however, cities 'occupy just 2 percent of the land surface of the Earth, but consume more than 75 percent of resources used every year' (Porritt, 2007, p315); more specifically, they are also centres of mobility, both within their boundaries and as hubs for national and international mobilities. Therefore, the 'sustainable city' cannot be seen as distinct from sustainable mobilities or sustainable development and, logically, nor can tourism. This, in turn, suggests that the answer to the question above is 'no'. It is not logical to separate tourism from sustainable development but, as we have already seen (and in danger of creating a circular argument), tourism cannot meet the requirements of sustainable development.

Nevertheless, there is a variety of social and economic practices, commonly considered to be or referred to as tourism, that undoubtedly brings benefits to both receiving (destination) and generating regions though, at the same time, giving rise to environmental consequences. There still remains the need, therefore, to seek ways of optimizing those benefits within the broader aim of environmental sustainability, though not bound by the rigid (and unworkable) guidelines of sustainable tourism development. As this book will go on to suggest, the way forward, perhaps, lies in refocusing away from tourism as a broad socio-economic phenomenon towards a more specific analysis of it as a form of capitalistic production and consumption and, in particular, of the 'capitals' that underpin the supply of tourism products and services to meet the needs of tourists. In other words, it will suggest that the identification and effective exploitation of these capitals, whether in the context of a destination or a particular sector of the production system, may provide a more appropriate basis for optimizing tourism economic developmental benefits within environmental parameters.

There is not, of course, anything radical in this approach. The concept of green capitalism, or combining economic growth with environmental sustainability, has been explored in depth by others (for example, Ekins, 2000) whilst, more specifically, rural resources have been re-conceptualized as 'countryside capital' as a basis for the more effective planning and management of rural tourism (Garrod et al, 2006). Nor is it the intention here to propose a new paradigm of tourism development. Rather, the purpose is to stimulate debate and research into ways of developing and promoting tourism that are disconnected from the concept and terminology of sustainable development. As a first step, it is necessary to explore in general the transformations – often referred to collectively as globalization – that are occurring in the world within which tourism exists and with which it interacts and, in particular, contemporary perspectives on development within an alleged 'post-development' era. It is to these issues that the next chapter turns although, perhaps by way of introduction, the following case study of tourism in Iceland provides an example of the implications of the inter-connectedness (or 'globalization') of the world economy, specifically the effects of the global financial crisis that, it is generally accepted, originated in the US sub-prime mortgage market.

Case Study: Iceland – national bankruptcy and tourism

According to the United Nations Development Programme's (UNDP's) most recent Human Development Report (UNDP, 2006), Iceland is the world's most developed nation, occupying, as it has done for a number of years, the top position on the annual Human Development Index (HDI). Riding on what has been referred to as an 'economic miracle' (Jónsson 2006) – since 1990, economic liberalization, privatization, tax cutting and other policies have underpinned dramatic economic growth in Iceland – its population now enjoy one of the highest levels of wealth in the world, an extensive welfare system, high life expectancy and low unemployment. However, the global financial crisis of 2008 served to demonstrate the fragility of that economic miracle. Concerns about the Icelandic economy being the most over-heated in the Organisation for Economic Co-operation and Development (OECD) countries had been expressed two years previously (Hall, 2006) but, as a result of the so-called 'credit crunch' and the subsequent collapse of its banking system, the International Monetary Fund (IMF) approved a US$2.1 billion loan to Iceland in November 2008, with further loans of US$2.5 billion from other Nordic countries to follow. The IMF loan, the first to a European nation since 1976, was significant not only for preventing national bankruptcy but also for signalling the end to Iceland's economic miracle. It also contributed to increased attention being paid to tourism and its potential contribution to economic growth.

Located in the north Atlantic some 800km northwest of Scotland and 287km east of Greenland, Iceland covers a land area of 103,000sq km. Geologically, it is a young country, situated on the mid-Atlantic ridge, the seam between the American and Eurasian plates; it continues to experience volcanic and geothermal activity. Much of its landscape reflects this continuing activity. The uninhabited interior consists of mountains and high plateaus and almost 12 per cent of the land area is glaciated; conversely, just 20 per cent is available for habitation and other use. Iceland is also socio-culturally a young country. Although visited by Irish monks and Norse settlers in the 7th century, the first permanent settlers arrived in 874 and the island continued to be settled by people of Celtic and Norse through to the 13th century. However, it is home to one of the world's first parliaments: the Alþing, still the country's parliament, first met in 930 at Pingvellir, now a major cultural tourist attraction on the island. More than 60 per cent of the current population of 313,000 lives in the capital, Reykjavik, and its neighbouring towns in the southwest corner of the island.

The location and geology of Iceland have long determined the characteristics of its economy. Not surprisingly, fishing has been the principal driver of economic growth. Since the mechanization of the fishing fleet in the early 20th century (Karlsson, 2000), commercial fishing and fish processing have remained the island's major export and an important source of employment. In 2006, marine products accounted for almost 34 per cent of exports of goods and services (56 per cent of exports of goods), although their contribution to export earnings has fallen in recent years as manufacturing's share has increased. In particular, the island's plentiful, relatively cheap and environmentally clean supply of geothermal power has been exploited to develop the energy-intensive production of aluminium and, collectively, manufacturing products now represent 25 per cent of exports of goods and services (34.4 per cent of goods). In 2005, 6.1 per cent of the working population of 161,000 was employed in fishing and fish processing and 10.1 per cent in manufacturing, but 71.8 per cent was employed in the service sector. However, tourism has also emerged in recent years as an important sector of the Icelandic economy. In 2006, tourism accounted for 4.2 per cent of total employment, contributed 4.1 per cent of gross domestic product GDP and almost 13 per cent of the export of goods and services (Statistics Iceland, 2008).

Iceland has long been a destination for tourists, drawn by its image of a place of natural extremes, a land of glaciers, volcanoes, fjords and geysers, yet also a place of long dark winters, cool summers and, frequently, unfavourable weather conditions. However, its relative inaccessibility and its reputation as an expensive destination (as Gössling (2006) notes, the prices of food, accommodation and local transport services are well above those in most other European destinations, whilst comparatively limited air services to the island further increase the costs of visiting the island) have, until recently, contributed to relatively low numbers of tourist arrivals. Between 1950 and 1970, tourist arrivals increased from just 4,300 to 53,000. By 1990, the figure stood at almost 142,000 but, since then, the number of tourists visiting Iceland has increased rapidly, particularly since 2000. Tourist arrivals reached 485,000 in 2007, representing an absolute rise of 60 per cent since the start of the decade (see Table 3.3).

As can be seen from Table 3.3, tourist receipts, which include tourist expenditure in Iceland on accommodation, food, transport and other related products, as well as air fares paid on Icelandic carriers, have also increased significantly. Nonetheless, it is interesting to note that, although tourism is often considered to be one of Iceland's fastest growing sectors, its relative contribution to the economy has, in fact, demonstrated limited growth between 1990 and 2006. For example, in 1990, tourism represented 3.7 per cent of GDP and 10.9 per cent of the export of goods and services; by 2006, these had increased to 4.1 per cent and 12.7 per cent respectively. This suggests that the growth in tourism has reflected the growth in the economy more generally, that tourism is, in a sense, 'holding its own' rather than out-growing other sectors.

This may be explained, in part, by the characteristics of tourism in Iceland, which may be summarized as follows:

Table 3.3 *Tourist arrivals: Iceland 1990–2007*

Year	Arrivals	Receipts* (IK mn)	Year	Arrivals	Receipts* (IK mn)
1990	141,718	13,572	1999	262,219	27,498
1991	143,413	14,158	2000	302,900	30,495
1992	142,561	13,363	2001	296,000	37,720
1993	151,728	15,742	2002	277,900	37,137
1994	169,504	17,804	2003	320,000	37,285
1995	177,961	19,918	2004	360,392	39,335
1996	195,669	20,755	2005	374,127	39,760
1997	210,655	22,006	2006	422,288	46,945
1998	232,219	26,336	2007	485,000	n/a

Note: * Receipts include tourist expenditure in Iceland and on air fares with Icelandic carriers.
Source: adapted from Statistics Iceland, 2008

- Highly seasonal: although tourist arrivals are spread throughout the year, particularly since Reykjavik has been promoted to the short-break market, tourist arrivals remain highly seasonal. This is, perhaps, not surprising given the short days and poor weather during winter which mean that July and August remain peak months. In 2007, for example, just over 50 per cent of total nights in hotels and guest houses were recorded in the summer season period of June to September. As a consequence, of course, hotel occupancy levels vary throughout the year, from an average high of 75 per cent in July (2007) to 25 per cent in January, though occupancy levels in hotels and guest houses in Reykjavik are higher than average throughout the year.
- Relatively limited markets: Iceland is dependent on a small number of key tourist markets. The Nordic countries provide, collectively, the largest number of visitors, accounting for around a quarter of all arrivals; however, the UK is the largest single market (approximately 16 per cent of total arrivals), with Germany and North America also important sources of tourists. Thus, the island's tourist economy remains susceptible to changes in those markets.
- Short length of stay: According to information provided by the Icelandic Tourism Board, the average length of stay is 10.4 nights in the summer and 5 nights in winter (ITB, 2005). However, a comparison of tourist arrivals against total nights in all types of accommodation suggests that the average length of stay is between three and four nights, although certain groups of tourists (for example, independent tourists staying in hostels or campsites) undoubtedly stay longer. Thus, the evidence suggests that Iceland is a relatively short stay destination, perhaps reflecting the high cost of tourism to Iceland and the fact that, for most visitors, many of the main attractions and activities can be undertaken within a five-day period
- Lack of geographical spread: related to the above point, tourism in Iceland is spatially restricted. That is, although accommodation and other facilities are available all around the island, the majority of overnights stays are

spent within the Reykjavik area and most tourist activity occurs within day trip distance from the capital. This is partly due to the fact that the largest proportion of Iceland's hotel and guest house accommodation is, unsurprisingly, to be found in the capital, although other areas offer a good supply of accommodation (Table 3.4). At the same time, however, many of the island's natural and cultural attractions can be visited in day trips from the capital, and activities such as boat trips and whale-watching also commence from Reykjavik harbour. Thus, in 2007, almost 75 per cent of all overnight stays in hotels and guest houses were in those located in Reykjavik.

Table 3.4 *Hotels and guest houses in Iceland by region 2007*

Region	No. of hotels & guest houses	No. of bedspaces
Reykjavik region	69	7248
Southwest	8	480
West	31	1465
Westfjords	27	905
Northwest	22	820
Northeast	53	2665
East	44	2004
South	57	3226
Total	311	18,832

Source: adapted from Statistics Iceland, 2008

The limited relative (as opposed to absolute) growth of tourism may also be explained by the fact that Iceland continues to be an expensive destination (though the collapse in the value of the Icelandic Krona in late 2008 resulted in a 20 per cent increase in tourism from the UK), that it attracts a niche market and that access to the island is restricted to the extent that the majority of flights to the island are operated by Icelandair and Iceland Express. Nevertheless, there are evident opportunities for the further development of tourism as an economic sector in Iceland, opportunities that have been recognized by the Icelandic Tourism Board within its policy for developing new products, reducing seasonality, opening new markets and improving the distribution of tourism around the island. Moreover, in 2008 state responsibility for tourism moved from the Ministry of Transport to the Ministry of Industry as evidence of a shift in perceptions of the role of tourism, whilst a projected growth in tourist arrivals to 1 million by 2017 is seen by some as an unofficial target for the development of the sector (Jóhannesson et al, forthcoming). However, although such growth could have significant environmental impacts (and given the centrality of the natural environment to the island's image and tourism product), there has been, and continues to be, a surprising lack of planning and control at the national level with respect to the environmental sustainability of tourism. The industry and, in particular, the tour companies that exploit the natural environment remain largely unregulated and few, if any, have achieved international certification recognition (Jóhannesson et al, forthcoming). Therefore, although tourism in Iceland may assume a more significant future role in the island's economy, a more comprehensive approach to planning and, perhaps, regulating tourism at the national level may be necessary.

4

Tourism, Globalization and 'Post-Development'

Tourism occurs within, and interacts with, a complex, multi-dimensional, multi-layered and dynamic world. In other words, the global tourism system's external environment comprises a variety of economic, political, cultural, technological, environmental and other elements that are not only inter-related themselves but that may also, individually or collectively, influence or be influenced by tourism. Moreover, these elements may interact with tourism at different levels. Political upheaval or natural disasters, for example, tend to have a local or regional impact (the events of '9/11', of course, being a notable exception), whereas economic factors may have more far-reaching implications. Certainly, the global financial crisis of 2008 is likely to have a major impact on tourism globally, at least in the shorter term (and, perhaps, may signal a fundamental change in the relationship between production and consumption more generally in the longer term). Only time will tell if the predicted zero or negative growth in international tourist arrivals materializes although, at the time of writing, there is widespread evidence of a dramatic downturn in tourism demand. For example, the demand for cruising has experienced a significant decline with some cruise lines reducing their operations, such as Royal Caribbean Cruises cutting several of its South American cruises as a result of poor levels of bookings (Starmer-Smith, 2008). Equally, the collapse of a number of airlines and tour operators during 2008 is attributable to the financial crisis and the problems associated with high oil prices earlier in the year.

More significantly, the global financial crisis is also evidence of trans-formations in the relationship between the different elements of tourism's external environment, of global political, economic and cultural change that is widely and collectively referred to as the process of 'globalization'. Over the last two decades, the 'phenomenon of globalisation – whether real or illusory – has captured the public imagination' (Held and McGrew, 2000, p1), although the term was first used in the 1960s at a time when political and economic interdependence between nations was becoming more evident.

However, it is since the late 1980s, a period that has witnessed momentous political and economic change (in particular, the collapse of communism and the virtually worldwide adoption of capitalism) as well as dramatic advances in and access to information and communication technology, that increasing academic and media attention has been paid to the concept of globalization. Seen as a potential 'analytical lynchpin' (Scholte, 2002) for exploring and explaining transformations in the contemporary social world, it refers generally to what many perceive to be increasing global interdependence and integration of trade, finance, communication, culture and technology or, as Wahab and Cooper (2001, p4) put it, to 'a world which, due to many politico-economic, technological and informational advancements and developments, is on its way to becoming borderless and an interdependent whole'. Nonetheless, globalization remains a highly contested concept. For some, it 'has become a pervasive instrument in the reorganization of the world' (Reid, 2003, p37); for others, it is just a convenient way of describing various political, economic and cultural transformations or a contemporary, fashionable term for the centuries old process of internationalization: 'globalisation, under other names, is not a new concept but rather an acceleration of trends that have been active for decades or even centuries' (Fayos-Solà and Bueno, 2001, p46). For yet others, globalization is a myth, for the simple reason that many of the processes and transformations that it purports to describe or explain do not occur at the global level (Hirst and Thompson, 1999).

Nevertheless, there are certain processes or activities that, since the 1960s, have become more global in scope, scale and, importantly, inter-connectedness, though whether these have contributed to or merely reflect what is referred to as globalization remains a matter of debate. For example, production and trade, financial services, flows of capital, technology, information and people all occur and are inter-related at the global level, whilst tourism in particular is seen by many to be a potent symbol of globalization. Specifically, it is interesting to note that in the early 1990s one of the major transformations identified with globalization was the internationalization of public debt in the US: 'Americans could enjoy through debt a higher level of consumption than their production would otherwise have paid for because foreigners were ready to accept a flow of depreciating dollars' (Cox, 1991, p338). It was, of course, the internationalization of US debt, specifically related to the sub-prime mortgage market, that sparked the 2008 'credit crunch'; a national, sector-specific debt problem became a globalized financial crisis.

Cox identifies five other transformations that are indicative of globalization: the internationalization of production; the internationalization of the state (that is, the dominant role played by supra-national bodies); uneven development, with some nations becoming relatively poorer; global migration patterns (both legal and illegal) from the less developed to the developed world; and, the 'peripheralization of the core' (Cox, 1991, p340), or increasing numbers of socially-excluded, powerless poor living amongst the affluent. Whether these transformations are indeed evidence of globalization, whether they are causes or outcomes of globalization, or whether it is even possible to consider them from a global perspective remains uncertain. For example, and as discussed later in the chapter in the context of tourism's development role, the inability of the world's poorest nations to achieve any measurable economic growth or development is largely attributable not to global influences but to national factors in general and to the failure of sovereign governments to fulfil their responsibilities to the citizens they purport to represent in particular (Ghani and Lockhart, 2008). However, there is clear evidence of such social and political-economic transformations (and others) in the contemporary world. Therefore, in the context of this book, it is important to explore the relationship between tourism and the alleged characteristics of globalization. In fact, according to Wahab and Cooper (2001, pxiii), '*globalisation* has begun to rival *sustainability* as an organising concept for the way we approach tourism' [emphasis in original]. This is, perhaps, to overstate the relevance of globalization to a social and economic activity that, as we shall see shortly, is primarily produced and consumed within national or local, rather than international, contexts. Nevertheless, when thinking about tourism, its economic developmental potential and its inter-relationship with the environment, it is important to consider the implications of globalization and, related to this, the notion of 'post-development' (many contemporary post-development strategies focus on challenges that have, perhaps, emerged from globalization) for the effective development of tourism.

The purpose of this chapter, then, is to highlight the key themes and issues related to globalization, to explore the extent to which tourism reflects or is influenced by the processes and outcomes of globalization and to consider tourism's developmental role within a 'post-development' framework. Collectively, the discussion of these issues will support the argument that viewing tourism within specific destinational or sectoral contexts as a form of capitalistic production and consumption provides the most appropriate and logical basis for exploring ways of enhancing or optimizing its economic contribution within environmental parameters. Evidently, therefore, it is first necessary to review briefly the globalization debate.

Globalization: Reality or myth?

The term 'globalization' is, like 'sustainability', widely used and applied in numerous contexts. In particular, it has become 'part of the linguistic currency of contemporary business' (Seaton and Alford, 2001, p97), not an altogether surprising assertion given that it is within the realm of production, trade and finance that material evidence of globalization (or, perhaps, international integration and interdependence) is most evident. However, and again as is the case with the concept of sustainability, although most people have some idea of what globalization means, there is no single, precise, universally agreed definition of it. In other words, although there is general agreement that there is an increasing degree of global inter-connectedness – the development of real-time information and communication through the internet being a notable example – there remains a lack of consensus over the extent to which globalization is a universal process which all societies and institutions are undergoing or whether it is simply a convenient label attached to the internationalization of certain spheres of social, economic and political life. Indeed, opinion remains divided between, on the one hand, those who consider globalization to be a real, identifiable and measurable influence to which all people and nations are subject (a group that Held et al (1999, p2) refer to as 'hyperglobalizers') and, on the other hand, the 'sceptics' , who deny the validity of the concept, arguing that it is 'essentially a myth which conceals the reality of an international economy ... in which national governments remain very powerful (Held et al, 1999, p2). In between these two extremes a third group can be identified, the so-called 'transformationalists', who recognize a process of global change, the bi-polar west and east centres of political economy having been replaced by a single, inter-connected, yet less certain, world to which societies and nations are having to adapt.

Even the alleged relationship between globalization and tourism in particular is contestable. Although information and communication technology, such as global distribution systems, on line booking (dynamic packaging), information sources and other services, from travel insurance and health advice to consumer rights and legal action sites, provides tourists with instant access to a borderless virtual world of information (epitomized, perhaps, by Google Earth); many of the characteristics of tourism claimed to be evidence of globalization are essentially an intensification of processes that have long defined the business and practice of international tourism. Certainly, more people are travelling across international borders, more countries have become major tourist destinations and the tourism production system has become typified by more numerous multinational corporations and increased transnational vertical and horizontal integration. Recently, for example, it was announced that British Airways, already negotiating a merger with the Spanish airline Iberian and possible collaboration with American Airlines, was in merger talks with Quantas. Though these negotiations subsequently failed, the potential nevertheless remains for creating a truly global airline. However, conducting business on an increasingly global scale does not necessarily imply a movement towards a socially, politically and economically borderless, inter-dependent world.

The relevance and implications of globalization to tourism will be considered shortly. Nonetheless, one of the difficulties with the concept more generally is that it means different things to different people (at least, to those who conform in principle with the idea that globalization is more than simply the internationalization of business): from the increasing mobility of people, goods, services, capital and information across a world in which political and geographic borders are of declining relevance, or so-called time-space compression (Harvey, 1989), whereby instantaneous communication and increasingly fast and inter-connected transport networks have reduced the constraints of space and time on human and economic activity, to more general notions of a process of forming a unified, global society. Irrespective of these differing perspectives, however, it is possible to identify a number of actual transformations in the contemporary world that may, in one way or another, contribute to a process of globalization. Such transformations include the following:

- Global production and consumption: not only is production becoming global with, for example, components manufactured in one country being assembled into the final product in another, but consumers and organizations have increasing access to international products. Thus, there is increasing mobility of material goods across national borders.
- Global financial markets: the emergence of global financial markets, speculation in and profits from the international circulation of money and increasing access to international finance, collectively encouraged by the liberalization of cross-border movements of finance, procedural standardization and other regulation (Scholte, 2005).
- Global politics: although national sovereignty remains, the role of the state has been transformed in as much as national governance is subject to sub-state, state and supra-state agencies and organizations, the latter including regional (for example, the European Union) and global bodies, such as the Bretton Woods institutions (International Monetary Fund (IMF), World Bank), the World Trade Organization (WTO), or various agencies of the United Nations (UN). In other words, state governments remain responsible for national populations; national territories are, however, subject to supra-national jurisdictions.
- Global information and communication: as already noted, advances in information and communication technologies, specifically the internet but also satellite-based mobile telephony, have increased access to and flows of instantaneous/real-time communication and information on a global scale.
- Global environment: awareness of and responses to environmental challenges have increasingly shifted from the local/national to the international, with issues such as climate change, water pollution, whaling and so on being recognized as global problems requiring global cooperation and action.
- Global society: the concept of the 'global village' has been enhanced by, for example: increasing migration, particularly 'south-north' but also 'north-north'; increased multi-culturalism; worldwide participation in and communication of sporting and cultural events; internationalization of consumer products, such as food, drink, automobiles; and, of course, the growth and spread of international tourism.

Whilst these transformations in themselves do not define globalization, collectively they point to a process whereby states and societies are becoming 'increasingly enmeshed in worldwide systems and networks of interaction' (Held and McGrew, 2000, p3). This, in turn, suggests that a degree of interdependence exists between states and societies such that events or developments in one society or state may have significant implications for other societies and states. Frequently cited examples of this phenomenon include: the Asian financial crisis of 1997; the wider impacts of '9/11' and the subsequent 'war on terror'; the Severe Acute Respiratory Syndrome (SARS) outbreak in 2003 and, of course, the 2008 'credit crunch' and global financial crisis. Consequently, Held and McGrew (2000, p4) define globalization as: 'the expanding scale, growing magnitude, speeding up and deepening impact of interregional flows and patterns of social interaction'. They go on to assert, however, that this does not imply a shift towards a single, harmonious, homogeneous global society. One of the contradictions of the concept is that awareness of increasing interdependence and inter-connectedness (that is, a threat to individuality, self-reliance and self-determination), may lead to animosity, conflict, xenophobia or counter-political movements, whilst a significant proportion of the world's population remains excluded from the process of globalization.

A similar position is adopted by Scholte (2002) who, revisiting the issue of definitions of globalization, rejects a number of existing broad definitions on the basis that they are redundant; that is, they do not provide a basis for extending existing knowledge or understanding that 'is not attainable with other concepts'. Thus, four existing definitions of globalization – globalization as internationalization (the intensification of an historical process that may be analysed from a variety of other perspectives); globalization as liberalization (a reworking of neo-liberal macroeconomic policy); globalization as universalization (the notion that everything – goods, services, culture – is becoming global reflects a centuries old process); and, globalization as westernization (western cultural modernization and imperialism, which have a much longer history than globalization) – are rejected in favour of a fifth definition. For Scholte (2002, p13), globalization is best conceived of as 'the spread of transplanetary – and in recent times more particularly supraterritorial – connections between people'. That is, people are increasingly able to engage with each other globally, or within one world, suggesting that globalization is, essentially, a spatial concept.

Nevertheless, Scholte goes on to suggest six qualifications to this definition of globalization, qualifications which to some extent reflect or support the arguments of the sceptics, or those who consider it to be a mythical concept. Specifically, Scholte accepts that:

- Globalization does not signify the end of territoriality; territorial (or national) boundaries still exist, encompassing territorial production, identities and political mechanisms. For tourists, of course, national boundaries still exist. At the practical level, there are many territories where visas are required (often through complex processes and at significant expense) to gain access whilst, culturally, barriers of language, custom, values and behaviour may exist.
- Globality, or the concept of global space ('one world') does not exclude the existence of other social spaces; 'the global is not a domain unto itself, separate from the regional, the national, the provincial, the local' (Scholte, 2002, p27). Thus, global space is a collection of spatial inter-relations within the whole. Similarly, tourist spaces are discrete, identifiable spaces, though inter-related (at least in the context of international tourism) as

elements of the global tourism system through the interaction of the local, national and international (local communities with international tourists, local business with international business, and so on).

- A binary divide does not exist between the global (distant, dominating and creating dependency) and the local (community, authenticity, empowerment); the global and local co-exist. This distinction, however, prevails within tourism, to the extent that community-based tourism is contrasted with globalized (mass) tourism.

- Globalization does not imply cultural homogenization. That is, enhanced global connectivity and interdependence does not necessarily reduce cultural diversity: indeed, it may serve to increase cultural diversity and pluralism. Tourism is frequently accused of encouraging acculturation and cultural commoditization, yet it may also be seen as a catalyst of cultural heterogeneity.

- Globalization is not universal; more people and societies are inter-connected, but not all people and societies and not to the same extent. In fact, some societies are totally excluded from globalization. Tourism, perhaps, is an exception in as much as most, if not all, states or territories are destinations for international visitors. Nevertheless, as will be discussed in more detail shortly, few could claim to enjoy global connectivity in terms of the nature of and benefits from their tourism sector.

- Globalization is political; social interaction inevitably involves power relations, from the level of the individual to that of society, the state and the international community. Globalization empowers some (for example, supra-national agencies, multinational corporations, national governments), but disempowers others. Certainly, dominant organizations or entrenched social structures may shape global inter-relations, but there is nothing certain or inevitable in this process. Power relations within tourism have long been seen to favour international corporations based in the metropolitan centre (Britton, 1991) yet such an analysis overlooks the power relations between other actors and the multiple political contexts within which tourism occurs. Thus, tourism in Cuba (see Chapter 2, case study) is characterized by a political economy distinctive from the dominant tourism-power relations discourse.

Thus, there are a number of challenges to the concept of globalization. Generally, sceptics argue that if it cannot be interpreted as a universal, global phenomenon (and much of the evidence suggests that this is the case) then globalization lacks the spatial specificity that it suggests. In other words, it becomes impossible, both spatially and in terms of process, to distinguish the international, transnational or regional from the global and, as a consequence, globalization is an ineffective basis for considering transformations in contemporary societies. More specifically, it is argued that what is conveniently labelled 'globalization' is, in fact, political-economic internationalization or regionalization, with cross-border flows of goods, services and people defined primarily by three main trading and financial blocs, namely, North America,

Europe and Asia-Pacific. Certainly, major international tourism flows remain regionalized within these three areas, with the more recent rapid growth in tourism activity in the Asia-Pacific region resulting largely, though not entirely, from an increase in intra-regional travel rather than in travel from Europe or North America.

Moreover, the formation of these blocs, requiring the regulation and promotion of cross-border activity, has been based upon the initiative, input and policies of national governments: '[national] governments are not the passive victims of internationalisation but, on the contrary, its primary architects' (Held et al, 1999, p6). Whether specific trading blocs, such as the Association of Southeast Asian Nations (ASEAN) or North American Free Trade Agreement (NAFTA), or political-economic unions, particularly the European Union, they remain the creations of their membership, although the counter-argument is that these organizations eventually become powerful in their own right, superseding national policies and interests. Equally, globalists also argue that, such has been the proliferation of international governmental organizations, non-governmental organizations (NGOs), pressure groups, treaties and so on that, again, national governments struggle to maintain a national focus, interest and influence.

The sceptical position also argues that internationalization 'dressed up' as globalization has been used to justify the continuance of western neo-liberal economic development or the so-called 'Washington Consensus', promoting and supporting deregulation, liberalization and privatization and thereby enhancing economic growth and development within the three regional blocs to the marginalization or exclusion of many less or least developed countries. In other words, it is argued that 'global' capital and investment flows remain primarily between and within advanced capitalistic economies or regions, thereby maintaining global inequalities and a global order that has changed little over the last century, hence underpinning the 'post-development' thesis that we shall turn to later in this chapter. In turn, the failure to address global inequalities or to make progress towards a unified global society is seen as driving the growth in nationalism and fundamentalism, most starkly evident in the activities of terrorist organizations, usually against symbols of western hegemony. Thus, as Held et al (1999, p6) observe:

> *The deepening of global inequalities, the realpolitik of inter-national relations and the 'clash of civilisations' expose the illusory nature of 'global governance' in so far as the management of the world order remains, as it has since the ... [nineteenth] ... century, overwhelmingly the preserve of Western states.*

It is not possible, of course, to do full justice to the globalization debate here; numerous books have been written that address issues that have only been touched upon, or not considered, here. Suffice to say that the concept of globalization remains highly contested, with powerful arguments presented on both sides of the debate (see Table 4.1 later for a summary of key points).

In a sense, therefore, it is difficult to explore the relevance of globalization to tourism if the very notion of globalization itself is questionable. Nevertheless, there is no doubt that tourism is becoming more global, if not globalized. Most countries are now destinations and so, in principle, compete within a global market for international tourists (but see below); they must also compete, to an extent, for the attention of multinational corporations or, at least, corporations based primarily in wealthier states, for investment, transport links and access to tourist markets. Thus, tourism must be considered in the context of its relationship to the concept of globalization, particularly with respect to its developmental role (see also Bianchi, 2002). Therefore, the next section considers the relevance of globalization to tourism both generally and in the context of key themes within the globalization debate, namely, the globalization of politics, culture and business.

Tourism and globalization

Tourism is frequently cited as a manifestation of globalization, in as much as reference is made to the constant and rapid growth in international tourist arrivals to support the argument of increased inter-connectedness between people on a global scale. At the same time, globalization is seen by some as a process to which tourism must respond. For example, Wahab and Cooper (2001, p5) refer to 'the impact of globalisation as a megatrend on tourism', essentially reifying it, or viewing it as a tangible phenomenon that influences the development of tourism (though, as already noted, Scholte (2002) argues that globalization is not a 'domain unto itself'). Similarly, others tacitly accept that tourism and globalization are inextricably linked (for example, Knowles et al, 2001), although the existence of a causal relationship between the two remains unclear.

To an extent, there is some validity in the suggestion that tourism contributes to, or is evidence of, a process of globalization. In addition to the greater international mobility of people, the existence of what has become (in principle) a global tourism marketplace, and the increasingly international, if not global, character of some travel and tourism organizations, information and communication technology has undoubtedly enabled inter-connectedness and interaction between all players in the tourism system on a global scale. Through the internet, for example, tourists are now able to communicate with relevant service providers around the world, to pre-purchase those services, to access official and unofficial information sources and to communicate with other tourists or friends and family 'back home'.

However, whilst the *virtual* world of tourism has become global or globalized, the same cannot be said for the *real* world of tourism. In other words, to refer to the 'globalization of tourism' or the challenges facing tourism in a globalizing world is to take a somewhat simplistic, uni-dimensional perspective on tourism and to overlook the historical development of international tourism of which current trends are, perhaps, merely an extension. That is, there has, of course, been an explosive growth in tourism since the 1960s, with more people travelling to more places and crossing international borders more frequently, utilizing services provided by an increasing number of travel and tourism businesses and organizations that facilitate such activity. However, it is less clear whether there has been, over the last two decades or so, a fundamental, qualitative transformation in tourism (its 'globalization') or whether it has simply been an intensification of a process that, in terms of the modern era of tourism, commenced some 150 years ago. This and other issues will be discussed shortly but, generally, a fundamental point relevant to the alleged globalization of tourism is the fact that tourism, for the most part, is not global. Although tourism occurs in most, if not all, countries and, hence can be thought of as a global phenomenon, most tourist activity does not involve travel across international borders – that is, the majority of tourism is domestic. As noted elsewhere in this book, over 80 per cent of tourist movements occur within national borders and, for many countries, the domestic tourism market is significantly more important in terms of both volume and value than incoming international tourism. For example, according to Seaton and Alford (2001, p103), domestic tourists in India outnumber international visitors by a factor of 45:1, whilst in France and Spain, over three-quarters of the holidaying population do so within their own countries. It is likely that a similar pattern exists in many other countries (only about 10 per cent of American citizens possess passports, for example) and, although domestic tourists are in all likelihood less valuable than international tourists in terms of per capita spend (particularly day-trippers, of course) and do not generate foreign exchange earnings, they are nevertheless of vital importance in terms of local economic development and regeneration. This also suggests that the tourism production system in many countries is concerned primarily with the domestic market. Again, Seaton and Alford (2001) refer to international research that found that, in the 12 countries surveyed, the domestic market was the most important, a phenomenon that is reflected across other sectors, such as accommodation, tour operations and travel retailing.

Of course, this is not the case in all countries or tourism destinations. In some not only is domestic tourism more limited in scale and economic contribution compared with the international tourism sector, but foreign tourists may significantly outnumber the local population. For example, Cyprus, with a population of 680,000, attracts around 2.3 million international tourists each year and tourism not only contributes over 25 per cent of gross domestic product (GDP) but also represents around 40 per cent of total exports. Nevertheless, the important point is that the concept of globalization is largely irrelevant to much of the tourism sector (both tourists and tourism service providers), functioning as they do within a national or even local domestic context. Moreover, even in those destinations which, in addition to significant domestic tourists, serve international markets, the alleged challenges of globalization may not, as the following sections suggest, be as intense as many would have us believe (see also Telfer and Sharpley, 2008, pp57–79). In fact, many of these challenges or consequences, such as the dominant power of multinational corporations or cultural homogenization, have long existed and been considered as negative aspects or consequences of tourism development: globalization just provides an alternative conceptual perspective on them.

Tourism and political globalization

According to the globalization thesis, the state is no longer able to effectively fulfil its responsibilities to its citizens, such as managing the economy, providing security and law and order, or implementing appropriate environmental policies, without engaging in and collaborating with supra-national forms and structures of governance and policy making. More specifically, individual states face a variety of policy decisions that demand cooperation and collaboration with other states on an international, if not global, scale. Such a situation has arisen as a result of, on the one hand, the emergence of certain global challenges in areas such as health, security and the economy and, on the other hand, the proliferation in international agencies and organizations which have become the focus of shared sovereignty and power and to which national governance has become subordinate. In short, from a globalist perspective, national state power and independence is in decline whilst international and global governance, underpinned by powerful agencies and a growing body of international law, is in the ascendency.

Sceptics, conversely, argue that a cornerstone of international relations is the legitimacy of national sovereignty, or recognition of the right of individual states to govern their territories and to adopt economic, social and political policies appropriate to national needs. Thus, there remains an unwillingness on the part of the international community to intervene in the domestic policy issues of individual states, irrespective of the extent to which such intervention is either necessary or desirable. A particularly tragic example was the 'stand-off' between international governments and aid agencies and the authorities in Myanmar following the devastating cyclone in that country in 2008.

In practice, nation-states probably find themselves lying, to varying degrees, somewhere between these two positions; whilst retaining national sovereignty, states must also give due recognition to, and act in accordance with, international policies, laws and agreements (though, in some cases, national governments may choose not to do so). To some extent, the same applies within the specific context of tourism in as much as, firstly, tourism may be affected by wider international protocols and agreements in policy areas such as climate change or law and order, or be one of a number of areas of concern of global agencies, such as the World Bank or the United Nations Development Programme (UNDP). Secondly, particular sectors or industries may be required to operate according to international policies, laws and conventions. For example, international commercial airline operations are subject to a wide variety of international regulations and codes of practice overseen by the International Civil Aviation Organisation (ICAO) whilst, since 1929, the Warsaw Convention has regulated the liability for the international air carriage of people, luggage and goods. Similarly, at the regional level, tour operations within Europe have, since 1990, been subject to the European Package Travel Directive which established a common set of rules for the sale of package holidays with a specific emphasis on affording a greater degree of protection to consumers of package travel (Grant and Sharpley, 2005).

However, there is no global or even regional policy framework which tourism development must respect or follow. The United Nations World Tourism Organization (UNWTO), the only 'worldwide' body concerned with tourism development, does not for the most part include developed nations amongst its membership and acts primarily in an advisory capacity whilst the World Travel and Tourism Council (WTTC), essentially a trade lobby for the travel and tourism sector, describes itself on its website (www.wttc.org) as the forum for the chairmen, presidents and CEOs of 100 of the world's foremost travel and tourism companies. It is, hence, an exclusive club (membership is by invitation) representing just a tiny proportion of the world's travel and tourism businesses, many of which are represented by regional, national or local organizations. Thus, most typically, it is the state, often in conjunction with sub-state agencies (or, in the case of the US, only sub-national agencies) that exercises power and control over the development and promotion of its territory for tourism. Further, the extent to which the state intervenes in tourism is dependent on domestic economic and political factors, varying from a more *laissez faire*, passive role, as is frequently the case in wealthier, developed countries where the state's involvement may be limited to national or regional marketing, the provision of infrastructure, managing attractions of national significance or, more generally, establishing a favourable political, regulatory and economic climate in order to enable tourism to flourish (Jeffries, 2001), to a more active, interventionist or entrepreneurial role often in evidence in less developed nations (Tosun and Jenkins, 1998).

It is also important to consider the extent to which the multinational corporations are able to exert political pressure within the tourism system. A common theme within the tourism literature has long been the issue of dependency arising from the ability of multinational corporations, usually based in the metropolitan centre, to dominate tourism development in the periphery. This issue has become crystallized within the tourism and globalization debate, the claim being that the tourism production system is becoming increasingly globalized – that is, a growing number of multinationals have a global presence – and, hence, that tourism development in the destination is increasingly controlled by global corporations. However, few, if any travel, tourism or hospitality organizations are truly global. As Fayos-Solà and Bueno (2001, p55) observe with respect to the corporate membership of the WTTC, 'most frequently, they are strongly identified – by origin, business culture, major operations and decision-making strategies – with one of the countries of the G3 triad ... with their presence in other countries being as subsidiaries, franchises, etc.' Some hotel corporations, such as Intercontinental, Marriott or Accor, have a widespread international presence (usually based on franchise or management contract operations) yet the international visibility of such groups belies their apparent domination. In Europe, for example, 90 per cent of all hotels are independently operated though, as evidence of the structure of the tourism sector in Europe, they account for roughly 70 per cent of rooms.

That is, the great majority of tourism-related businesses in Europe are small to medium size enterprises; indeed, Seaton and Alford (2001) refer to a study undertaken in the late 1990s that found that 95.5 per cent of enterprises in the then 15-member state European Union had between zero and nine employees, with 15 per cent of businesses being 'one man' enterprises. There is little reason to suppose the picture is any different in other regions. That is, the great majority of tourism businesses, whether hospitality, catering, travel retail, tour operating or attractions, are small-scale enterprises with a primarily domestic focus and limited political influence, although exceptions inevitably exist. For example, the Gambia Experience is a relatively small UK-based operator specializing in tours/holidays to The Gambia. However, the company accounts for 60 per cent of the UK market to The Gambia or roughly 30 per cent of all tourist arrivals in the country and, hence, enjoys considerable influence within The Gambia's tourism sector (Sharpley, 2009; see also case study below). Overall, however, it is erroneous to describe tourism as a globalized sector and the power and influence of multinational corporations is overstated. As will be considered in the next chapter, this also has implications for the one global issue related, in part, to tourism, namely climate change.

Tourism and cultural globalization

Tourism, as a global (or globalized) activity, is frequently associated with the globalization of culture, itself conceptualized as the emergence of a popular global (western/American) culture and a corresponding decline in national political and cultural identities. Driving this globalization of culture is, according to globalists, the increasing worldwide diffusion of cultural information and knowledge through information and communication channels which are controlled not by states but by commercial organizations which have, in effect, become global cultural brokers.

Conversely, sceptics argue that not only are national or local cultures resistant to the transforming cultural messages conveyed by the global media, but also that global information and communication systems enhance an awareness of difference and strengthen national and local culture. In other words, the perceived threat of a homogenized global culture communicated through contemporary information channels is countered by a resurgence of interest in traditional cultures. Moreover, national media remain powerful influences and, even within political-economic groups such as the European Union, national identities have not been subordinated to a European identity and culture, despite the efforts of so-called 'Eurocrats' to create one.

The extent to which tourism reflects these contrasting positions remains debatable. As a social activity defined primarily by the 'on-site' consumption of experiences, tourism inevitably brings together different cultures within the context of the destination. The consequences of this cultural interaction, sometimes referred to generically as host-guest relationships, have long been explored within the literature (Smith, 1977; Reisinger and Turner, 2003; Wall and Mathieson, 2006), the focus frequently being upon the more immediate consequences (both negative and beneficial, though emphasis tends to be placed on the negative) of tourism on social practice and structures within destination communities, as well as longer-term cultural transformations that may be related to tourism development. At the risk of over-simplifying complex processes, a variety of social consequences can be directly linked to tourism, whereas the relationship between tourism and cultural transformation, resulting perhaps from cultural assimilation or cultural 'imperialism', is less clear. Not only may cultural change result from broader influences, such as the global media and communication channels, rather than tourism in particular, but much also depends on the nature and scale of tourism development, the cultural distinctions between local communities and tourists and the strength or resilience of local culture to change, as well as the behaviour of tourists themselves. For example, recent anecdotal evidence suggests that an increase in the number of Russian tourists in Greece has actually reduced the potential for negative cultural impacts as the Russians tend to demonstrate a preference for staying in resorts rather than visiting cultural sites or local communities. At the same time, cultural change may be manifested in greater cultural diversity and awareness amongst both local communities and tourists, countering the globalists' claim of increasing cultural homogeneity around the world. Either way, the important point is that the relationship between tourism and cultural transformation is not a uniform, global process, but must be considered on a 'case-by-case' basis.

Tourism and business globalization

Reference has already been made to the alleged globalization of the tourism production system, reflecting the globalization of the world's economic and financial systems more generally. As was pointed out, not only are the majority of tourism-related enterprises small scale enterprises but, in many cases, they operate in and serve a domestic market. However, a further and final point with the 'globalization of tourism' debate that deserves attention is the claim that, as tourism has become globalized, tourism businesses and destinations now operate in a global competitive market – that is, competition within tourism has also been globalized. There is a degree of validity in this argument. Most, if not all, countries are now tourist destinations and, therefore, compete with each other to attract tourists who, as we have seen, are not only able to access information and services via the internet, but who are also able to travel further more frequently, easily and cheaply as a result of technical and business-model innovation in international air transport as well as fewer political barriers to international travel. Though a 'borderless' world is, in practice, unlikely to evolve because of security issues, cross-border travel has become greatly simplified and, as a consequence, established destinations with stable markets are having to compete internationally. For example, long-weekend domestic breaks within the UK now compete with (often cheaper) short-break trips to European cities, whilst the short-haul two-week holiday competes with two-week holidays virtually anywhere in the world.

Nevertheless, as Seaton and Alford (2001) argue, despite the undoubted increasingly global *competition* within tourism, the existence of a global tourism *consumer* is less certain. In other words, although destinations compete in a global market, they tend to attract and rely on tourist arrivals from a small number of key, traditional markets, usually reflecting geographical proximity and ease of access, cultural homogeneity, a population's propensity to travel internationally and historical and political ties. Thus, for example, Cyprus has long depended upon the UK as its main tourist market, reflecting historical political ties between the two nations as well as the fact that Cyprus is familiar to British visitors: English is widely spoken; until the adoption of the Euro in January 2008 the local currency was the Cypriot pound; and cars are driven on the left, as in the UK. Similarly, The Gambia, a former British colony in West Africa, also depends upon the UK market whilst the main tourist market for neighbouring Senegal, a former French colony, is France. In fact, the resorts of the French-based group, Club Med, in Africa are located primarily in former French colonies, including Senegal, Tunisia and Morocco.

Consequently, again, the point is that although the tourism system is located within a world that, according to some, is undergoing a process of globalization, in many respects tourism remains separate or immune from that process. That is, tourism is not a globalized socio-economic activity and its contribution to globalization is, perhaps, limited. Table 4.1 summarizes the globalization debate both generally and with specific reference to tourism. In turn, this conclusion reinforces the position that uniform, global approaches to tourism development cannot meet the diversity of contexts within which tourism occurs and that a more focused 'unit of analysis' is required.

This argument is developed further in Chapter 6. In the context of this chapter, however, it is also important to consider post-development, a concept related to globalization in as much as the sceptic school argues that global inequity remains as evident as ever, whilst globalists similarly predict increasing inequality within and between societies. In other words, from either perspective, development as a global project has failed, an argument that defines the post-development position.

Post-development and tourism

> *The idea of development stands like a ruin in the intellectual landscape ... it is time to dismantle this mental structure.* (Sachs, 1992, p1)

As noted in Chapter 2, by the 1990s a development 'impasse' had been reached. That is, it had become recognized that the 1980s had been, for many developing countries, a lost decade, an assessment that, according to Schuurman (1993, p1) could equally be applied to development studies and development theory. It had become apparent that a vacuum in development theory had emerged – against a background of meta-theories, development had, for many countries, failed to materialize yet no new theories or approaches had emerged

Table 4.1 *The globalization debate and tourism: A summary*

	Globalists	Sceptics	Tourism
Concepts	Deepening and intensification of global inter-connectness and interdependence facilitated by extensive and rapid flows of people, goods, capital and information	Intensification of historical process of internationalization; regionalization as intensification of western political-economic hegemony	Socio-economic activity that occurs on a global scale but primarily defined by territorial boundaries
Politics	Diminishing role and relevance of the state and national sovereignty; growth in multilateralism and international governance	International system based upon respect for national sovereignty. International cooperation driven by nation-states	Sector-specific laws, agreements and protocols; nation-state responsible for territorial development and promotion of tourism
Culture	Emergence of a global popular culture; cultural homogenization or cultural hybridization	Greater awareness of national distinctions; growth in nationalism	No universal role of tourism as an agent of cultural transformation; local factors determine cultural consequences
Economy	Emergence of a global economy; global financial and informational flows; multinational corporations and global competition	Development of regional blocs with economic flows within and between them; increasing inequality between global rich and poor	Limited evidence of a globalized tourism economy; a global, but not globalized, economic sector; no global competition

Source: adapted from Held and McGrew, 2000

to address this problem. Indeed, some questioned the relevance of development studies to the practical social and economic problems facing many nations (Edwards, 1996) whilst, more radically, the post-development school began to challenge the very concept of development. Some commentators such as Sachs, quoted above, argue that the notion of development is fundamentally flawed, inherently unjust and has never worked – in short, the global development project has failed:

> *Development has failed to meet the needs and preoccupations of those at the bottom of the social ladder. Often, it has turned them into their own enemies, once they have internalized the developers' perception of what they need. This has served to exacerbate social tensions everywhere. It has made the bad rich richer and the good poor poorer. It has destroyed the old fabric of communal societies. And it has created needs, envies and services that can only make people more dependent on development, while systematically dis-possessing the excluded from their means of sustenance.* (Rahnema, 1997, p391)

Others, conversely, suggest that development was 'a hoax, never designed to deal with humanitarian and environmental problems, but simply a way of allowing the industrialized North ... to continue its dominance of the rest of the world' (Thomas, 2000b, p19). Irrespective of these two viewpoints, however, supporters of the post-development thesis argue that development, as a process and a goal, should be abandoned, that the 'end of development' should be recognized, though not the idea of change and progress towards a better world. As Rahnema (1997, p391) suggests:

> *The end of development should not be seen as an end to the search for new possibilities of change, for a relational world of friendship, or for genuine processes of regeneration able to give birth to new forms of solidarity. It should only mean that the binary, the mechanistic, the reductionist, the inhumane and the ultimately self-destructive approach to change is over.*

The basis of post-development thought lies in the argument that, prior to the emergence of international development processes and policies implemented by western institutions from the 1950s onwards, many countries, though lacking in health care, educational opportunities, sanitation and so on, were not, by their own perceptions, poor. It was only when external (western) expectations and norms were introduced through the intervention of international agencies that these countries came to be seen, both by the outside world and themselves, as poor or undeveloped and, hence, in need of 'development' (see Escobar, 1997). Thus, development, as experienced by less developed countries of the South, is seen as a western-centric philosophy that, manifested in the imposition of western socio-economic values and systems, has 'destroyed indigenous cultures, threatened the sustainability of natural environments and has created feelings of inferiority among people of the South' (Willis, 2005, p8). In fact, according to Escobar (1997), one of the leading proponents of the post-development school, western-inspired development policies are simply mechanisms for the imposition of economic control over less developed countries to an extent that is equally, if not more, pervasive than the preceding colonial system.

Recognizing the need for change, though not western-centric development, post-development theorists see the answer lying in alternative conceptions of change that emanate from people themselves deciding how they wish to live their lives. In other words, rather than local communities engaging (or being seen to engage) in projects overseen by international agencies, the driving forces should be 'local thinking and local actions' (Esteva and Prakash, 1997, p281), though with the invited cooperation of external agencies if necessary. Thus, post-development is, in a sense, a reaction against globalization:

> *Local initiatives, no matter how wisely conceived, seem prima facie too small to counteract the 'global forces' now daily invading our lives and environments ... [there is] ample proof*

that local peoples often need outside allies to create a critical mass of political opposition capable of stopping those forces. But the solidarity of coalitions and alliances does not call for 'thinking globally'. In fact, what is needed is exactly the opposite: people thinking and acting locally, while forging solidarity with other local forces that share this opposition to the 'global thinking'.
(Esteva and Prakash, 1997, pp281–282)

This focus on locally-based 'anti-development' is criticized by some for espousing romantic visions of pre-industrial societies and, hence, being regressive and overlooking the fact that most developed countries have experienced an industrial age. At the same time, the post-development school's principal concern for the less developed world suggests anti-capitalist, revolutionary undertones whereas its fundamental thesis is, ironically, of equal relevance to the notion of development-as-regression in the developed world. Moreover, with an emphasis on the discourse of development and an eclectic philosophical underpinning, post-development offers little by way of a solution to the development 'impasse': 'the quasi-revolutionary posturing in post-development reflects both a hunger for a new era and a nostalgia politics of romanticism, glorification of the local, grassroots, community with conservative overtones' (Pieterse, 1998).

Nevertheless, for all intents and purposes it presents a radical perspective on, rather than an outright rejection of, development and also highlights important issues with respect to understanding and addressing poverty and other challenges on a global scale. It also points to an alternative perspective on tourism development for, if tourism is to bring benefits or change to destination communities (even if such benefits are not described as 'development'), then tourism development should, as far as possible, be driven by destinational needs (as perceived by the destination) and resources (or capitals) in cooperation with external actors. This is not the same as 'community tourism' with its emphasis on the local and the small-scale. The destination may be a resort; equally, it may be a region or a nation-state and the community the national population. However, the principle remains the same: thinking and acting locally, though engaging positively with national or international networks to optimize tourism's benefits according to identified locally defined (rather than externally imposed) needs. This, in turn, points to the need for a conceptualization of tourism that provides a framework for establishing how tourism should be developed to satisfy those needs: tourism as (sustainable) development, tourism as economic growth or, as this book suggests, tourism as a function of capitalist supply and demand.

Of course, one of the problems with the post-development thesis is that it assumes implicitly that local political, economic and social structures operate efficiently and effectively in the interests of all local people; development and change has failed because of external intervention and, thus, the solution lies in local action. However, it has become increasingly recognized that in many of the world's poorest countries, particularly the so-called least developed countries (LDCs), poverty, inequality and a more general lack of development or progress is as much, if not more, the outcome of internal, domestic factors as it is the result of international or global forces. Therefore, the final section of this chapter considers the challenges facing LDCs as a specific tourism system context, followed by a case study of tourism in The Gambia.

Least developed countries and tourism

The countries that comprise the less developed world may be divided, albeit somewhat simplistically, into two groups: developing countries and LDCs. Developing countries, or those that are making tangible advances against accepted measures of human development, collectively comprise around two-thirds of all countries not formally recognized as 'developed' and are notable for their diversity with respect to land area, topography, population, economic and technological development, health care, education and so on. LDCs, conversely, are those countries that, according to accepted yardsticks, are not making progress; that is, they are not developing but maintaining a static or worsening socio-economic condition relative to other countries.

Forming a relatively homogeneous group comprising the world's least socio-economically developed countries, LDCs have, since 1971, been formally recognized and categorized by the UN as being least developed and facing major obstacles in achieving even limited development (UN, 2008). It is both interesting and salutary to note that, since the first list of LDCs was officially complied, only two countries have graduated from LDC status, namely, Botswana in 1994 and, most recently, Cape Verde in 2007, reducing the number of LDCs on the current triennially-reviewed list to 49 (Table 4.2). This alone, perhaps, is stark evidence of the failure of development, as claimed by the post-development school, to meet the needs of the world's poorest people and societies, those at the bottom of the world's social ladder or what Collier (2007) refers to as the 'bottom billion'. Whereas developing countries, as defined above, collectively achieved average annual economic growth of 4 per cent during the 1980s and 1990s, accelerating to 4.5 per cent in the early years of the new millennium, per capita income in LDCs declined by 0.5 per cent per annum during the 1990s; by 2000, 'they were poorer than they had been in 1970' (Collier, 2007, p9). As a result of this lack of economic growth and development, it has been suggested that LDCs should more appropriately be referred to as 'non-viable national economies' (de Rivero, 2001). He does in fact argue that 'more than forty years into the myth of development, reality shows that the rule is the non-development of at least 130 countries' (de Rivero, 2001, p127), vastly expanding the list of countries that are not, in his terms, developing. Whether this is the case or not remains debatable but his point is that many countries, particularly LDCs, do not possess the capacity to achieve the consistent growth in their national economies necessary to underpin development or to maintain their position in the global economic order.

Inevitably, perhaps, tourism has long been seen as a potential catalyst of economic growth and development in LDCs (Cater, 1987) whilst, more

Table 4.2 *Least developed countries: Selected development and tourism indicators*

Country	HDI rank	GDP per capita (US$) 2000	GDP per capita (US$) 2005	Aid (as % of GDP) 2005	Poverty (% of pop. below $1/day) 1990–2005	Tourist arrivals 2005 ('000)	Tourist arrivals (av. ann. growth) 2000–2005	Tourist receipts ($mn) 2005	Tourist industry (% of GDP)
Afghanistan	–	n/a	n/a	n/a	n/a	n/a	n/a	n/a	n/a
Angola	162	430	1350	6.6	n/a	210	32.7	66*	2.1
Bangladesh	140	390	470	2.4	41.3	271	8.1	n/a	1.5
Benin	163	340	510	9.4	30.9	174*	n.a.	106**	3.0
Bhutan	132	540	870	10.9	n/a	9	5.0	n/a	n/a
Burkina Faso	176	250	400	12.7	44.9	222*	n.a	n/a	1.2
Burundi	167	120	100	54.3	54.6	148	38.5	2	1.8
Cambodia	131	280	380	10.3	34.1	1055	22.7	840	9.3
Cape Verde	102	1280	1870	14.7	n/a	198	11.5	123	10.9
Central African Rep.	171	270	350	8.0	66.6	8	n.a	4*	1.0
Chad	170	180	400	8.8	n/a	21**	n/a	n/a	1.0
Comoros	134	400	640	6.7	n/a	18*	n.a	10*	2.8
DR of Congo	168	80	120	29.1	n/a	61	-9.9	1	1.3
Djibouti	149	780	1020	8.8	n/a	30	8.5	7	n/a
Equatorial Guinea	127	650	710	4.8	n/a	n/a	n/a	n/a	n/a
Eritrea	157	180	220	28.4	n/a	83	3.5	66	n/a
Ethiopia	169	130	160	18.9	23.0	210*	16.7***	173*	4.5
Gambia	155	320	290	16.4	59.3	111	7.5	n/a	8.1
Guinea	160	400	370	7.5	n/a	45	6.4	30*	2.2
Guinea-Bissau	175	160	180	29.4	n/a	n/a	n/a	n/a	n/a
Haiti	146	490	450	6.3	53.9	96	-9.0	93**	n/a
Kiribati	–	1030	1390	12.6	n/a	n/a	n/a	n/a	7.2
LAO PDR	130	280	440	11.3	27.0	236	5.5	147	4.2
Lesotho	138	630	960	6.1	36.4	304	0.1	30	2.0

Liberia	–	130	130	52.8	n/a	n/a	n/a	n/a	n/a
Madagascar	143	240	290	29.8	61.0	229*	43.6***	105*	2.2
Malawi	164	150	160	25.6	20.8	471*	5.0***	26	2.7
Maldives	100	2010	2390	3.7	n/a	617	7.2	287	31.1
Mali	173	220	380	12.1	72.3	143	10.6	130*	2.9
Mauritania	137	460	560	11.1	25.9	n/a	n/a	n/a	n/a
Mozambique	172	210	310	22.0	36.2	470	n/a	130	n/a
Myanmar	132	n/a	n/a	n/a	n/a	242	3.9	84*	3.2
Nepal	142	220	270	6.4	24.1	385		132	2.7
Niger	174	160	240	17.6	60.6	55**	-4.6***	28**	1.2
Rwanda	161	250	230	26.0	60.3	n/a	n/a	44	3.0
Samoa	77	1350	2090	8.6	n/a	98	2.8	77	n/a
Sao Tome & Principe	123	300	390	61.8	n/a	14	n/a	n/a	11.3
Senegal	156	450	710	14.1	17.0	769	14.6	209**	3.3
Sierra Leone	177	140	220	34.6	57.0	40	20.1	83	3.3
Solomon Islands	129	650	590	47.1	n/a	n/a	n/a	n/a	3.1
Somalia	–	n/a	n/a	n/a	n/a	n/a	n/a	n/a	n/a
Sudan	147	310	640	4.4	n/a	61	n/a	89	1.0
Timor-Leste	150	480	750	31.7	n/a	n/a	n/a	n/a	n/a
Togo	152	270	350	3.0	n/a	81	6.2	15**	1.6
Tuvalu	–	1170	1890	36.0	n/a	n/a	n/a	n/a	n/a
Uganda	154	260	280	17.3	n/a	468	19.4	266*	5.0
UR of Tanzania	159	260	340	15.5	57.8	556*	2.5***	796	4.1
Vanuatu	120	1240	1600	12.4	n/a	61	1.5	52**	16.4
Yemen	153	410	600	2.1	15.7	336	35.7	262	1.9
Zambia	165	290	490	21.6	63.8	515*	-10.9***	161*	1.1

Notes: * 2004 data; ** 2003 data; *** growth on previous year; HDI = Human Development Index.
Sources: World Bank/UN, 2006; UNDP, 2007; UNWTO statistics; WTTC statistics

recently, the potential contribution of tourism to the economic development of LDCs has become the focus of more specific attention: 'when the importance of tourism is recognised [in LDCs], all dimensions of the tourism economy should be regarded as an integral part of the development strategy' (UNCTAD, 2001, p18). In fact, at a 'high level' meeting in preparation for the Third UN Conference on Least Developed Countries in 2001, the delegates agreed that they were:

- *Conscious of the serious socio-economic situation of the LDCs, many of which are increasingly marginalised from the global economy;*
- *Aware of the valuable economic opportunities which international tourism has already brought to several LDCs [and] the catalytic impact tourism activities can have on the development process;*
- *Convinced that, for a large majority of LDCs, tourism development can be an avenue to increase participation in the global economy, alleviate poverty, and achieve socio-economic progress for all the people of these countries.* (UN, 2001)

In practice, many LDCs have developing tourism sectors whilst economic data appear to support tourism's developmental role. For example, tourism now represents over 70 per cent of service exports in LDCs, whilst it is amongst the top three export industries in almost half of them (UNCTAD, 2001, p4); it has also been suggested that, in 2004, international tourism was the primary source of foreign exchange earnings in 46 of the then 49 nations on the LDC list, though this contradicts the assertion that one-third of LDCs experience limited tourism activity (UNCTAD, 2001). What is certain is that in some LDCs, such as the Maldives and Nepal, not only has tourism become the dominant economic sector, but also growth rates in tourist arrivals and receipts have been achieved that are significantly higher than the world average, particularly in Cambodia, Tanzania and Uganda.

Nevertheless, the fact remains that even those LDCs that have developed relatively successful tourism sectors have been unable to translate this into broader economic growth and development. In other words, those factors that have served to restrict the development of LDCs appear to have imposed similar barriers to tourism's economic growth potential and, as a consequence, the achievement of 'socio-economic progress for all the people of all these countries' would seem to be a highly optimistic objective. The questions to be asked, therefore, are: does this reflect the increasing marginalization of LDCs within a globalized world economy, or are there nation-specific, domestic forces that contribute to the maintenance of LDC status? And, what are the subsequent implications of the development of tourism, sustainable or otherwise?

The UN lists three criteria, or structural handicaps, that define LDC status, at least two of which must be overcome for a country to graduate to 'developing' status (UN, 2008):

1   Low per capita income (under US$750 for inclusion; over US$900 for graduation);
2   Human resource weaknesses related to health, nutrition, education and adult literacy;
3   Economic vulnerability, based upon a complex combination of a number of indicators, such as the instability of agricultural production and the relative economic importance of non-traditional activities.

To this list, de Rivero (2001, pp118–31) adds a number of challenges in LDCs to support his argument that many, if not all, of them should more accurately be referred to as non-viable national economies. These challenges emanate, in part, from a colonial history and a position of dependency within the global political economy that has long existed and from which it has been impossible to escape. More specifically, however, LDCs also suffer a number of domestic, inter-related challenges, principally a lack of technological resources: 'the main disease ... that is infecting, with increasing virulence, the vast majority of the misnamed developing countries, is scientific and technological poverty' (de Rivero, 2001, p118). In a world with an increasing demand for highly technological products, the likelihood of LDCs being able to break into these markets becomes ever more remote. Furthermore, stagnant economic growth, widespread poverty, rapid population growth, mono-production and the export of primary products, dependency on energy and food imports, limited international investment and, last but most certainly not least, a dependence on international aid, all contribute to a situation where, according to de Rivero, any form of development or progress is unlikely to occur.

These are, however, symptoms of under-development and not necessarily the causes. Thus, Collier (2007) suggests that there are four main factors, or what he refers to as 'development traps', which go some way to explaining why conditions of extreme poverty persist for the world's 'bottom billion'.

Internal conflict

Both civil wars and coups d'état are costly and relatively common in LDCs and other less developed nations. According to Collier (2007, p18), 'seventy-three percent of people in the societies of the bottom billion have been through a civil war or are still in one'. Moreover, in addition to the economic cost of civil wars (equivalent to an annual reduction in economic growth of about 2.3 per cent per year), their legacy (political instability, displaced peoples, health care, and so on) further undermines the potential for economic stability and growth. Internal conflict also, of course, has a direct impact on tourism. Since 1983, for example, Sri Lanka's tourism sector, which directly and indirectly supports around 1 million people, consistently suffered from the effects of the recently concluded conflict between government forces and the Tamil Tigers in the northeast of the country.

Dependence on a natural resource

Paradoxically, wealth created by an abundant natural resource, such as oil, may enhance poverty in the longer term. Local resources may be diverted to its production, traditional exports become uncompetitive and collapse and, frequently, the proceeds may enhance corruption.

Geographical isolation or 'landlockedness'

Geographical isolation itself may not retard growth, particularly in the age of global information and communication (though access to those networks is, of course, a necessity). However, international transport links are essential for trade and economic growth in general, and the development of tourism in particular. The tourism sectors in many LDCs owe their existence to the establishment and maintenance of air links by and with the main tourism generating regions. However (though of less relevance to tourism, perhaps), being landlocked, or surrounded by other poor countries with limited transport infrastructure, frequently impacts on growth and development through the extra costs incurred in transporting exports.

Poor governance

'Terrible governance and policies can' according to Collier (2007, p64) 'destroy an economy with alarming speed'. The rapid economic collapse of Zimbabwe since 2000 and a corresponding collapse in its tourism sector is a powerful, if extreme, example, yet in many LDCs, poor, inefficient or corrupt governance is seen as a major barrier to economic growth and development. This issue is explored in detail by Ghani and Lockhart (2008) who argue forcefully that widespread poverty, a lack of respect for human rights, political instability and a lack of a legal framework to ensure law and order is the direct result of what they refer to as the 'sovereignty gap'. That is, there exists a

> disjunction between the de jure assumption that all states are 'sovereign' regardless of their performance in practice and the de facto reality that many are malfunctioning or collapsed states, incapable of providing their citizens with even the most basic services, and where the reciprocal set of rights and obligations are not a reality. (Ghani and Lockhart, 2008, p21)

In other words, states are failing because their governments neither respect the rights of their citizens nor fulfil their obligations to them; in effect, the state and the population operate independently of each other, the ruling elite frequently enriching themselves whilst the majority of the population live in extreme poverty. Nevertheless:

> Prosperity is ... within the reach of all humanity, but to attain this goal we must first address its necessary pre-condition – effective states that perform the necessary functions for their citizens in our complex world, as well as an international community with the stamina to tackle the challenge of making the world a whole – a genuine international community that agrees to create a collective well-being. (Ghani and Lockhart, 2008, p31)

What this appears to suggest is that global prosperity requires globalization, a process that, as already discussed, is seen by both supporters and critics of the globalization thesis as enhancing global inequalities. Irrespective of this conundrum, however, ineffective or inappropriate policies (or even a complete lack of policies) may impact significantly on tourism development in particular. Indeed, the policy arena is one of a number of recognized challenges to tourism development in LDCs listed by UNCTAD (2001, pp8–13):

- Geographical characteristics: smallness, remoteness and 'land-lockedness' may limit access and investment.
- Vulnerability to external shocks: these include both natural disasters and external political or economic factors.
- Structural handicaps: limited transport and accommodation facilities; poor telecommunications; limited access to global distribution systems; human resources weaknesses; and, high leakages and inter-sectoral weaknesses.
- Policy environment: an absence of appropriate domestic policies for and investment in tourism development may be exacerbated by a lack of international recognition of the specific challenges facing LDCs.

The extent to which these challenges are evident in practice is explored in the following case study of tourism development in The Gambia but the important point that emerges from both the globalization debate and the specific issue of tourism in LDCs within the broader post-development context is that tourism is a global phenomenon, in that few places do not attract tourists or support a tourism sector. That is, it occurs on a global scale. However, tourism is not globalized; there is little evidence of global, or even international, inter-connectedness or interdependence except, perhaps, in the case of some multinational hospitality organizations and the major strategic alliances in the airline sector, nor is competition within the tourism market truly global. In fact, for the most part, tourism is national or local in terms of both demand and supply. Thus, there is no single, uniform external environment to the tourism system. Each tourism development context presents a unique combination of socio-cultural, political, economic and environmental factors with which tourism interacts and which must be understood if the benefits of tourism are to be optimized. For example, community-based tourism is frequently promoted as a means of enhancing tourism's benefits to local people yet, in the case of LDCs, the 'sovereignty gap' may limit the success of such a policy – indeed, where the poor are disenfranchised, interventionist policies, such as pro-poor tourism, may offer the best solution.

If each tourism development context is unique, so too must be the desired outcomes of tourism. In other words, tourism is described as an agent of development, but 'development' must be interpreted according to the needs of individual destinations. It may mean, for example, economic diversification, regeneration or, for LDCs perhaps, little more than a subsistence activity. A common theme in all tourism contexts, however, is that tourism is a business. It is, usually, a function of capitalist supply and demand, whereby resources are exploited to support the production of services and experiences sold, preferably for a profit, to tourists. It is through the sale of tourist services that employment is created, income is generated, supply chains developed and so on. Therefore, it is logical to suggest that the most appropriate basis for exploring ways of optimizing tourism's benefits according to the needs of the destination is to start with an analysis of the resources, or capitals, available to that destination, an argument that is pursued in more detail in Chapter 6. Nevertheless, key to any tourism development is (physical) environmental sustainability, both as defined by specific destinational contexts and in terms of broader (global) challenges, particularly climate change. Thus, the following chapter turns to the environmental side of the tourism development equation.

Case study: Tourism development in The Gambia

The Republic of The Gambia, situated in West Africa, is the smallest country on the African continent. Following the course of the River Gambia, it is bordered by Senegal to the north and south, and by the North Atlantic Ocean to the west. It has a total land area of 11,300 sq km and is 350km long and just 48km wide at its widest point (see Figure 4.1). Lying equidistant between the equator and the Tropic of Cancer, some six hours' flying time from northern Europe, The Gambia experiences a tropical climate of a hot rainy season from June to November and a cooler dry season from November to May.

The country's present borders were established in agreement with France in 1889, the year that it became a British Crown Colony; however, Britain first gained possession of The Gambia in 1783 under the Treaty of Versailles and established a military post in Bathhurst (now Banjul, the capital) in 1816.

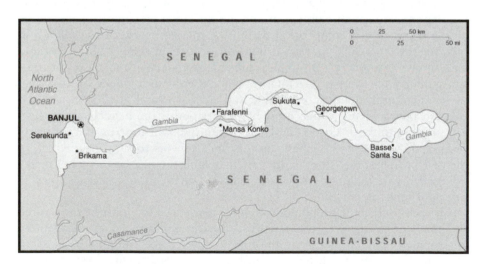

Source: CIA World Factbook

Figure 4.1 *The Gambia*

Independence was achieved in 1965 and The Gambia became a republic in 1970. The country enjoyed what was claimed to be multi-party democracy until a military coup in 1994. Two years later, presidential elections were held and the new President, Yahya Jammeh, was subsequently re-elected in 2002 and his party, the Alliance for Patriotic Reorientation and Construction (APRC), maintained a strong majority in the 2002 National Assembly elections which were boycotted by opposition parties. In 2006, President Jammeh was re-elected to a third term, though there are doubts over the extent to which democratic principles were upheld.

The population of The Gambia is approximately 1.6 million and comprises a number of ethnic groups, each maintaining its own language and traditions. About 90 per cent of Gambians are Muslims and some 60 per cent of the population lives in rural villages. The official or natural population growth rate currently stands at 2.7 per cent per annum, although this is boosted to some 4.2 per cent per annum by immigration from less politically stable neighbouring states. With one of the continent's highest population densities (142 per sq km), managing future population growth represents a significant challenge.

The economy of The Gambia

The Gambia has few natural resources. Consequently, the dominant activity is subsistence agriculture, accounting for almost 75 per cent of employment but just 35 per cent of GDP which, in 2002, amounted to US$356 million (www. worldbank.org). One of the principal agricultural sectors is the production of groundnuts and groundnut products which, prior to the development of tourism, was the country's main source of foreign exchange earnings. Groundnut production currently represents 7 per cent of GDP, whilst other agricultural activity is based on crops, fishing, livestock and forestry. A limited industrial sector accounts for 12 per cent of GDP whilst services, including tourism, account for 53 per cent. Tourism itself is estimated to contribute 12 per cent of GDP although, according to WTTC data, the wider tourism economy in The Gambia accounts for 23 per cent of GDP. Some 10,000 people, or 2.5 per cent of the working population, are employed directly and indirectly in tourism; however, it is suggested that, given the high level of subsistence agriculture and other informal economic activity, tourism accounts for 20 per cent of formal employment.

With its limited resources, its small industrial base and principally agrarian economy, not only does the country suffer a significant balance of payments deficit and high levels of external debt, but it also has a narrow tax base that limits revenue generation opportunities. Thus, economic progress remains largely dependent on international aid which, in 2003, amounted to almost US$60 million.

Development indicators

The Gambia is one of the poorest countries in the world. It is one of 49 officially recognized LDCs, and is ranked 155th out of 177 nations on the UNDP's

Human Development Index (HDI) (UNDP, 2007). With a per capita GDP in 2006 of US$310, average household income falls below the US$1 per day poverty threshold; with over half the country's wealth owned by just 20 per cent of the population, between 50 per cent and 70 per cent of the population are estimated to live in extreme poverty. Despite efforts to address this, little progress has been made and, according to the country's first Millennium Development Goals Report (Republic of The Gambia, 2003), there is a high risk that the goal of reducing the incidence of extreme poverty in the country by 50 per cent by 2015 will not be met. Table 4.3 provides other selected indicators of (under)development in The Gambia.

Table 4.3 *The Gambia: Selected development indicators 2005*

Population under 15 years old (% of total)	41.2
Population over 65 years old (% of total)	3.7
Life expectancy at birth	56
Under-five mortality rate (per 1000 births)	137
Adult literacy rate (% of over 15 year olds)	30.9 (female)
	45 (male)

Source: adapted from UNDP, 2007

Tourism development in The Gambia

Tourism was first considered as a means of fostering socio-economic development in The Gambia in the mid-1960s. At that time, the country was largely dependent on the export of groundnuts and groundnut products and the global markets for these were becoming increasingly unstable. Thus, there was a recognized need to diversify into other sources of foreign exchange earnings. With its attractive winter climate and undeveloped coastline, the potential existed to market The Gambia as an exotic winter sun destination. The first tourists arrived in 1965, initially on Swedish organized tours, though limited growth was experienced. Five years later, the supply of hotel beds had grown from an initial 162 to 300 and arrivals had increased from 300 to 2600 in 1970–71, but it was not until 1972 that a major effort was made by The Gambia to develop tourism.

Since then, there have been two distinct phases in the development of tourism in The Gambia: a period of relatively stable growth up to 1994 and, following the military coup, a decade that has experienced erratic arrivals figures and no overall growth.

Phase 1: 1972–1994

As noted above, relatively few tourists visited The Gambia in the years immediately following its 'discovery' by the Swedish tour operator Vingressor. However, once proactive steps were taken to develop the sector, the country experienced a rapid increase in the annual number of tourist arrivals, although a number of fluctuations demonstrated the sector's vulnerability to both

Table 4.4 *Tourist arrivals (air charter) in The Gambia 1972/3–1994/5*

Year	Arrivals	Year	Arrivals
1972–73	15,584	1984–85	45,861
1973–74	20,383	1985–86	47,926
1974–75	18,651	1986–87	45,759
1975–76	21,116	1987–88	47,734
1976–77	19,505	1988–89	54,149
1977–78	15,769	1989–90	47,012
1978–79	25,907	1990–91	58,026
1979–80	23,822	1991–92	65,771
1980–81	19,209	1992–93	63,940
1981–82	13,331	1993–94	89,997
1982–83	26,745	1994–95	42,919
1983–84	39,491		

Source: Central Statistics Department, 2005 (www.gambia.gm/Statistics/Publications.htm)

internal and external events (see Table 4.4). For example, arrivals in 1981–82 fell dramatically as a result of a failed coup attempt. It should be noted that, for the purpose of comparison, these figures are for air charter arrivals only; figures for non-charter air arrivals are not available from 1996 onwards. However, virtually all leisure tourists travel on package/charter flights from Europe. It should also be noted that, during this first period, arrivals figures relate to a 12-month tourism season (July–June) as opposed to a calendar year.

During this period, two principal characteristics of tourism to The Gambia immediately emerged. Firstly, the country became dependent on a small number of key tourist markets, specifically the UK and Scandinavia. From the mid-1980s, the UK became the dominant market, accounting for well over 50 per cent of annual arrivals throughout the period. Secondly, tourism became highly seasonal – as a winter sun destination, the majority of visitors arrived during the peak season of November to April, with over 80 per cent of arrivals occurring during this six-month period. Although efforts were made to develop a summer market, the country remained uncompetitive compared with Mediterranean summer sun destinations.

With respect to accommodation supply, the number of bed spaces increased rapidly. By the late 1970s, tourist bed capacity had reached around 3000 and by the mid-1990s some 5000 bed spaces were available. The great majority of these were in hotels and guest houses located in a 15km strip of land along the coast designated in 1974 as a Tourism Development Area. Most hotels were of tourist, mid-range quality; by 1994, the country boasted only one five-star hotel, the 312-bed Kairaba Hotel. The government of the day provided a variety of incentives and controls for hotel development, as well as establishing a number of specific bodies responsible for policy development and implementation. However, the influence of the public sector was limited by inefficient administration and a lack of funding to support tourism development and promotion. In the country's first five-year development plan, for example,

Dalasi 16.8 million, less than 4 per cent of the national budget, was allocated to tourism development; in the second five-year plan (1980–85), this sum was halved. Consequently, tourism development was largely driven by the overseas-dominated private sector, with grants from international agencies funding some infrastructural developments, whilst the Gambia Hotels Association became the country's marketing body.

As tourism to The Gambia grew, particularly during this period, so too did its economic importance. By 1992, it was estimated that tourism was accounting for around 10 per cent of GDP, or about US$26 million to the economy. However, the contribution of tourism to the economy was limited by the fact that most tourists were on pre-paid package tours and, as a result, spent as little as $8 per day within the country (reflecting few spending opportunities outside the hotels). Moreover, as the majority of food and drink consumed by tourists had to be imported, the tourism sector suffered significant leakages, to the extent that only around 20 per cent of the holiday price paid by tourists remained in The Gambia. Nevertheless, the tourism sector accounted for some 7000 direct and indirect jobs.

By 1994, then, tourism had evolved into a major economic sector in The Gambia, although the sector displayed the typical characteristics of dependency – high leakages, significant foreign ownership of tourism assets, dependency on two principal but highly seasonal markets and on international tour operators both for the supply of tourists and for air links with northern Europe. Such dependency was evidenced in the collapse of tourism following the 1994 coup yet, by the following year, the country was optimistic about the future development of tourism. However, this optimism was misplaced.

Phase 2: 1995–2005

In the year following the coup, the tourism sector recovered well and by 1998 pre-coup figures had been exceeded. In 1999, a record 96,000 tourists visited The Gambia but, since then, annual arrivals figures have fluctuated. As noted in the most recent tourism development plan (DSTC, 2005, p26), the tourism industry 'completely lost momentum in the period 2000–2005', although recent years have witnessed something of a resurgence (Table 4.5).

The UK market remains dominant though its share has declined in recent years, accounting for 42 per cent of all arrivals in 2006. Scandinavia remains

Table 4.5 *Tourist arrivals in The Gambia 1995–2006*

Year	Arrivals	Year	Arrivals
1995–96	72,098	2001	75,209
1996	76,814	2002	78,893
1997	84,751	2003	73,000
1998	91,106	2004	90,098
1999	96,122	2005	107,904
2000	78,710	2006	124,800

Source: GTA, 2003; GTA, 2007

an important market, representing almost 12 per cent of arrivals, but the Dutch, German and Spanish markets are of growing importance. Against this background of variable tourist arrivals, a number of developments during this second phase are of significance:

- There has been an increase in the supply of accommodation. By 2007, 32 recognized hotels and guest houses offered almost 6400 bed spaces, including a new 200-room Sheraton Hotel, supplemented by a number of houses/apartments available for private rent. In addition, new developments away from the coastal strip, such as the Mandina eco-lodges at the Makasutu Forest, a small up-market project developed according to ecotourism principles, have added to the supply of accommodation which is now estimated to total 7000 bed spaces. The majority of hotels remain under foreign ownership, however; despite favourable terms in acquiring land within the Tourism Development Area, a 31 per cent bank lending rate discourages local investment.
- Infrastructural developments have included a US$10 million beach recovery project funded by an African Development Bank loan, a US$150,000 street lighting system in the main tourism development area, a new road bypassing Serrekunda, the country's largest urban connurbation, that has dramatically improved access to the tourist area and the upgrading of the coastal road south to the Senegalese border. The international airport has also benefited from a new terminal building although facilities remain basic. Landing and handling fees at the airport are some 50 per cent higher than at Gatwick, reflecting the low level of traffic yet acting as a major disincentive to airlines and tour operators.
- There has been a reduction in the number of tour operators offering The Gambia as a winter sun destination. According to one report, some 43 European operators brought tourists to The Gambia in 1994 but, by 2002, the number of operators had more than halved. Just eight major UK operators now feature the country in their winter sun brochures, one of which, the specialist Gambia Experience, offers a year-round programme. This company now accounts for some 60 per cent of all UK arrivals as well as operating a weekly 'scheduled charter' flight from Gatwick throughout the year – the only scheduled air link between The Gambia and Europe is a weekly flight to Brussels. Thus, tour operators remain highly influential in the development of tourism in The Gambia and, through their dominant role, are able to negotiate low contract prices with hotels. The average per person contract price (bed and breakfast) is £10–£12 (US$13–US$16) per night and, as a consequence, few hotels are profitable and in a position to reinvest in upgrading facilities.
- It is also suggested that the decline in arrivals in 2001 and 2002 (Table 4.5 above) resulted from a German operator, Frosch Touristik International, that had been running four flights a week into the country, cutting its programme to The Gambia in response to a policy decision to ban all-inclusive holidays in The Gambia, a major market for the operator. The extent to

which the decline in arrivals is fully attributable to the loss of this business is uncertain, though it serves to demonstrate the country's continuing and total dependency on overseas tour operators and the consequential fragility of the tourism sector in The Gambia.

• A continuing problem (and one recognized by the country's tourism authorities) is the lack of data, particularly with respect to the economic value of tourism to the country. Thus, although reliable and contemporary arrivals figures are available, only general statistics, such as tourism's contribution to GDP, are regularly provided. However, specific studies provide additional data which contribute to the overall 'picture'. In 2004, the tourism sector accounted for 13 per cent of The Gambia's GDP, with net foreign exchange earnings estimated to be US$40 million. Leakages are estimated to be 45 per cent of gross expenditure, although this may well be a conservative figure. Despite the 'Gambia is Good' project, which links local farmers with hotels, relatively little progress has been made in developing backward linkages in the local economy and one-third of the country's total imports of food and beverages go to hotels to meet the needs of tourists. Most hotels, for example, import eggs because it is cheaper than using domestic sources (the feed for hens must also be imported at high cost).

Additionally, relatively few opportunities still exist for significant levels of additional expenditure outside the hotels (hence the short-lived policy of banning all-inclusive holidays in 2000). For example, a survey in 2000–01 found that tourists spent, on average, Dalasis 596 per day (£25 at the prevailing exchange rate), although almost two-thirds is spent on food, drinks and excursions in the formal sector. A pro-poor tourism project running since 2001 has significantly increased the earnings of specific groups within the informal sector (see Bah and Goodwin, 2003) although this has had little overall impact on spreading the economic benefits of tourism throughout the local economy. Conversely, a significant number of overseas charities have been established, often by people who have visited The Gambia as tourists, usually to assist the development of schools and education, whilst some tour operators, such as Gambia Experience, have established charitable funds to support local education projects. However, no comprehensive record of the activities and spending of these organizations exists.

A further source of revenue for the government is the 15 per cent tax imposed on all sales within the formal tourism sector. In 2004, this provided Dalasis 54 million (£1.08 million/US$1.45 million) in revenues, augmented by a £5 arrivals tax that is imposed on all international air arrivals. In 2004, this boosted government revenues by £450,000 (US$600,000).

• Over the last decade, there have also been a number of developments with respect to the institutional organization of tourism in The Gambia. At the governmental level, tourism has, since 1995, been the responsibility of the Department of State for Tourism and Culture (DSTC), the principal tourism policy and planning body. Implementation and operational activities are undertaken by the Gambia Tourism Authority (GTA), which was set up in 2001 by an act of the National Assembly as a statutory body to develop, regulate and promote the Gambian tourism sector. Although an executive arm of the DSTC, the GTA is funded by annual fees paid by the formal private tourism sector, principally hotels and the four major ground-handlers in the country. Therefore, the relationship between the GTA, the DSTC and the private sector remains unclear.

In addition to these two bodies, the Responsible Tourism Partnership, members of which include representatives of the public, private and voluntary sectors, and the Association of Small Scale Enterprises in Tourism (ASSET) have been established in recent years. These two organizations work towards developing a more responsible approach to tourism development, particularly with respect to helping small-scale businesses benefit more from their participation in tourism.

Over the last decade, then, a number of positive developments have occurred that, in principle, have laid the foundations for the further growth and development of tourism and for increasing its contribution to wider economic development. However, further research has revealed a number of barriers to tourism-induced development. These fall under three main headings.

Characteristics of tourism in The Gambia Tourism is spatially constrained to the small coastal strip, thereby limiting employment, income and other opportunities to the western margins of the country. There are few, natural/cultural sites or places of interest to justify tourism developments beyond the coast. Even there, the tourism product is focused primarily on a limited mid-range hotel sector. Tourism in The Gambia is also highly seasonal, with a significant degree of dependency on overseas tour operators.

Structural challenges Structural handicaps, such as poor international/domestic transport and telecommunication links, limited tourism facilities and infrastructure and limited human resources, are prevalent in The Gambia. However, it is inter-sectoral weaknesses and high levels of leakages (hence a high level of imports to support tourism) in particular that remain significant barriers to tourism-induced development and economic growth/poverty alleviation.

The tourism policy environment

- The financial exploitation of tourism: tourism is seen as a valuable source of government revenue yet there is little, if any, re-investment in the sector, any infrastructural improvements usually being dependent upon international aid. Moreover, high levels of taxation limit the ability or incentive for local operators to invest. At the same time, efforts to optimize government revenues from tourism have undermined the success of specific programmes, such as a pro-poor tourism initiative.

- Inappropriate policies: the development and growth of tourism in The Gambia is, to some extent, restricted to inappropriate policy decisions. For example, it is now recognized that the focus should be on increasing the volume of traditional, mass winter sun tourism, yet current government policy concentrates on small, ecotourism developments. At the same time, the allocation of scarce resources to inappropriate marketing schemes, as well as a high degree of patronage within the political system, further restricts the development of the sector.
- Lack of knowledge/information: the Gambia Tourism Authority has limited information or statistical data at its disposal. There is, therefore, a lack of knowledge and understanding of tourist markets, tourist behaviour and needs and the contribution of tourism to the economy and development. As a consequence, policy decisions are taken on the basis of assumptions rather than evidence (Sharpley, 2007b; 2009).

5

Tourism Environments

So far, the main focus of this book has been on tourism within the broader context of development. In particular, the potential contribution of tourism to the socio-economic development of destination areas has been explored within the context of contemporary concepts and processes related to development including, of course, sustainable development. A number of principal themes have emerged from this discussion.

Firstly, tourism brings recognized economic benefits to destination communities as well as to generating regions, in the latter case through employment in outbound tourism organizations, transport operators and other services. However, the extent to which such economic benefits act as stimuli to wider development remains unclear but is generally overstated. Secondly, each tourism developmental context is unique with respect to, for example, the characteristics of the destination, the nature and scale of tourism and, in particular, the needs and expectations of local communities as perceived by themselves. Thirdly, tourism occurs on a global scale but is not globalized. Both the demand for and supply of tourism is, for the most part, domestic, whilst the flows and production of international tourism remain distinctively geographically or politically regionalized. Consequently, although certain sectors, such as international airlines, play a pivotal role in international tourism mobility and destination development, the assumed subordination of local or national influence over tourism development to global forces in general, and all-powerful multinational corporations in particular, is not so widely manifested in practice as is frequently claimed. Finally, and reflecting the main thrust of this book, sustainable tourism development has been shown to be a failed concept. That is, although contemporary policies refer to tourism being developed in accordance with the principles of sustainable development, this represents an unworkable marriage – the production and consumption of tourism are, collectively, unable to meet the requirements and objectives of sustainable development.

This is not, of course, a new argument; since the idea of sustainable tourism development first emerged it has been hotly debated and widely criticized (Weaver, 2004). Nevertheless, the preceding chapters suggest that an alternative framework is now required for considering ways of optimizing tourism's economic contribution to destination communities, the concept of sustainable tourism development having run its course. However, this is not to suggest that the environmental sustainability element of the sustainable (tourism) development equation should also be rejected. The environment, however defined, remains intrinsic to the continuing success, or sustainability, of tourism destinations. Tourism, like any economic activity that is resource dependent, must sustain or maintain its resource base as a prerequisite to its long-term health, but particularly because the environment is intrinsic to the tourism experience or 'part of tourism's product' (Mieczkowski, 1995, p112). That is, tourists consume environments, either simply by 'gazing' upon them, as Urry (2002) famously puts it, or interacting with them more intimately. Indeed, the environment is more often than not the principal attraction of the destination, whether the physical natural/built environment or the socio-cultural environment, whilst the significance of climate (or, more specifically, climate change) both to the immediate tourist experience – adverse weather conditions can, for example, ruin a holiday – and to longer-term transformations of destination environments has become of greater concern (Hall and Higham, 2005; Hamilton et al, 2005; Becken and Hay, 2007).

The issue of climate change and its links with tourism are explored in more detail later in this chapter. Nonetheless, the point here is, as noted in Chapter 1, that the relationship between tourism and the environment, in particular the physical natural and built environment, has long been recognized. Concerns were first raised over the exponential growth of tourism and its consequential impacts on host environments in the late 1960s and early 1970s (Mishan, 1969; Young, 1973; Turner and Ash, 1975). At that time, environmentalism more generally was framed by neo-Malthusian concerns over population growth (Ehrlich, 1972) and the 'Limits to Growth' school (Meadows et al, 1972) and consequently, although international tourism was still then in its infancy, certainly relative to its contemporary scale and scope, there were calls for restraint in its development:

> *Travel on this scale ... inevitably disrupts the character of the affected regions, their populations and ways of living. As swarms of holiday-makers arrive ... local life and industry shrivel, hospitality vanishes, and indigenous populations drift into a quasi-parasitic way of life catering with contemptuous servility to the unsophisticated multitude.* (Mishan, 1969, p142)

Since then considerable effort, manifested in innumerable books, journal articles and other publications, has been dedicated to exploring the factors influencing tourism's environmental impacts. Initially, these principally adopted a tourism-centric, linear 'cause-effect' approach (Mathieson and Wall, 1982) but, just as understanding of the tourism-environment relationship has advanced from the 'advocacy' position, which viewed tourism and environmental protection/conservation as separate issues, through the 'cautionary' and 'adaptancy' to the 'knowledge' position (Jafari, 1989), so too have perspectives on the causes of and responses to the environmental consequences of tourism development evolved and broadened, albeit to a limited extent. For example, Mieczkowski (1995) observes that, generally, it is difficult to differentiate between environmental transformations resulting from tourism activity and those associated with either changing biophysical conditions, including climate change, or other socio-economic factors. More specifically, he also asserts that the environmental impacts of tourism are, in fact, a manifestation of the broader consequences of mainstream, western-centric development (see Chapter 3) that subordinates people and environmental resources to profit and economic growth (Southgate and Sharpley, 2002, p256).

This theme is expanded upon by Brockington et al (2008) who argue that, far from representing a challenge to the advance of capitalism, contemporary approaches to conservation – particularly the establishment of protected areas – and capitalism work together; 'conservation and capitalism are shaping society and nature, often in partnership' (Brockington et al, 2008, p5). In other words, solutions to environmental problems are promoted in ways that enhance capitalist consumerism, but that also frequently result in unintended consequences for landscape and wildlife conservation and for people, the displacement or eviction of local communities from areas that become formally designated as protected being seen as a common outcome. In particular, they consider ecotourism to be a specific example of the interdependency between environmental conservation and neo-liberal capitalism. That is, ecotourism is often seen as a vehicle for protecting wildlife, empowering communities and providing much needed income to local people although, frequently, the development of ecotourism may actually negatively transform local lifestyles and exclude local communities from economically important landscapes to allow tourists to consume what they perceive to be 'authentic' experiences. More generally, of course, the conservation-capitalism partnership is also implicit within the sustainable tourism literature in as much as tourism, as a manifestation of neo-liberal economic activity, is promoted as a potential means of preserving and enhancing physical and cultural environments. In short, perspectives on the tourism-environment relationship have, to an extent, shifted from a confrontational approach that considers tourism, particularly mass tourism, as an inevitably destructive activity that must be contained and managed (though this argument is still evident in journalistic treatments of the subject), to one which views tourism and conservation within a context of mutual dependency and benefit, albeit within a (western) neo-liberal framework.

Nevertheless, the tourism literature continues, for the most part, both to locate the analysis of the environmental consequences of tourism development within a tourism-centric, destination-specific context and also to adopt a deterministic, cause-and-effect approach to tourism's impacts. As Wong (2004, p452) observes, early research into tourism's environmental impacts tended to focus on 'one particular environmental component' and most analysis was 'post factum' and hence lacking baselines against which both past and future environmental change could be assessed. Moreover, according to Wong (2004, p452), little has changed: 'Overall, research [into tourism's environmental impacts] has been relatively poorly developed and not truly multidisciplinary, lacking coherence and being relatively fragmented and unstructured'.

Whilst this is, to an extent, both logical and inevitable, especially from a destination management perspective, it does not allow for an exploration of other factors, both intrinsic and external to the destination, that may influence perceptions of and attitudes towards the environment with respect to its protection or exploitation or that determine the focus and philosophy of planning and management policies both generally and for tourism in particular. Moreover, nor does it allow for temporal transformations. That is, attitudes towards the environment, the needs of societies or local communities and environment management policies all change over time. For example, the building of numerous railway viaducts in the English countryside during the 19th century was opposed by groups concerned about the visual impact on the landscape; when those same viaducts were threatened with demolition in the late 20th century, conservation groups sought to protect them as part of the rural heritage.

In short, within the context of the tourism-environment relationship, the natural or built destination environment is typically seen as a single, discrete, given entity that must be managed or conserved yet, at the same time, exploited for touristic consumption. However, as hinted at in previous chapters, there is no single environment, even within the context of a particular destination. Just as there is no single nature, but multiple 'natures' (Macnaghten and Urry, 1998), so too are there multiple environments; the destination environment is defined by the varying perceptions of different local groups, the attitudes and expectations of visitors, regional and national policy makers and so on (Holden, 2000). At the same time, of course, specific destinational environments do not exist in isolation from wider national or global environments – from the tourism system perspective, the broader environment is an exogenous factor with which the tourism system interacts, the global atmosphere or climate system being an obvious example. Thus, tourism environments are diverse, complex and, in a sense, multi-layered.

The purpose of this chapter, therefore, is to conceptualize the complexity and diversity of tourism environments as a contribution to an alternative approach to tourism development discussed in the following chapters. That is, it does not set out to propose strategies for managing tourism's environmental consequences; these are considered at length in the extant tourism literature. Rather, focusing specifically on the physical environment, it seeks to develop a conceptual model of the tourism-environment relationship as a framework for identifying issues that support the argument for a resource- or capitals-based approach to tourism development at the destinational level. A number of these issues are then exemplified in the case study of the English Lake District at the end of the chapter.

Tourism environments: Towards a conceptual model

To develop a conceptual model of the relationship between tourism and the environment may seem an ambitious, if not impossible, task (Meyer-Arendt, 2004). Each and every tourism development context, whether local, regional or national, is unique. Not only are destinations defined by a particular combination of environmental resources, natural or man-made, but the robustness or fragility of those resources, their significance or centrality to the tourism experience, and the scale, scope, character and stage of development of the tourism sector more generally represent parameters within which the tourism-environment interface may be perceived and, consequently, appropriate policies for the management and development of tourism considered.

Moreover, distinctions exist between the ways in which local communities, tourists and other stakeholders perceive or value the destination environment, distinctions which may also be influenced by the broader socio-economic and political context within which the destination is located. Thus, local communities may view the environment as a legitimate resource for development, particularly where tourism plays a relatively important role in the local economy, whereas tourists may value highly a pristine or undeveloped traditional environment. Conversely, the cultural significance of a resource may, for local communities, outweigh any potential economic value arising from its exploitation as a tourist venue or attraction, Uluru (Ayers Rock) in Australia being a notable example (Brown, 1999).

Equally, as observed in Chapter 1, tourists themselves vary enormously in terms of their attitudes towards particular environments, their degree of understanding of their impacts on the local environment and their consequential behaviour (Hillery et al, 2001) whilst, according to Carrier and Macleod (2005), ecotourists in particular travel in what they refer to as an 'ecotourist bubble'. That is, they consume constructed or commodified ecotourism experiences from within a 'bubble' that obscures the social, economic and political processes that enable them to enjoy such experiences (see also Brockington et al, 2008, pp144–6). More simply, particular environmental resources may be used in different ways by different tourists. For example, it has been found that visitors to rural areas place varying degrees of importance on the rural environment and the activities they are able to participate in, true 'ruralists' seeking to enjoy 'traditional' rural environments and activities being in a minority compared with those exploiting the environment for non-traditional or 'urban' activities (Kastenholz, 2000).

The tourism-environment interface within particular destinational contexts may also be influenced by a variety of factors beyond, or external to, the destination. As already observed, the broader socio-economic and political context, such as the degree of regional or national economic development or the institutional structures, ideologies and robustness of governance, may impact directly upon the ways in which the environment is perceived, managed and exploited. For instance, there are numerous examples of existing environmental protection measures, such as national park status, being overlooked or abused for financial gain. One such example occurred in Thailand in 1998 when the national government, in the hope of boosting the country's image and, hence, tourism revenues, approved the use of Maya Beach in the Phi Phi Islands National Park as the location for the movie 'The Beach'. Despite protests from campaigners who pointed out that Thai national parks were not for sale, the production of the movie went ahead, with significant environmental alteration and damage occurring (The Beach War, n.d.). Restorative work was undertaken by the film production company once the shooting of the movie was completed although, somewhat ironically, the Phi Phi Islands were subsequently devastated by the 2004 Indian Ocean tsunami.

Of course, more often than not national park designation and other environmental protection measures are observed, establishing the extent to which environmental adaptation or exploitation may occur or the nature and scale of development, if any, within the boundaries of protected areas (Eagles and McCool, 2002). Conversely, where no formal landscape designation exists, national planning laws may determine or restrict the scale and nature of tourism developments in order to maintain environmental integrity. In Cyprus, for example, reflecting similar restrictions in many other destinations, planning laws stipulate that hotels should be built at least 300m from the shoreline and be no more than five storeys high (Sharpley, 1998). At the same time, informal influences, such as national cultural identity needs, may also dictate how environmental resources are perceived and, hence, managed. For instance, it is claimed that the development of national parks in the US reflected 'powerful nation-building forces ... and that country's own search for features adequate to portray its greatness' (Brockington et al, 2008, p47). Conversely, and as explored in more detail in the case study at the end of the chapter, the designation and subsequent management policy of national parks in England reflects an atavistic, romantic vision of pre-industrial rurality.

Other exogenous influences on the tourism-environment relationship can also be identified, including international private and public sector organizations concerned with supporting and promoting tourism development, as well as pressure or activist groups that seek to limit tourism development. For example, it has been found that grassroots activist groups in southern Europe, specifically in Greece, Spain and Portugal, have increasingly engaged in demonstrations and other forms of protest against environmentally damaging tourism developments (Kousis, 2000). At the same time, of course, global environmental forces, in particular climate change, are of direct relevance to the integrity and sustainability of environmental resources at the local, destinational level. Becken and Hay (2007), for example, look in some depth at climatic changes in Alpine Europe since the 1980s noting that, if current global warming trends continue, the winter tourism industry in that region will face significant challenges with shorter skiing seasons and diminished snow-reliability, new patterns of demand favouring higher altitude resorts and increased potential for catastrophic events, such as major avalanches or flash flooding.

Interestingly, in late 2008, the Alps had, at an early stage in the skiing season, experienced one of the best snowfalls for some 30 years. Along with other climatic events occurring at the same time, including significant and early ice cover in the Arctic and extensive snowfalls over Canada and the northern half of the US, this served to demonstrate the uncertainty surrounding climate change predictions and to support the argument of some that, although there have undoubtedly been measurable increases in greenhouse gas (GHE) emissions, the extent to which these directly influence climate change is less certain.

The complex climate change debate is beyond the scope of this chapter, though a useful overview can be found in Henson (2008). The point is, however, that although the principal focus on the tourism-environment relationship must, inevitably, be on local, destinational issues, influences and outcomes, it should also be considered within a framework that embraces wider political, cultural and environmental influences. In other words, and as the conceptual model in Figure 5.1 below attempts to demonstrate, the relationship and interaction between tourism development and the environment, the factors that may influence the nature of that relationship and, consequently, the ways in which the environment is perceived and managed must be viewed from a multi-dimensional (and, implicitly, a multi-disciplinary) perspective, giving due recognition to broader forces and influences that may impact upon or shape tourism development at the destination.

Inevitably, the model in Figure 5.1 over-simplifies the complex and dynamic relationship between tourism and the environment and the multitude of situations within which it occurs. As already observed, each tourism development context is unique, a particular amalgam of physical, social, cultural, political and economic resources that collectively provide experiences for tourists who themselves are individually unique with respect to their needs, expectations, values and behaviour. Thus, no single model can possibly conceptualize the virtually limitless diversity of tourism-environments relationships or, more succinctly, the innumerable tourism environments that exist within the tourism system.

Nevertheless, the model does serve to demonstrate not only the extent to which multiple environments exist, even within the context of certain destinations, but also the complex and multi-dimensional factors and influences that create those multiple environments. It also suggests that the way in which the destination environment is protected, managed or exploited for tourism requires the effective interplay between the different environments or, more precisely, agreement or compromise between differing, competing perceptions of the most appropriate use of that environment. This, in turn, suggests that the environment, as a specific form of capital that is exploited through tourism development, is inextricably linked to the extent to which other capitals – social, political, economic – are possessed by individuals, groups, communities or organizations both within and outside the destination. Thus, for example, the owners of valuable or scenic landscape may possess significant environmental capital, but if that landscape is protected by planning restrictions or protective designations, as in the case of the English Lake District described later in this chapter, the landowners' lack of political capital limits their ability to utilize or exploit their environmental capital as they might wish.

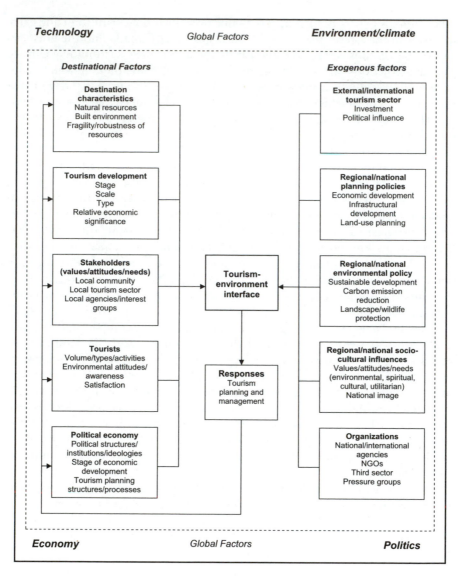

Figure 5.1 *A conceptual model of the tourism-environment relationship*

The notion of capitals as a basis for an alternative approach to tourism development is returned to in the following chapter. For the purposes of the present chapter, however, Figure 5.1 provides a useful framework for highlighting issues that are significant to the tourism-environment relationship. In particular, it proposes that there are three layers or levels at which influences on that relationship and, hence, the management of tourism environments, should be considered. Firstly, of course, it is essential to locate the analysis of the interface between tourism and the environment within the context of the destination:

the destination environment is one, usually significant, element of the tourism product or experience and must be managed in such a way that it not only meets the needs and expectations of tourists but also continues to attract tourists (and maintain the tourism sector) into the future. At the same time, the use and management of the destination environment should also reflect, as far as possible, the needs of local communities and other stakeholders, optimizing not only the benefits that accrue to them through tourism but also meeting other needs.

In some instances, particularly small island micro-states and sub-national island jurisdictions (Baldicchino, 2006), the destination is synonymous with the state. That is, the destination is perceived to be the state as a geographical entity in its entirety (even though tourism development may be focused on specific resorts) and, with tourism frequently playing a dominant role in the local economy, national environmental policies may be directly related to tourism development. More commonly, however, the destination – for example, a coastal resort, a wilderness area or national park, an historic city, or a smaller, attraction-based destination – exists within a broader, more diverse national context in which 'external' (to the destination) state policies, environmental and otherwise, may impinge upon the tourism-environment relationship within the destination. These may have a direct influence through, for example, planning regulations, national conservation or land designation processes and, of course, national tourism development structures and policies, or an indirect influence through, for example, transport policies. Thus, the second level highlights what are referred to in Figure 5.1 as exogenous factors, which may include the environmental ideologies of international organizations, such as development agencies or non-government organizations (NGOs), which become 'internalised' in destination development (Brockington et al, 2008).

Thirdly, all tourism destinations interact with and are influenced by factors at the global level. Principal amongst these in the tourism-environment context is, of course, climate change, to which tourism may contribute directly through the emission of greenhouses gases from transport (land, sea and air) and indirectly through the consumption of energy by tourism-related businesses and operations. Other localized environmental consequences of tourism may also be of global significance, such as damage to marine environments arising directly from tourism activity (Orams, 1999), whilst destination environments are themselves at risk from climate change and its associated consequences, such as transformations in weather patterns, extreme weather events, global warming and rising sea levels. At the same time, however, the relationship between tourism and the environment may also be influenced by other global factors, such as technological innovation in, for example, air transport, economic recession and political processes. The latter includes events such as the United Nations Conference on Climate Change held in Poznań, Poland in December 2008, which accelerated the progress towards a potential new global agreement on climate change in general, and reductions in carbon emissions in particular, with evident implications for the tourism sector (www.unfccc. int/meetings/cop_14/ items/4481.php).

The remainder of this chapter is concerned with highlighting the key issues for tourism development that emerge from each of these three levels of analysis of the tourism-environment relationship as conceptualized in Figure 5.1.

Tourism environments: Destinational factors

Inevitably, it is at the level of the destination that the interface between tourism and the environment is most evident. Not only are environmental resources exploited, developed, transformed or enhanced for (or, conversely, protected from) tourism and tourists, but the presence of tourists 'on site' as they consume tourism experiences adds an additional dimension to the tourism-environment relationship. At the same time, it is at the destinational level that the differing perceptions of/attitudes towards the environment of different stakeholder groups are most likely to be in evidence, that conflicts between these differing perceptions are most likely to occur and, to complicate matters further, that two different 'types' of tourism environment can be identified. These can be categorized, perhaps somewhat simplistically, as follows:

- The direct tourism environment: environmental resources, under either private or public ownership and over which the tourism sector has some degree of control or influence, that are exploited and consumed as core elements of the tourism product or experience. These include natural resources, such as beaches, mountains, national parks, lakes, marine parks and so on, and built resources and heritage, including historical structures, museums, constructed public spaces, and purpose-built attractions and infrastructure.
- The indirect tourism environment: environmental resources, including 'public goods' such as the climate, that lie beyond the control or influence of the tourism sector yet are incidental to (or, in marketing terminology, 'augment') the tourism product experience. Thus, rural landscapes, including traditional rural built heritage, such as farms and villages, augment the experience of specific attractions or activities in rural settings – during the foot and mouth crisis in the UK in 2001, for example, which resulted in a massive cull of cattle and sheep, it was found that people were less willing to visit an 'empty' countryside devoid of livestock (Sharpley and Craven, 2001).

These two broad tourism environments can be combined with the destinational factors identified in Figure 5.1 to create an adapted version of a model first developed by the Organisation for Economic Co-operation and Development (OECD) in the late 1970s, yet still relevant today, for conceptualizing the relationship between tourism and the destination environment (Figure 5.2). This model originally provided a framework for assessing tourism's environmental impacts, identifying a number of tourism-generated stressor activities (for example, resort construction, generation of wastes and tourist activities), the nature of the stresses themselves and the primary (environmental) and

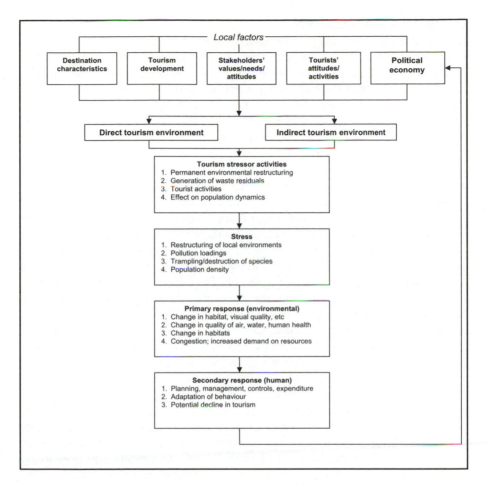

Source: adapted from OECD, 1981

Figure 5.2 *The tourism-environment relationship: The destination*

secondary (human) responses to this environmental stress. These stresses and management responses are considered widely in the literature, the most comprehensive review remaining Wall and Mathieson (2006). For the purpose of this chapter, however, it is the issues related to the local, destinational factors and their influence on perceptions and use of the physical environment that are of most relevance. Though discussed here separately, these factors are inevitably inter-related: the manner in which a particular destination environment is perceived and exploited for tourism will most likely reflect a combination of all the factors identified in Figure 5.2. Nevertheless, reviewing them individually serves to reveal the underlying complexity of destination environments.

Destination characteristics

Destination environments vary considerably, of course, in terms of their physical resource base. At a basic level, they can be divided into either natural or built environments but, within these two broad categories enormous diversity exists with respect to their character, their attraction to tourists, the type and scale of tourism they are able to support, their fragility or susceptibility to damage or degradation and their perceived value, both intrinsically and as potential resources for tourism development. Built tourism environments may, on the one hand, comprise robust, purpose-built attractions, facilities and amenities that are designed to meet the needs of planned volumes and activities of tourists. On the other hand, other built resources, such as historic cities, ancient monuments, cathedrals and so on, may be more fragile and culturally significant and, thus, require appropriate management in order to balance conservation and other needs with their role as tourist attractions. For example, visitor numbers at Hill Top, the Lake District home of Beatrix Potter, are limited by time-ticketing and the house is closed over winter for restorative work. Moreover (and in contrast to the Phi Phi experience referred to earlier), the National Trust, which owns the property, did not permit the house to be used for the filming of the recent movie 'Miss Potter' in order to prevent damage to the building or its contents.

Equally, natural environments vary from fragile wilderness areas that benefit from significant biodiversity or high scenic/landscape value and are, hence, attractive to tourists in their own right (yet are able to support limited tourism development) to those with little intrinsic value but with the potential to be developed for tourism. In the latter case, for example, many coastal tourism resorts have been developed in areas of limited ecological and landscape value and with little or no potential to support other economic activities, such as agriculture. Thus, tourism may be seen as an appropriate and potentially lucrative use of otherwise unproductive resources. One frequently cited example of this is Cancún, a large-scale resort complex developed in an area of swamp and jungle on the northern tip of Mexico's Yucatán peninsula. Similarly, previously unattractive and unproductive land bordering beaches near Monastir in Tunisia has, since its designation as a 'zone touristique', been developed into a thriving tourism area. Of course, such developments are not without controversy with respect to environmental and other impacts that result from tourism development – Cancún's development has been criticized for its significant environmental and social impacts (Hiernaux-Nicolas, 1999; Telfer and Sharpley, 2008, p65), whilst tourism development in Tunisia has been similarly criticized (Poirier, 1995). Nevertheless, the point is that, subject to prevailing socio-cultural, economic and political factors (it is interesting to note, for example, that Yellowstone National Park in the US was initially designated in 1872 to optimize opportunities for commercial gain through providing a 'pleasuring ground for the benefit and enjoyment of the people' (McNamee, 1993, p20) and it was not until 1918 that conservation policies came into force (Albright and Cahn, 1985)), the specific characteristics of both natural and built environmental resources are significant in setting the parameters of their use for tourism.

Tourism development

The tourism-environment relationship and, indeed, perceptions of the manner of and extent to which environmental resources should be developed or exploited for tourism, is very much dependent upon the scale, scope, type and, in particular, the stage of tourism development at the destination. Quite evidently, certain forms of tourism, such as small-scale, community-based, 'non-consumptive' tourism, may have relatively limited impact on the local environment; conversely, large-scale tourism developments, or those that result in significant exploitation of or alterations to natural environments, the development of large-scale skiing resorts being a specific example (Hudson, 2000), may result in major and irreversible environmental consequences, both directly in terms of permanent restructuring of the environment and damage to flora and fauna related to tourist activities, and indirectly through, for example, excessive demands on water or the development of associated infrastructure.

However, although there is undoubtedly widespread evidence of the negative environmental consequences of large-scale tourism developments, such as those along the Spanish 'costas', the relationship between the scale and type of tourism and the environment cannot always be assumed to be predictable. That is, mass or larger-scale tourism developments may not always be environmentally destructive; equally, smaller-scale, 'appropriate' forms of tourism development may incur relatively high environmental costs. For example, all-inclusive, club-style resorts, pioneered by Club Méditerranée in the early 1950s with the opening of their first holiday village on the island of Mallorca and which, since then, have become more popular and widespread, particularly in the Caribbean, have been criticized for exploiting destination environments with little return to local communities. However, though catering to the mass sun-sea-sand market, as self-contained units their environmental impact is relatively limited compared with that of other mass tourism resorts. Conversely, so-called ecotourism developments, such as that in Belize, have been found to have significant negative impacts on the natural (particularly marine) environment (Duffy, 2002).

With respect to the stage of tourism development, the more established a destination or resort is, the more likely it is that concern about the environmental consequences of tourism will be less in evidence than in newer, emerging destinations. On the one hand, this may simply reflect the belief that, in established resorts, the 'damage has been done' and that the principal focus of environmental management should be on 'operational' issues, such as reducing pollution and waste production or undertaking remedial work to damaged or degraded resources. In emerging destinations, conversely, the opportunity still exists to manage or control development and, hence, the extent to which the environment is exploited. On the other hand, in long established destinations, such as some British seaside resorts which evolved during the

19th century, there is, in effect, no tourism-environment relationship. That is, the entire environment may be perceived as a tourism environment and, again, environmental concerns are likely to be limited to operational issues. Thus, overall, no general assumptions can be made about the nature of the tourism-environment interface in the context of the characteristics of tourism development; it is likely to vary on a case-by-case basis.

Stakeholders

Perhaps the most significant factor in the creation or perception of different environments at the level of the destination is the differing perceptions of and values attached to the environment, or differing attitudes regarding how and to what extent environmental resources should be exploited or protected/conserved, amongst different stakeholder groups. In turn, the extent to which the attitudes of a particular group prevail within tourism planning and development at the destination will be dependent on the degree of influence, or political capital, they possess within the local community, which itself will reflect the effectiveness or otherwise of local democratic processes. Indeed, it has long been recognized that, in a tourism planning context more generally, 'consideration should be given to each stakeholder group, regardless of the relative power or interest held by each' (Sautter and Leisen, 1999), not only to appreciate their differing roles and influence but also as a basis for developing effective, democratic decision-making processes (Bramwell and Lane, 2000). Therefore, recognizing the perceptions and influence of different stakeholder groups is fundamental to understanding in particular the tourism-environment relationship at the destination.

However, it is surprising that little or no research has been undertaken into local community attitudes towards 'their' environment as a resource for tourism development, either generally or across different stakeholder groups within destination communities. Certainly, although a number of studies have focused on host community perceptions and attitudes, these have focused primarily on attitudes towards tourists and tourism development in general, exploring differing attitudes amongst different population groups (Mason and Cheyne, 2000) and different determinants of local community support for tourism (Gursoy and Rutherford, 2004), and perceptions of the socio-cultural consequences of tourism in particular (Brougham and Butler, 1981; Milman and Pizam, 1988; King et al, 1993). Typically, such studies suggest that those who depend more on tourism view it more favourably than those less involved, but that, generally, local residents favour tourism for the benefits it brings, despite the social consequences experienced (Akis et al, 1996).

Nevertheless, the existing research points towards the way in which environmental attitudes and values might vary amongst different stakeholder or interest groups within the destination community. It is likely, for example, that those benefiting directly from tourism – that is, those whose livelihoods depend on tourism – view the environment as a legitimate resource for exploitation and would resist policies that reduce those benefits. For instance, a plan to restrict, on environmental grounds, car access to a popular valley in the English Lake District with a regular bus service provided as an alternative, was opposed by local shop-keepers and accommodation providers who feared losing business as a result. Conversely, those not involved in or dependent upon tourism might be more ambivalent whilst others with positive environmental values or strong conservation interests, whose enjoyment or use of environmental resources is affected by tourism development, or for whom the cultural or spiritual value of the environment outweighs any potential economic benefit derived from its development for tourism, would most likely oppose the exploitation of the environment.

The number and influence of different stakeholder groups varies, of course, according to different destinations and broader political and economic policies (Sheehan and Ritchie, 2005): increasingly, for example, the rights and needs of indigenous populations take precedence over economic or business interests. As previously noted, however, the important point is that each tourism destination comprises a number of different environments, depending on the needs and values of different stakeholders, and that appropriate processes are required to ensure that these are taken into account in tourism planning.

Tourists

As Holden (2000) observes, tourists do not represent an homogenous group of consumers. That is, they are likely to perceive, interact with or use destination environments in different ways according to their differing needs, attitudes, motivations and behaviours. Thus, a particular destination may be consumed in varying ways by different groups of tourists, sometimes creating conflict between different tourists groups or sometimes challenging differing perceptions of how those environmental resources should be used. Again, the English Lake District provides a useful example of this. Until 2005, powered boats were able to use Windermere, the largest lake in the national park, for water skiing and other activities. However, in March of that year, a 16kph speed limit was imposed, effectively banning the use of powered boats on the lake. Despite the size of the lake (it is over 16km long and 1.5km wide) and the fact that it was the only one of about 15 major lakes in the park to permit powered boating activity, the speed limit was introduced, against much opposition, to preserve the tranquillity of the area and other visitors' enjoyment of that tranquillity.

Distinctions may also exist, of course, between the environmental attitudes of tourists and members of the local destination community. Reference was made earlier in this chapter to Uluru (Ayers Rock) in Australia, for tourists an iconic symbol and an attraction to be seen and, perhaps, climbed. Indeed, from a semiotic perspective, Uluru is symbolic of Australia, a sign of 'Australian-ness' that must be visited (Culler, 1981). Thus, tourists are perhaps more likely to visit Uluru for its symbolism, as a place famous for being famous, rather than to discover or understand its cultural significance to the indigenous population. Conversely, local communities may consider their environment a legitimate resource for exploitation and development whereas tourists may be seeking pristine, undeveloped, traditional or 'authentic' places and environments.

In fact, academic attention has long been focused on the relevance of authenticity to tourist experiences. MacCannell (1989), for example, considers the modern tourist to be a secular pilgrim on a quest for authenticity, or tourism a search for the authentic: 'sightseeing is a kind of collective striving for a transcendence of the modern totality, a way of attempting to overcome the discontinuity of modernity' (MacCannell, 1989, p130). For the tourist, such authenticity may be revealed by traditional societies and cultures; equally, it may be manifested in undeveloped natural or traditional built environments which reflect traditional cultures. Moreover, this desire or search for the authentic is recognized by the tourism industry, which 'only markets those images that it anticipates will be verified during travel, for tourists authenticity is not necessarily determined by gaining a genuine appreciation for another culture, but rather by verifying a marketed representation of it' (Silver, 1993). As a consequence, significant distinctions may exist between destination environments desired by local communities and those anticipated by tourists. In other words, an environmental paradox exists in as much as the touristic appeal of many destinations – their authentic or traditional environment – may be challenged by the outcome of tourism, namely, modernization and development. Thus, not only do these differing perceptions of the destination environment raise issues of equity and sustainability (Cohen, 2002) but also a balance must be achieved in meeting the needs of local communities and maintaining an environment that is attractive to tourists.

Political economy

The final key factor in determining the nature of the tourism-environment relationship at the destinational level is, broadly, the local political economy or, more specifically, the stage of socio-economic development, the nature of local political structures and institutions and, related, the institutional planning and organization of tourism at the local level. It is, of course, difficult to generalize, the political economy of particular destinations reflecting both a unique combination of endogenous economic and political characteristics and structures (which may also reflect the character of the local environment and/or natural resources) and also differing exogenous relationships with the international community. Consequently, the influence of the local political economy on perceptions and use of environmental resources for tourism can logically only be assessed on a case-by-case basis.

Nevertheless, some general observations can be made. For instance, in less economically and socially developed societies, where there is a greater need for and dependence upon tourism as a source of income and employment, it is likely that the natural and built environment will not only be considered as a valid resource for exploitation but also that it will suffer from over-exploitation, a situation that may be exacerbated by inappropriate or ineffective political intervention. A notable example of this is the Angkor Wat temple complex, Cambodia's principal tourist attraction. According to Smith (2007), Angkor Wat is currently facing the fastest growth in tourist numbers of any United Nations Educational, Scientific and Cultural Organization (UNESCO) World Heritage Site: in 1993 just 7650 tourists visited the site; in 2006 almost 900,000 visitors, or roughly half of all international tourist arrivals in Cambodia, paid a total of US$25 million in ticket sales to enter the complex. With tourism to Cambodia expected to increase to around 3 million arrivals by 2010, the already significant damage to the temples' infrastructure caused by the sheer volume of tourists is only likely to increase. Moreover, the development of nearby Siem Reap, with over 250 hotels and guest houses providing accommodation for tourists along with associated attractions and facilities, is not only destroying the historic identity of the city but excessive demands for water are lowering the ground water table. As a consequence, the fragile foundations of many of the temples are sinking, potentially threatening the long-term survival of Angkor Wat (Sharp, 2008). This over-exploitation of the site is, perhaps, inevitable given the potential for earning tourist dollars in a country with a per capita annual income of approximately US$600 but, despite various plans to relieve pressure on the site, including the introduction of a reservation system, the promotion of alternative temple sites and the exploitation of alternative ground water sources, there is little evidence of efforts on the part of the authorities to address the significant environmental consequences of the rapid and unplanned growth of tourism at the site (see also Winter, 2007).

In other instances, the political economic power of particular social or cultural groups may influence the nature and direction of tourism development in general and the use of environmental resources in particular (Din, 1982), or changing socio-economic circumstances may influence perceptions towards specific environments. In Europe, for example, tourism has been widely promoted as a means of counteracting the social and economic challenges facing rural areas, primarily those associated with the decline of traditional agrarian industries (Cavaco, 1995; Hoggart et al, 1995; Williams and Shaw, 1998). Thus, rural environments have increasingly become seen as a resource for tourism and leisure rather than agricultural production, a role enhanced by more recent shifts in European agricultural policy towards subsidy payments based not on production but environmental conservation. At the same time, the extent to which tourism policies and plans are implemented is also an important factor. In Cyprus, for example, policies have long existed to control the quality and scale of tourism accommodation development, though attempts to translate policy into practice have proved ineffective. As a consequence, much of the island's coastline has been developed, or earmarked for development, resulting in both an over-supply of accommodation and significant environmental consequences (Sharpley, 2000b).

Numerous other examples can be provided to demonstrate the influence of political and economic factors on the relationship between tourism and the destination environment. The point is, as already noted in this chapter, there potentially exist numerous perceived environments within specific destinational contexts. However, the manner in which the relationship between tourism and these environments is manifested in practice, or the way in which environmental resources are exploited or protected, depends upon a number of destinational factors and the relationship between them. Equally, as the next section will summarize, a variety of factors or influences external to the destination may also play a role in determining the tourism-environment relationship within the destination.

Tourism environments: Exogenous factors

Many tourism destinations exist within a broader, national political, socio-cultural, economic and legislative context. Thus, whilst local economic and political structures, planning policies and procedures, socio-cultural institutions and the local tourism sector all have a direct influence on the nature and extent of the use of environmental resources, destinations are not, of course, immune to a wide variety of exogenous factors. As with the local political-economic issues considered in the previous section, not only are these exogenous factors too numerous and diverse to discuss in detail here, but also their relevance and influence will vary according to destinational contexts. For example, tourism development in fragile or sensitive natural environments is likely to be subject to national policies with respect to wildlife conservation, landscape protection and designations, as well as policies relating to agriculture, forestry, water supply, transport development and so on. Conversely, urban or city tourism destinations may be required to respect or respond to national policies on employment, leisure, transport or urban regeneration. In short, the environmental capital of the destination, though largely determined by local, destination-related factors and influences, is also defined to varying extents by exogenous factors. These are categorized in Figure 5.1 above.

Dominant amongst such exogenous factors are regional or national policies and legislation, imposed either directly or through appropriate quasi-governmental agencies with respect to land-use planning, infrastructural development and socio-economic development in general and environmental/sustainable development policies in particular. In terms of tourism environments, such policies are most commonly manifested in national park and other landscape/wildlife designations and protection measures, as well as policies and legislation for the protection of built heritage, restricting the extent to which, in principle, environmental resources of national or international significance may be exploited or adapted for tourism. At the same time, national tourism development policy and investment, such as the designation of tourism development zones, the provision of fiscal incentives to encourage overseas investment in tourism facilities and infrastructure, or direct national investment, also represent an externally imposed policy framework for the tourism-environment relationship. Equally, the activities and influence of pressure groups and third-sector organizations, especially regional or national conservation/environmental groups, but also of lobby groups or those representing particular activities or interests that depend upon access to and use of environmental resources, may also be significant. Thus, in short, the tourism-environment interface at the level of the individual destination cannot be divorced from the wider policy, legislative and institutional framework within which it exists.

Tourism environments: Global factors

Despite the traditional focus of concern for and research into the environmental consequences of tourism at the level of the destination, attention has more recently turned to the tourism-environment relationship within a global context. In other words, it is now recognized that although the consequences of the interaction between tourism and the natural/built environment are, inevitably, most evident (and, perhaps, most easily managed) within the context of the destination – it is the destination environment that is transformed, adapted, exploited or protected to meet the needs of tourism, and where tourists consume the environment – a relationship exists between tourism and the global environment. More specifically, increasing attention is now being paid to the inter-relationship between tourism and climate change in terms of both responses to the risks and challenges that transformations, trends and extreme events in global weather patterns pose to destinations and the potential mechanisms for mitigating tourism's impact, through carbon emissions, on the global climate.

This is not to say that climate change is the only global factor that is of relevance to the tourism-environment relationship. Just as the tourism system in its entirety is embraced and influenced by global political, economic, technical and, of course, environmental factors, so too is the tourism environment as a specific element of the tourism system. Thus, for example, global economic and political forces may influence, albeit usually on a temporary basis, the direction and volume of international tourist flows, with consequential environmental implications. For instance, for three days following the '9/11' attacks in the US in 2001, no commercial flights were permitted in American airspace; during that short period of time, a significant reduction in aircraft emissions was recorded, resulting in 'cleaner' skies and more extreme day and night time temperatures. Equally, global environmental policies and schemes may impact upon the development and management of environmental resources at the local level, a notable example being UNESCO's World Heritage List. First established in 1972, the purpose of the list is to identify and protect natural and cultural heritage sites around the world which are considered to be of outstanding value to humanity and which, incidentally, tend to be major tourist sites and attractions. There are currently 878 World Heritage Sites, 679 of which are cultural, 174 are natural and 25 are mixed natural-cultural sites (see http://whc.unesco.org/en/list).

However, it is the challenge of climate change that is of most relevance in the context of this chapter and, arguably, one of the most significant issues facing the future development of tourism on a global scale. As the United Nations World Tourism Organization (UNWTO) claims:

climate is a key resource for tourism and the sector is highly sensitive to the impacts of climate change and global warming, many elements of which are already being felt ... the tourism sector must rapidly respond to climate change ... and progressively reduce its Greenhouse Gas (GHG) contribution if it is to grow in a sustainable manner. (UNWTO/UNEP, 2008, p25)

Undoubtedly, such concerns have, to an extent, been prompted by increasing public awareness of the causes and impacts of climate change, awareness which itself has been enhanced by increasing media attention paid to climate change in general and by well-publicized reports and media events, such as Al Gore's controversial film 'An Inconvenient Truth', in particular, and by an increasing body of scientific evidence, such as that compiled by the Intergovernmental Panel on Climate Change (IPCC). The latter's reports consistently demonstrate that climate change or, more precisely, global warming, is a measurable phenomenon: 'Warming of the climate system is unequivocal, as is now evident from observations of increases in global average air and ocean temperatures, widespread melting of snow and ice and rising global average sea level' (IPCC, 2007, p2). Moreover,

most of the observed increase in global average temperatures since the mid-20th century is very likely due to the observed increase in anthropogenic GHG concentrations. It is likely that there has been significant anthropogenic warming over the past 50 years averaged over each continent. (IPCC, 2007, p5)

Thus, it is now generally accepted that there is a trend towards global warming, that there are more numerous extreme climatic events and that there are increasing concentrations of so-called GHGs in the earth's atmosphere. What remains less certain is the extent to which anthropogenic emissions of GHGs are directly related to climate change and global warming: although compelling scientific evidence is presented, there are still many who claim that contemporary global warming is a natural climatic event, whilst the IPCC's use of terms such as '*likely*' and '*very likely*' reflects this uncertainty. '*Likely*', for example, translates as up to 60 per cent certainty.

It is not the intention to engage in the climate debate here. However, there are undoubtedly clear connections between tourism and the characteristics of and transformations in the global climate. Therefore, whilst a causal relationship is more difficult to establish – 'the open and complex nature of [both the tourism and the climate] systems means that it is extremely difficult to predict, manage and control future changes with any level of practical significance and relevance' (Becken and Hay, 2007, p9) – there are a number of issues that are of relevance to tourism development at both the destinational and global levels, as attested by the increasing academic attention paid to the subject (Hall and Higham, 2005; Hamilton et al, 2005; Viner, 2006).

These issues fall under two broad headings related to tourism's interaction with climate and climate change. On the one hand, tourism destinations may be affected by and must respond to both gradual climatic transformations related to global warming, such as changing weather patterns and rises in sea level, and extreme events, such as hurricanes. On the other hand, tourism is a potentially significant source of GHGs, particularly through carbon emissions generated by land, sea and air travel but also, to a much lesser extent, through power consumption in tourism facilities and attractions. According to Gössling (2002), 90 per cent of tourism carbon emissions are generated by transport, 6 per cent by accommodation providers and 4 per cent by tourist activities. Therefore, the need exists to reduce tourism's overall 'carbon footprint', both through seeking ways of reducing emissions and engaging in carbon offset schemes.

This two-way relationship is explored at length in the literature (for example, Viner and Agnew, 1999; Becken and Hay, 2007; UNWTO/UNEP, 2008). In particular, many commentators explore the potential impacts of climate change on destinations, focusing on the environmental consequences and the likely transformations in patterns of tourism demand that may result from both warmer, or more extreme, climatic conditions and changes to the physical environment. Table 5.1 summarizes the possible impacts and the implications for tourism.

As is evident from Table 5.1, the most likely outcome of climate change in the longer term will be a transformation in tourism flows, typified by a shift in travel to cooler destinations (i.e. more northerly) or higher destinations, with significant implications for local destination economies. Thus, although there is no certainty with regards to the extent of climate change and its likely impact on destinations, there is a need for all destinations (whether potential 'winners' or 'losers') to anticipate and, as far as possible, develop strategies to meet the potential challenges of climate change.

With respect to carbon emissions, attention is primarily focused on transport in general and air transport in particular. This is not surprising given that transport accounts for the major share of tourism's overall carbon footprint which is estimated to be between 5 per cent and 6 per cent of global GHG emissions (Gössling, 2002). Estimates of aviation's share of global GHGs (based on carbon emissions) vary from around 2 per cent to 5 per cent; importantly, however, it is claimed by some that the warming impact of high altitude aircraft emissions may be two to four times greater than that of carbon emissions alone and, therefore, that the environmental impact of aviation is significantly higher than most estimates suggest (see, for example, www.greenskies.org). Interestingly, despite the fact that the great majority of tourism is domestic and that most tourism trips are taken by car, less attention is paid to the contribution of car-based tourism to GHGs and climate change. This reflects, perhaps, the difficulty in identifying leisure and tourism travel as a specific form of car-based travel, yet it is likely that the contribution of land-based transport for touristic purposes (particularly taking into account broader definitions of tourism to include day trips and either leisure-related

Table 5.1 *Climate change impacts, implications and tourism outcomes*

Impact	Implications	Tourism outcomes
Warmer temperatures	Altered seasonality, heat stress for tourists, cooling costs, increased likelihood of infectious diseases	Shift in demand towards cooler (more northern) destinations
Decreasing snow cover and shrinking glaciers	Lack of snow in winter sport destinations, increased snow-making costs, shorter winter sports seasons, aesthetics of landscape reduced	Focus on higher altitude resorts; development of alternative products, markets (climbing, hiking, etc)
Increasing frequency and intensity of extreme storms	Risk for tourism facilities, increased insurance costs/loss of insurability, business interruption costs	Reduced demand for tourism in 'at risk' areas
Reduced precipitation and increased evaporation in some regions	Water shortages, competition over water between tourism and other sectors, desertification, increased wildfires	Diminished attraction/ increased risks, hence reduced demand and increased travel to cooler, safer destinations
Increased frequency of heavy precipitation in some regions	Flooding damage to historic architectural and cultural assets, damage to tourism infrastructure, altered seasonality	Reduced demand; high costs of repairs to infrastracture
Sea level rise	Coastal erosion, loss of beach area, higher costs to protect and maintain waterfronts	Loss of amenity; decline in tourism
Sea surface temperatures rise	Increased coral bleaching and marine resource and aesthetics degradation in dive and snorkel destinations	Reduced demand
More frequent and larger forest fires	Loss of natural attractions; increase of flooding risk; damage to tourism infrastructure	Reduced demand
Soil changes (e.g., moisture levels, erosion, acidity)	Loss of archaeological assets and other natural resources, with impacts on destination attractions	Reduced demand

Source: adapted from UNWTO/UNEP, 2008, p61

mobility) is significantly higher than estimated. Some 10 per cent of global GHGs are accounted for by car transport and, when other environmental costs associated with the motor car, including car manufacturing, the building of roads and other infrastructure, car disposal and the human costs in terms of deaths and injuries, the overall environmental impact of car-based tourism is likely to be significant (Alvord, 2000).

Calculating the 'true' climatic impact of tourism-related transport and tourism activity more generally is, undoubtedly, a highly complex task. What is likely, however, is that, in the future, there will be increasing political pressure to reduce travel and tourism-related carbon emissions. Therefore, as a consequence, tourism planning at the destination will have to take into account not only the means of reducing the local carbon footprint through, for example, encouraging greater efficiency or alternative energy use amongst the local tourism sector as well as sustainable local transport, but also the likely shifts in demand that may result from both climate change itself and transport policies that aim to mitigate the climatic impacts of travel.

Tourism environments: A summary

Overall, this chapter has attempted to conceptualize the tourism environment, exploring how the interaction between tourism and the environmental resources upon which it depends directly and indirectly may be influenced by different perceptions and values towards those resources on the part of stakeholders, tourists and other groups. At the same time, a variety of other factors, both within and external to the destination, may determine perceptions and use of the environment. In other words, and as the following case study of the English Lake District demonstrates, tourism destinations are defined by numerous different environments as perceived by different groups or stakeholders, with the actual interaction between tourism and the environment resulting, in effect, from 'negotiation' between these different environments. Two further points require emphasis. Firstly, destination environments (other than public goods, such as the climate) 'belong' to destinations and destination communities; the environment is defined by their values, perceptions and needs and, within the parameters of external factors, the manner in which the environment is exploited for tourism should reflect those values, perceptions and needs. Secondly, the environment is a basic element of the tourism product. It is a resource, or a type of capital, which is exploited by the tourism sector and from which benefits (usually economic) accrue. Consequently, the development of tourism, itself fundamentally an economic or capitalistic activity, should be based upon an analysis of the supply of environmental and other capitals within and as perceived by individual destinations, rather than on overarching policies and principles such as those proposed by the sustainable development paradigm. It is to this idea of tourism development based upon tourism capitals that the next chapter turns.

Case study: The multiple environments of the English Lake District

Situated in the northwest of England within the county of Cumbria (Figure 5.3), the Lake District, covering an area of some 2280sq km, is England's largest national park. It is renowned for its unique juxtaposition of lakes, tarns, valleys and mountains, the result of 500 million years of complex geomorphology and glacial activity, and within the boundaries of the national park can be found England's highest mountain (Scafell Pike, 977m), and her longest (Windermere, 20km long) and deepest bodies of water (Wastwater, 70m depth). But although the Lake District's outstanding and unique landscape owes much to natural forces and processes, particularly during the last Ice Age, it has also been nurtured and shaped by centuries of human activity. The relative wildness of high peaks and the glacial lakes that occupy many of the valleys combine with semi-natural woodlands, fellside fields divided by dry-stone walls and more intensively cultivated farmland in the valleys, whilst even some of the lakes are, in fact, man-made: there are 17 reservoirs in the Lake District. Moreover, settlement patterns and built heritage reflect the agrarian socio-economic tradition of the area and, currently, some 55 per cent of the national park's area is registered as agricultural land.

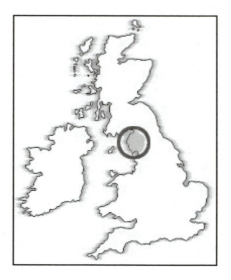

Figure 5.3 *Location of the Lake District*

The contemporary Lake District is, therefore, a living, working landscape. According to latest data, the total resident population within the national park is 41,650, representing 8.5 per cent of the population of the county of Cumbria as a whole. Approximately 37 per cent of the park's population lives in the main urban centres, which include the principal tourism 'honeypots' of Windermere/Bowness, Ambleside and Keswick. These towns provide a significant proportion of the Lake District's tourism facilities, amenities and attractions and are the main focus of tourism activity. Not surprisingly, perhaps some 43 per cent of all employment in the national park is tourism related. Other important sources of employment include manufacturing (9.3 per cent of all employment), agriculture and forestry (7.6 per cent) and education (8.09 per cent). In 2004, total tourist spending in the national park amounted to £602 million; estimates of tourism's contribution to the national park's gross domestic product (GDP) are not available, although by way of comparison agricultural holdings within the park generated a total income of £59 million in 2002, roughly one-tenth of the value of tourism that year. It is also important to note that over one-fifth of the housing stock in the Lake District is accounted for by second or holiday homes.

Thus, despite the evidence of farming and other agrarian activity, the environment of the Lake District is very much a tourism environment. In other words, it is the development of tourism that, since the early 19th century, has arguably had the greatest influence on the Lake District's environment and built heritage. In 1769, the poet Thomas Grey undertook a short ten-day excursion in the Lake District and is commonly regarded as the first genuine 'tourist'. His narrative was to inspire writers and artists alike to visit the region; visitors included J.M.W. Turner, John Constable and Thomas Gainsborough, capturing the sublime beauty of the mountains and lakes in their paintings. However, it was the Romantic poets, particularly William Wordsworth, who did most to create an enduring 'place-myth' of the Lake District, producing an imagined, literary landscape that remains an attraction for present-day tourists. As a consequence, the Lake District became, and for many visitors still is, a literary environment, whether that of Wordsworth, Arthur Ransome (*Swallows and Amazons*) or Beatrix Potter.

Nevertheless, the Lakeland fells also attracted early walkers and climbers, the first recorded ascents of many peaks being made in the 1790s, though it was not until a century later that fell walking and rock-climbing became more popular, also establishing the Lake District as a sport/activity environment. In the early 19th century, inns for tourists opened in the less accessible dales whilst the development of the three main tourist centres was accelerating. However, tourism was, at this time, relatively limited; it was the arrival of the railways in the mid-1800s that was to have the greatest impact on the Lake District, providing opportunities for tourists to visit in their thousands rather than hundreds, transforming the built environment and establishing the foundations of the contemporary tourism industry. Moreover, although the railways opened up the area to day-trippers from the northern industrial towns – on Whit Monday (Pentecost Monday) in 1883, over 10,000 day-trippers visited Windermere – 'the expansion of the Lake District tourist market came to depend increasingly on the growing band of middle-class visitors who were holiday-makers first, sight-seers second and devotees of romantic mountain solitude hardly at all' (Marshall and Walton, 1981, p186).

In other words, the Lake District also developed as a 'playground' environment. Indeed, throughout the latter half of the 20th century, tourism to the Lake District grew rapidly, the principal factors being greater mobility underpinned by a rapid increase in car ownership along with increases in leisure time and disposable income and the growing popularity of outdoor recreation. By the early 1960s, not only had mass tourism arrived in the Lake District but also, as one commentator at the time observed, 'tourism is becoming the dominant industry in the area ... today the visitor is beginning to own the place and, if we are not careful, the whole area will be turned into one vast holiday camp' (Nicholson, 1963, p181). Recent history demonstrates that this fear was misplaced although tourism remains a significant activity in the Lake District. It is estimated that between 15 and 20 million visitor days are now spent in the Lake District annually. The great majority of visitors are on day trips, with just 16 per cent of tourists staying for at least one night, although they account for 42 per cent of visitor days and 65 per cent of tourist revenue. Over 80 per cent of all visitors arrive by car and continue to use their cars to travel around the park. In fact, a recent survey of tourist behaviour in the Lake District found that, although the natural beauty of the area is a major attraction, the majority of visitors participate in more passive activities, such as 'visiting towns, shopping, visiting restaurants and pubs and driving around by car' (Creative Research, 2002, p10). Hence, tourist activity is centred primarily on the main honeypots referred to previously. Those who are more active go on short walks or visit an attraction, with literary 'shrines', such as Wordsworth's Dove Cottage or Beatrix Potter's home at Hill Top, being particularly popular; fewer than 10 per cent of visitors venture into the fells. Thus, despite the natural attractions of the Lake District and the opportunities for outdoor recreational activities they offer, these are not the principal draw for the 'typical' Lake District visitor.

The different tourist environments of the Lake District – the literary/cultural environment, the sport/activity environment and the playground environment – may be compared with various stakeholder environments, principal amongst which is the 'national park' environment. The Lake District was designated as a national park in 1951, its statutory purpose being to preserve and enhance the natural beauty of the area and to promote its enjoyment by the public. Since designation, however, these two purposes have increasingly come into conflict and, as a consequence, subsequent governmental reviews and legislation have redefined the purposes of national parks, giving precedence to conservation over tourism and recreation. This is translated into rigorous application of planning laws and, when necessary, the passing of byelaws to maintain the 'natural' environment (despite it being largely adapted by human activity) and its quiet enjoyment by the public. In practice, this has resulted in the national park becoming almost a living museum, an environment being maintained at a particular point in history and, arguably, becoming ever further removed from the needs of contemporary residents and tourists. It is interesting to note that the Lake District, as all other national parks in England and Wales, is not formally recognized as such in the International Union for Conservation of Nature's (IUCN's) official worldwide list of national parks, calling into question both the appropriateness of its designation and the parameters within which its development is restricted.

However, numerous other commercial, public and voluntary sector stakeholders also play a role in, and seek to impose their values on, the management of the Lake District. These include:

- The local tourism sector: shops, restaurants, hotels, guest houses, local transport and tour operators, activity centres and other facilities and attractions, all of which seek to exploit the environment, directly or indirectly, for commercial gain.

- The regional tourism authority (Cumbria Tourist Board) which, financed by the Regional Development Agency, a semi-autonomous agency responsible for social and economic development, views the Lake District environment in terms of place marketing.
- The National Trust – Europe's largest conservation organization – which owns 25 per cent of the park's land area and which seeks to maintain the physical and cultural environment of the Lake District for the benefit of both local communities and visitors.
- Local authorities: local government bodies with responsibilities within the national park.
- Farming and forestry industries: hill farmers seek to maintain an agrarian socio-cultural lifestyle based on government subsidy to preserve the landscape.
- Friends of the Lake District: a charitable body that seeks to promote the sustainable development of the Lake District.

Thus, there are varying perceptions of the Lake District's environment and how it should be protected or exploited. Through the central role played by the national park authority, some consensus is achieved between these yet it is uncertain to what extent the resultant environment meets the needs of tourists or, indeed, those who live and work within the park's boundaries.

6
Tourism as Capitalism

Some years ago, I attended an international tourism conference held to mark the advent of the new millennium. The theme of the conference was *Tourism 2000: A Time for Celebration?*, and the paper I presented was titled, somewhat confrontationally, 'In defence of (mass) tourism' (Sharpley, 2006b). The purpose of the paper was to challenge what had become, during the 1990s, a tourism development debate polarized between, on the one hand, allegedly unsustainable, mass ('bad') tourism and, on the other hand, sustainable, alternative ('good') tourism, a dichotomy that, as observed elsewhere in this book, has long characterized the concept of sustainable tourism development. Drawing on a number of case studies, the paper argued that, far from being the destructive force that many considered and still consider it to be (for example, Hickman, 2007), traditional 'mass' tourism may be a more effective vehicle of economic growth and development than tourism developed according to the 'typical' principles of alternative or sustainable tourism. For example, from the mid-1970s, Cyprus experienced rapid economic and social development based on the no less rapid development of its (mass) tourism sector; as a consequence, by the late 1990s Cypriots enjoyed the third highest standard of living of all Mediterranean countries after France and Italy. Although the intensive development of tourism on the island was criticized by some as unsustainable (and more recent problems facing the tourism sector have stemmed primarily from an over-supply of accommodation facilities), there is no doubt that mass tourism has been a positive force in the economic and social development of Cyprus (Sharpley, 2003). In fact, the experience of Cyprus and other successful mass tourism destinations, such as the Canary Islands and the Balearics (Mallorca, Menorca, Ibiza and Formentera), suggests that the problems that are widely associated with mass tourism development are more to do with ineffective local planning and management than with a reified 'mass tourism'.

The paper also suggested that, given its restricted focus on the supply of tourism at the destination, the concept of sustainable tourism does not recognize the important economic and social role of (mass) tourism in generating regions in terms of both the significant contribution to employment provided by the outbound tourism sector (tour operators, transport operators, travel retailers and associated service providers) and the potential social benefits of widespread participation in international travel and tourism amongst generating country populations. In short, the paper argued for the adoption of 'a more pragmatic approach to the global role and contribution of tourism' (Sharpley, 2006b, p280) that, whilst seeking to minimize its negative environmental consequences, celebrates the contribution of all tourism, including mass tourism, to economic growth and development.

Though criticized by some, perhaps justifiably, for its somewhat simplistic approach, the paper not only highlighted many of the inherent weaknesses of the concept of sustainable tourism development, weaknesses that, in preceding chapters in this book have been explored and expanded upon within a more rigorous theoretical framework, but it also pre-empted the recent shift in 'official' conceptualizations of sustainable tourism development. That is, it proposed that *all* forms of tourism should be considered for their potential contribution to economic development, albeit within the parameters of environmental sustainability. Similarly, rather than focusing on specific, niche or alternative forms of tourism, such as ecotourism, the United Nations World Tourism Organization (UNWTO) now defines sustainable tourism as a condition applicable to *all* forms of tourism, or tourism that is developed according to the principles of sustainable development (UNWTO, 2008e). The only difference, of course, is that the UNWTO considers sustainable development to be the most appropriate development framework whereas the conference paper argued that, irrespective of the type of tourism to be developed, sustainable resource use should be a guiding principle.

The implicit theme of 'In defence of (mass) tourism' was, therefore, that tourism is, first and foremost, a global economic activity; it is, fundamentally, big business, a form of capitalist endeavour that, over the last half century, has become increasingly pervasive around the world. Moreover, through enabling ever more people to consume tourism services and experiences, that capitalist endeavour has brought substantial economic benefits to many destinations and, of course, tourism generating regions. Indeed, whilst tourism is often thought of as a social phenomenon – for example, it was once described, somewhat dramatically, as accounting for 'the single largest peaceful movement of people across cultural boundaries in the history of the world' (Lett, 1989, p77) – it is essentially a capitalist phenomenon; the growth in tourism has, to a great extent, been underpinned by the evolution and development of a sophisticated and innovative commercially driven travel and tourism sector. In other words, since 1841, when Thomas Cook organized his first trip (admittedly for altruistic as opposed to commercial reasons), taking 570 people by train from Leicester to a temperance meeting in nearby Loughborough, UK (see Brendon, 1991), the travel and tourism 'industry' has grown into one of the world's largest economic sectors, both creating and satisfying, for profit, the needs of ever increasing numbers of tourists. Similarly, destinations seek to profit from tourism, producing and selling tourist experiences for income, foreign exchange earnings and employment generation. In a sense, therefore, destinations can also be thought of as a tourism 'business'; equally, sustainable tourism development, as a prescriptive set of principles, can be considered in some cases to be a disruptive intervention in that business.

Thus, the most logical starting point for proposing an alternative (to sustainable tourism development) approach to the development of tourism is, in a sense, to 'go back to basics'; that is, to recognize and accept that tourism is, in practical terms, a manifestation of capitalist production and consumption that produces economic benefits, or profits, for destinations and tourism businesses. This is not to play down the importance of understanding and seeking to manage the negative consequences, or what economists refer to as the 'externalities', of tourism development. An assumption throughout this book is that tourism should be developed within the parameters of environmental sustainability whilst an appreciation of what may be described collectively as the socio-cultural impacts of tourism – that is, the consequences of tourist-local community interaction – is fundamental to the longer-term 'health' of destinations. Nevertheless, the principal purpose of developing tourism at the destination, and for businesses to engage in the commercial provision of tourism services, is to achieve economic benefits, whether income, employment or, more specifically, profit.

The purpose of this chapter, therefore, is to consider tourism as capitalist endeavour. In other words, it sets out to relate tourism to the defining characteristics of capitalism in general before going on to identify the different types of inputs, or productive capitals, in particular that are exploited to produce the outputs of the tourism production system: that is, the services and experiences that tourists consume. These capitals then form the basis for an alternative approach to tourism development that is proposed in the following, final chapter. It is not the intention of these two chapters to establish a set of principles or guidelines for tourism development; rather, they seek to build a conceptual framework to stimulate further debate and research. The first task, then, is to attempt to define capitalism as the now dominant global economic system of which tourism is a part.

What is capitalism?

Capitalism is a term that, to an extent, defies precise definition. Over half a century ago, Dobb (1946, p1) observed that:

> It is perhaps not altogether surprising that the term Capitalism, which in recent years has enjoyed so wide a currency alike in popular talk and in historical writing, should have been used so variously, and that there should have been no common measure of agreement in its use.

On the one hand, according to Dobb (1946, p5), capitalism can be thought of as a 'spirit' that distinguishes 'pre-capitalist man', who engaged in economic activity to satisfy his immediate or natural needs, from the capitalist who 'sees the amassing of capital as the dominant motive of economic activity'.

Consequently, capitalism is defined by a spirit of adventure or entrepreneurship combined with Weberian rationality and calculation. On the other hand, capitalism can be thought of as a particular system of production, whereby the ownership of the means of production is concentrated in the hands of a small social group – the capitalist class or bourgeoisie – whilst the labour provided by the working class, or proletariat, becomes a commodity that is bought and sold. For Karl Marx, the difference between the value of labour (the wages paid to a worker) and the value of commodities produced is the surplus value (or profit) that is extracted from workers through a process of exploitation, hence his prediction that, as the conditions of the working class continued to worsen, capitalism would eventually collapse.

More generally, capitalism can be defined – and, in all likelihood, is most commonly thought of – as a particular type of economic system and the society that is built upon it (Lekachman and Van Loon, 1981). It is also an economic system that, traditionally associated with the capitalist economies of the developed countries or 'First World', is becoming more widely adopted, particularly since the demise of the centrally-planned socialist systems of the so-called Eastern Bloc from the late 1980s onwards. According to Saunders (1995), the roots of the capitalist economic system can be traced back as far as the 11th century, when commercial trade routes were opened up and rudimentary systems of money and credit established through 'the use of bills of exchange' (1995, p2). By the 16th century, the feudal agricultural system in many parts of Europe had been replaced by a system of production and labour being rewarded by monetary payments, but it is with the rapid economic and technological developments of the 19th century, particularly in England, that the emergence of capitalism is most commonly associated. As Saunders (1995, p1) observes, 'The Crystal Palace exhibition [in 1851] was the first great party to celebrate the emergence of a new social and economic system which was destined to revolutionise life on this planet – the system we know today as capitalism'.

It is no coincidence that it is also the 19th century in which the roots of contemporary mass participation in tourism lie. The new industrial age brought with it not only the means of travel (the railways, steamships) for increasing numbers of people, but also the emerging social and economic capitalist system generated both the desire and, over time, the ability (increasing income and socially-sanctioned free time) to engage in tourism. For example, many British seaside resorts owe their existence to the development of the railways during the mid-19th century, whilst holidays, such as 'wakes weeks', when factories, mills or even entire towns closed for a week, not only provided the business for the resorts but were also a manifestation of the organization of leisure time within the capitalist system (Clarke and Critcher, 1985; Rojek, 1993). At the same time, of course, the capitalist spirit that underpinned the burgeoning capitalist system generally was also revealed in a nascent travel industry in particular. Reference has already been made to Thomas Cook, probably the world's oldest and certainly longest-surviving travel organization, but a number of other commercial travel companies and other tourism service providers were also founded during the latter half of the 19th century to facilitate (and profit from) the public's increasing desire and ability to participate in tourism. Thus, in short, contemporary tourism can be seen primarily as a manifestation, or outcome, of 19th century capitalism.

Even when defined as an economic system, contemporary capitalism varies significantly from one system to another, and from one society or country to another. National economies vary, for example, in size, structure, rate of growth, position in the economic cycle and their relationship with other economies, and experience varying degrees and forms of monetary, fiscal and regulatory intervention on the part of governments (Kantor, 1995). Moreover, it is a dynamic phenomenon; the nature of capitalism and capitalist systems change over time. Technological advances, global information and financial systems and alleged globalization more generally (see Chapter 4) have fundamentally transformed national and international capitalist systems, whilst the financial crisis of 2008 is seen by some as a turning point in the history of capitalism from where a 'new capitalism' may evolve (Peston, 2008). Nevertheless, there are a number of characteristics or elements common to all capitalist systems. These are usefully considered in the context of sustainability (or, more precisely, sustainable capitalism) by Porritt (2007) though, for the present purposes, the three defining elements of capitalism identified by Saunders (1995) are appropriate for establishing the relationship between tourism and capitalism.

The private ownership of property

The first key feature of capitalism is that it involves the private ownership of property, including land, buildings, machinery and the raw materials, that are utilized or exploited in the production of goods and services. From a classical economics perspective, these collectively represent the stock of capital from which monetary returns can be gained and are usually sub-divided into two forms of capital, namely, productive capital and non-productive capital. The former comprises plant and machinery which is used directly to produce products and services, whilst the latter, such as land, are considered real assets in as much as they are not directly used in production but, nonetheless, possess a value which may be realized when sold (Gerrard, 1989, pp77–78). Within the context of tourism, this distinction between productive and non-productive assets is, in some instances, rather fuzzy. Areas of land, such as a beach or a mountain (if privately owned), may be directly exploited by the tourism sector, either by simply being used by tourists (sunbathing/swimming at the beach, or walking/climbing in the mountains, for example) or by being physically developed (building hotels alongside beaches or chair lifts at ski resorts, for example). In the first scenario, the land is productive in the sense that monetary gains, that is, tourist expenditure in the local economy, result from its use. In the second scenario, greater, more direct gains may be earned through the lease or sale of the land to developers, as well as enhanced tourist expenditure in the local economy (see Kantor, 1995, p3).

The significance of private ownership lies in the fact that the owners of property enjoy three important rights: 'the right of exclusive control and use of the property; the right exclusively to benefit from the exploitation of that property; and the right to dispose of the property as one sees fit' (Saunders, 1995, p3). It is in this context that capitalist systems differ significantly from socialist, centrally-planned systems. In Cuba, for example (see Chapter 2 case study), the state owns most of the country's assets and productive resources. This is certainly the case in the tourism sector where all tourism facilities are fully or, in the case of some hotels, majority owned by the state. Thus, those working in the Cuban tourism sector enjoy none of the rights of private ownership; they are poorly paid state employees with little reason or incentive to seek to optimize the monetary returns from those facilities. This points to another form of private ownership, namely, the individual's ownership of their own bodies and their labour. Hence, unlike feudal systems, where individuals are permanently obligated to others, some traditional social or caste systems, which limit how and where individuals may work, or socialist systems, where work and remuneration are controlled by the state, individuals in capitalist societies are, in principle at least, free to choose for whom they work and to negotiate the terms and conditions of their employment. Thus, employers have access to labour only through voluntary contract.

For the most part, of course, the tourism sector or industry, comprising hospitality providers (accommodation, food and beverage), transport operators, attractions, tour operators, travel retailers, activity organizers and other services, is privately owned. Certain services, such as airports or local or national tourism marketing and information, may be provided by the public sector either by necessity or reflecting political ideology whilst, in those less developed countries with limited private financial capital, some elements of the tourism sector, such as hotels, may also be owned by the state. At the same time, of course, some resources, such as the sea, the atmosphere and the climate, are not owned by anyone but, implicitly, have some value if exploited by tourism, whilst in some destinations, such as national parks or nature reserves, the land and infrastructure may be owned by the state. Nevertheless, travel and tourism businesses are primarily private and, consequently, enjoy the rights and benefits of private ownership, although the extent to which they are free to exploit their property as they wish may vary according to external influences, such as planning regulations, employment laws, health and safety regulations and so on. Thus, the tourism sector reflects capitalism more generally for, as Saunders (1995, p4) notes, 'capitalism does not ... preclude a role for the state, but it does entail as little use as necessary of the political process'.

The pursuit of profit

As observed above, Dobb (1946) suggested that capitalism may be defined as a spirit of entrepreneurship focused on the generation of profit. More specifically, 'the very purpose of wealth creation in capitalist economies is to generate profits' (Porritt, 2007, p82). It is the private ownership of property, described in the previous section, which both enables and motivates the pursuit of profit, whether at the individual or corporate level, the second key feature of capitalism. Throughout history, of course, individuals have sought to increase their wealth, whether legally, illegally or through coercion; capitalism, however, is distinctive in that most, if not all, economic activity is geared towards the continual pursuit of profit. In other words, capitalist production of goods and services is not motivated by immediate satisfaction of individual needs, but in the hope of making a profit. Moreover, profit (and year-on-year increases in profit) is the most common measure of success in capitalist systems: a successful business is one that not only makes a profit but increases it, thereby enabling investment to further grow the business (and profits) and to reward shareholders (themselves participants in the capitalist system) through dividend payments.

Thus, as Saunders (1995) notes, in capitalist systems, production is a means to an end (that is, profit) rather than an end in itself. As a consequence, the production of particular goods and services occurs not necessarily where a particular need or demand exists, but where profits can be made. This, in turn, suggests that where particular needs cannot be satisfied profitably, the production of goods and services must be either subsidized or undertaken by the public sector. For example, the provision of public transport services (air, rail or bus) in remote or rural areas is frequently unprofitable and, thus, requires public financial support. Conversely, products that are not 'necessary', or not required to fulfil immediate needs, are still produced if a profit is to be made – and if immediate demand does not exist, then the existence of those products or services, or the effective marketing of them, may create demand. One example here is the manner in which rapid advances in communication technology, such as mobile phones or personal computers, leads to the continual development and production of new products that, whilst offering additional capabilities and features, may not reflect actual consumer needs. In a sense, the existence of the product creates a perceived need, rather than vice versa. Within the tourism sector, the mass production of trinkets or souvenirs, sometimes referred to as 'airport art', is a similar example; tourists do not 'need' such products, but purchase them, frequently on impulse, to remind them of their holiday.

However, production that is driven by profit maximization and growth is problematic in two ways. Firstly, as Porritt (2007, pp92–93) argues, businesses may seek to 'cut corners if they can get away with it and to externalise as high a proportion of their costs as they are legally permitted to do'. In other words, the environmental and social costs of production are, as far as possible, externalized or, more simply, not paid for by either the producer or consumer. Further, efforts to require the 'internalization' of such costs may meet resistance or be unsuccessful. For example, in 2001 the regional government of the Balearic Islands approved the introduction of an 'eco-tax' to be levied on the 9 million tourists visiting the islands each year, the aim being to raise up to £50 million for an eco-fund for environmental improvements. After just one year, however, the tax was dropped: viewed simply as a direct 'tourist tax', it was blamed for a drop in visitor numbers and, hence, a decline in profits of tourism businesses. Had the tax been imposed on businesses and passed on to consumers through marginally increased prices, the outcome may have been different. Secondly, the profit motive drives accumulation and constant growth, leading to the excessive exploitation of resources and waste. Successful capitalist economies are those that are growing; per capita wealth increases, business profits increase but so too do the demands on the environment and natural resources.

Tourism, as a specific economic sector, directly reflects capitalism's drive for profit. All tourism businesses at all levels in the tourism system, from large organizations such as airlines, tour operators and hotel chains, to the innumerable small businesses (restaurants, guest houses, shops, craft/souvenir producers) that typically comprise the tourism sector, are in business to make money, to generate profit. New products and services – new destinations, new experiences – are generally introduced not to satisfy customer demands, but to remain competitive, to attract new customers and to maintain and enhance profits. Indeed, it could be argued that capitalism has fed the continual growth in tourism, a notable example being the development of low-cost airlines. Exploiting the liberalization or deregulation of airline operations, particularly in Europe and the US, these have, in their drive for market share and profitability, grown rapidly by continually opening up new routes and new destinations at very low prices. As a result, some are not only examples of successful capitalist endeavour (Ryanair, for example, is the world's largest international carrier in terms of passenger numbers), but they have also been instrumental in feeding the growth in independent travel, international short-break travel and, particularly in Europe, tourism based upon second-home ownership. And destinations themselves are in a sense profit driven; as argued throughout this book, tourism is developed principally for its potential economic benefits or returns, that is, the income (direct earnings from tourists, indirect earnings to related businesses and sectors, tax revenue derived directly and indirectly from the tourism sector and so on) and employment that is generated through the exploitation of local resources or capitals.

As a consequence, of course, resources may be over-exploited; McKercher's (1993) well-known 'truth' that tourism has such a tendency directly reflects this drive for profit. Thus, an increasing number of businesses, such as those contributing to the 'Tour Operators Initiative for Sustainable Tourism Development' (www.toinitiative.org), are seeking to internalize some of the costs of tourism production. Certainly, what is referred to as 'corporate social responsibility' is becoming increasingly prevalent within the tourism sector. Nevertheless, profit remains the lifeblood of tourism.

Markets and market prices

Although the private ownership of property provides both the means and the motivation for engaging in capitalism, and profit provides its objective, capitalist systems cannot function without their third and perhaps most important element, namely, markets. In other words, capitalist economic systems depend upon the ability to exchange goods and services; without the marketplace, such exchanges would not occur and capitalism could not exist. Of course, there have always been markets, traditionally local meeting places where people gathered to trade or exchange products. However, the expansion of markets beyond the local to the national and international, as well as the expansion of the range of goods and services that could be exchanged, became possible through the development of a common value equivalent, specifically: money. Thus, capitalist systems are essentially money systems; it is money that drove the development of the capitalist system by separating producers from consumers, and it is the increasingly sophisticated, technology-based means of transferring money more rapidly over time and space, often within technology-based markets, such as the internet, that has enabled the development of a truly global capitalist system. This is certainly the case in international tourism, where both tourism businesses and tourists themselves have benefited from simpler and more effective transfer of and access to money. Not so long ago, for example, exchanging travellers' cheques was the safest, yet sometimes cumbersome, way of accessing local currency abroad; now, debit or credit cards provide instant access to local currency. Similarly, it is now a relatively simple and quick process for an individual tourist to book and pay for all the elements of a holiday – transport, car hire, accommodation, visits to major attractions – as well as purchasing guide books and additional services, such as insurance, online from their home computer.

Within capitalist markets, goods (raw materials and finished products) and services are exchanged for money in markets that are *relatively* free: most markets are subject to some form of government intervention or control, such as import duties, subsidies, product quality regulations, taxes or price controls, and so are not entirely free. International air travel, for example, is subject to a variety of taxes and additional charges which, certainly in the case of flights with low-cost airlines, may collectively be significantly higher than the actual cost of the flight itself. Entry visa costs or departure taxes (in Cuba, for example, international tourists are required to pay US$25 on departure) are, similarly, forms of intervention in the market for international travel.

Importantly, however, within capitalist systems the exchange price of goods and services is, by and large, determined by the market. That is, 'a key feature of capitalism is that exchange occurs at a price which is principally determined by the point at which supply meets effective demand' (Saunders, 1995, p7). Therefore, in competitive markets, if supply exceeds demand then prices fall until such time as supply matches demand. A specific example of this in the tourism sector, as mentioned earlier, is Cyprus, where a failure on the part of the authorities to limit the number of hotels being built resulted, by the late 1990s, in an over-supply of hotel rooms relative to demand. Consequently, international tour operators were able to negotiate from a position of strength with the result that, in effect, four-star hotels were selling rooms at two-star prices. This in turn led to Cyprus being, during the early years of the new millennium, in the curious (and economically unsustainable) position of experiencing an increase in tourist arrivals but a decrease in overall tourist receipts.

Conversely, of course, where demand exceeds supply, prices rise or a relatively high price can be charged. Thus, tourist destinations with unique attractions or 'scarcity value' are able to charge a higher price than might otherwise be the case. The unique environment and culture of the Himalayan Kingdom of Bhutan, for example, has long attracted international tourists. However, a policy of restricting the number of annual visitors to the Kingdom (primarily to limit the impacts of tourism on the local environment and culture) has enhanced the scarcity value of Bhutan as a tourist destination, with the result that tourists are willing to pay a relatively high price set by the authorities for the experience of visiting the country.

Given its scope and complexity, it is in fact difficult to explore fully the role of the market and market prices within the tourism production system. Indeed, an analysis of the tourism system from an economic perspective is fraught with difficulty (Bull, 1995; Sinclair and Stabler, 1997). Not only are there different product markets, from the almost 'perfect' competitive markets of the so-called Mediterranean 'identikit' summer sun destinations where price is the dominant factor and, consequently, where there is high elasticity of demand, to 'monopolistic' destinations with unique selling points and low demand elasticity, but also, given the multi-sectoral character of tourism, innumerable markets exist within markets. Moreover, some resources or products within tourism markets, such as attractive landscapes, are not exchanged for money: they are, in a sense, free inputs into the tourism product. The point is, however, that all tourism (domestic and international) is a function of capitalist supply and demand; that is, tourism occurs because of the effective functioning of innumerable markets within the tourism system. Even in the case of Cuba, referred to earlier, where all the factors of production in tourism are state owned and, hence, no internal market exists, international tourism to the island operates within an international market. Cuba competes with other destinations in that market and, despite its unique cultural and political attributes – its 'unique selling points' – the price of tourism to Cuba is, to a great extent, determined by the market.

The example of Cuba also points to the variety of tourism markets and the inherent difficulty in understanding their complex functioning. For a Caribbean destination Cuba is relatively cheap, partly reflecting the mass, resort-based character of much of its tourism sector, partly reflecting the lower standards of quality and service which, ironically, result from the inherent inefficiencies of a centrally-planned economy. Thus, generally, the inter-relationship of supply and demand in tourism, and the consequential market price, is more complex than with many other products and services. For example, the demand for tourism at the level of the individual tourist is affected by a variety of economic factors (see Table 6.1), to say nothing of the various social and cultural influences that may determine the needs, expectations and behaviour of tourists (Sharpley, 2008).

Nevertheless, the fundamental point in the context of this book is that tourism, at both the level of individual businesses and the destination, is a form of capitalistic endeavour. Consequently, for destinations, in particular, to

Table 6.1 *Economic influences on tourism demand*

Tourism generating areas	• Levels of personal disposable income • Distribution of incomes • Holiday entitlements • Value of currency • Tax controls/controls on tourist expenditure • Company competitive environment
Tourism destination areas	• General price level • Quality of tourism products • Economic regulation of tourists
'Link' factors	• Comparative prices in generating and destination areas • Promotional effort by destination in generating area • Exchange rates • Time/cost of travel

Source: adapted from Bull, 1995 in Evans, 2002, p374

optimize the benefits from tourism – in a sense, to optimize their profits – it is necessary to utilize or exploit their available resources effectively in order not only to meet their own objectives or needs, such as maximizing employment creation, increasing income, government revenues or foreign exchange earnings and so on, but also at the same time to remain competitive within the tourism marketplace. This, in turn, suggests that the starting point for planning and development of tourism at the destination should be the identification and assessment of local resources, or capitals, which, as in any capitalist system, are inputs in the production of goods and services. Therefore, this chapter now identifies and considers what will be referred to as 'destination capitals'; that is, the stock of productive resources or assets possessed by a destination that individually or collectively can be exploited to generate a flow of benefits to the destination.

Tourism destination capitals

Capitalism is, by definition, the ownership and use of capital. Indeed, according to the Oxford English Dictionary, the origins of the term can be traced back to the work of the novelist William Makepeace Thackeray who, in 1854, used 'capitalism' to refer to the ownership of capital. Similarly, Karl Marx, Friedrich Engels, Benjamin Disraeli and others referred to capitalists as owners of capital, although it was not until the early 20th century that Max Weber first used capitalism more generally to describe an economic system. Nevertheless, as Porritt (2007, p138) observes, 'the core concept of capitalism, from which it derives its very name, is the economic concept of *capital*' [emphasis in original]. It is from the ownership and use of capital that profits are generated, and it is those profits that accord value to the capital from which they are generated.

From a classical economic perspective, capital is thought of in terms of assets that have the potential to generate a return. That is, they are seen as *productive* capital in as much as they are utilized in the production of other goods and services. At the same time, capital is itself produced, as opposed to naturally occurring (or non-productive) assets such as land or minerals, and is not 'used up' in the production process. Consequently, capital traditionally refers to plant and machinery and is one of three principal factors of production, the others being land and labour.

Since the 1960s, however, not only have other types of capital, such as human capital or intellectual capital, been considered by economists as important factors of production, but also the concept of capitals has been embraced by other social sciences and applied to other, non-economic contexts. For example, the French sociologist Bourdieu (1986) argues that individuals possess three forms of capital, namely, financial capital (possession of economic resources), social capital (resources based upon social relationships and networks) and cultural capital (the skills, knowledge and education possessed by an individual that, collectively, may reflect family background, social class and so on). Moreover, according to Bourdieu, cultural capital may take three forms: embodied (that is, inherited by socialization from the family or acquired through education); objectified in material objects and, hence, appropriated through financial capital or symbolically through embodied capital; or, institutionalized through academic qualifications or credentials. Importantly, for Bourdieu, these capitals do not possess value in the economic sense; rather, they empower the individual with the knowledge to achieve a particular status, identity or position in society.

Bourdieu's work and other sociological interpretations of capitals are explored in depth elsewhere (for example, Portes, 1998). However, the concepts of social and cultural capital and, indeed, other capitals have provided the foundation for a number of other models and applications. For example, the Sustainable Livelihoods Approach (SLA), which 'centres on the objectives, scope and priorities for development from the perspective of poor people' (Carney, 2002, p13), focuses upon five distinctive capitals – natural, social, human, physical and financial capital – as the basis for understanding and analysing the livelihoods of the poor. In a similar way, Forum for the Future (www.forumforthefuture.org) offers the 'Five Capitals Model' as a basis for sustainable development within a capitalist framework. In other words, it identifies five distinctive capitals that any organization uses to deliver its products and services. These products and services contribute, in turn, to improvements in people's quality of life but, in order to continue to do so, stocks of them must be sustained and enhanced (Table 6.2).

In both the SLA and the Five Capitals Model, capitals are seen from the more traditional perspective as assets from which particular benefits can be derived. It can be similarly argued that all tourism destinations also possess a variety of capitals which, to varying degrees, have the potential to generate a flow of benefits to both the destination (or, more specifically, destination communities) as producers of goods and services and to tourists as consumers of those goods and services. Therefore, the remainder of this chapter identifies and explores these capitals which then form the basis of an alternative approach to tourism

Table 6.2 *The Five Capitals*

Natural Capital is any stock or flow of energy and material that produces goods and services. It includes:

- resources – renewable and non-renewable materials;
- sinks – that absorb, neutralize or recycle wastes;
- processes – such as climate regulation.

Human Capital consists of people's health, knowledge, skills and motivation. All these things are needed for productive work.

Social Capital concerns the institutions that help us maintain and develop human capital in partnership with others; e.g. families, communities, businesses, trade unions, schools and voluntary organizations.

Manufactured Capital comprises material goods or fixed assets which contribute to the production process rather than being the output itself; e.g. tools, machines and buildings.

Financial Capital plays an important role in our economy, enabling the other types of Capital to be owned and traded. But unlike the other types, it has no real value itself but is representative of natural, human, social or manufactured capital; e.g. shares, bonds or banknotes.

Source: Forum for the Future, 2009

development proposed in the following chapter. Although the selection and interpretation of capitals relevant to tourism destinations might appear to be somewhat arbitrary, the following capitals, listed below and then individually considered in more detail, arguably reflect the productive assets of any tourism destination:

- Socio-cultural capital: in the context of tourism destinations, socio-cultural capital is used to refer to the structures, sociological institutions, cohesion, adaptability and openness of destination communities and their cultural characteristics and practices.
- Human capital: human capital refers to the supply and capabilities (knowledge, skills, motivation, innovative/entrepreneurial capacity) of individuals to contribute to the production and delivery of touristic services and experiences.
- Environmental capital: the environmental capital of destinations is defined broadly to include both the natural environment (that is, natural capital: resources, sinks and processes) and the built environment (facilities, attractions and infrastructure).
- Financial capital: the availability of financial capital (private and public sector) within destination economies determines the extent to which other capitals may be owned, developed and traded.
- Political capital: although a subset of social capital, the type and extent of political capital possessed by a destination determines its power relationship with external actors and, hence, its ability to self-determine its tourism development.

- Technological capital: tourism markets (the supply-demand interface) are increasingly dependent upon information and communication technology. Access to, ownership of and skill in the use of such technology is a key destination capital.

Importantly, the purpose here is to not to reflect the reality of any particular destination; nor is it to consider each capital in any depth: to do so is well beyond the scope of this chapter, whilst future research may reveal the significance and inherent challenges of applying them to the processes of tourism destination planning and development. Rather, the purpose is to highlight the nature and inter-connectedness of destination capitals as a basis for analysing the potential for optimizing the benefits flowing from the development of tourism within the context of destinational objectives and market opportunities.

Socio-cultural capital

Social and cultural capital are most usually considered in the literature as separate, identifiable forms of capital, the concept of social capital, in particular, attracting significant attention from a variety of social science disciplines. According to Adler and Kwon (2002, p17), 'a growing number of sociologists, political scientists, and economists have evoked the concept of social capital in the search for answers to a broadening range of questions confronted in their own fields'. As a consequence, social capital is subject to various and often competing definitions and is applied in a 'multitude of guises ... to analyse and explain various phenomena' (Woodhouse, 2006, p84), to the extent that agreement over a single definition and application is never likely to emerge. Moreover, some question the extent to which social capital can justifiably be referred to as a capital, in economists' sense of the word, although Robison et al (2000) suggest that social capital shares some conceptual similarities with physical capital and, like more traditional notions of capital, can provide a flow of benefits. For example, an empirical study by Woodhouse in two towns in regional Australia (2006) found a positive link between social capital and levels of economic prosperity whilst, conversely, Putman (1995) associated a decline in social capital in America with growing individualism, less civic engagement, a rise in ethnocentrism and a decline in social cohesion.

What, then, is social capital? Adler and Kwon (2002, p17) define it as 'the goodwill that is engendered by the fabric of social relations and that can be mobilised to facilitate action' whilst Coleman (1988, S98), a notable proponent of social capital, states that:

> Social capital is defined by its function. It is not a single entity but a variety of different entities, with two elements in common: they all consist of some aspect of social structures, and they facilitate certain actions of actors ... within the structure.

In other words, social capital is a resource that arises from relationships or interaction between people or groups of people – that resource being manifested in, for example, trust, mutual support and cooperation, or a collective will to work towards particular objectives – and that creates value through actions which result in benefits for society. In a sense, therefore, social capital may be thought of as a form of collective or community spirit embodied in a society generally, or within specific organizations, groups or institutions, which underpins positive actions for the benefit of society.

Definitions of cultural capital, conversely, typically reflect Bourdieu's notion of cultural capital as the knowledge and skills possessed by an individual. However, Throsby (1999, pp6–7) adopts an alternative conceptualization, suggesting that, in an economic as opposed to sociological framework, cultural capital can be thought of as the 'stock of cultural value embodied in an asset. This stock may in turn give rise to a flow of goods and services over time, i.e., to commodities that themselves have both cultural and economic value'. He goes on to distinguish between tangible cultural capital, such as buildings, monuments or works of art (that is, cultural heritage), which may generate income flows, and intangible cultural capital, or 'the set of ideas, practices, beliefs, traditions and values which serve to identify and bind together a given group of people'.

This particular perspective on cultural capital is of evident relevance to tourism destinations. That is, a destination's stock of cultural capital, including both that which is physical or tangible, such as historical buildings or art collections, and intangible, such as festivals, ceremonies or, perhaps, a 'traditional lifestyle', are assets or attractions that may directly or indirectly generate income. Moreover, intangible cultural capital may be enhanced or accumulated through its supply to tourists, cultural practices being strengthened or revitalized through their (re)presentation as a tourist attraction although, as widely discussed in the tourism literature, the process of commoditization may reduce the cultural significance or meaning to the local community. Social capital, conversely, can be thought of as the cohesion, cooperation and collective willingness to support and adapt to tourism, to welcome tourists and, as a community, to embrace tourism for the flows of benefits that it generates.

Human capital

The value of human capital as a factor of production in capitalist economies has long been recognized. For example, Adam Smith, in his book *The Wealth of Nations* (1776), referred to the abilities and talents of people as a form of capital, the costs of the acquisition of which, through education, apprenticeships and so on, are repaid through the profits generated by the application of those abilities and talents in the workplace. Thus, human capital is traditionally seen as labour or, more precisely, the skills and knowledge that people are able to apply to a production process to produce economic value. Consequently, from an economic perspective, the value of human capital has traditionally been measured in terms of the economic value produced by labour, or the profit after wages, training, education and other costs have been taken into account. In other words, human capital has been seen in a similar light as other forms of productive capital, such as machinery; investment in additional human capital (that is, employing more staff), increases output, as may investing in individuals through training to enhance their productivity.

In many respects, this is still the dominant interpretation of human capital. Although business organizations now have 'human resource' as opposed to 'personnel' departments, and despite the emergence of terms such as 'intellectual capital', the 'knowledge economy' and 'lifelong learning' as an investment in human capital – in other words, the increasing focus on knowledge as the basis of human capital – it is probably true to say that human capital is still measured in terms of productivity and productive value. When organizations seek to 'rationalize' or enhance profitability through efficiency gains, it is the cost of labour that is usually first addressed. Such an approach overlooks, of course, alternative and less quantifiable values of human capital, such as an individual's character or personality. Moreover, Porritt (2007) argues that human capital should not be thought of in economic terms. He suggests that human capital should be defined in terms of physical capacity (health and well-being), intellectual capacity, emotional capacity and spiritual capacity, factors which not only contribute to an individual's development and life chances but collectively contribute to the development of a more sustainable society: 'when thinking about the flow of benefits and "free gifts" from people's human capital in such broad terms, it is clear that it cannot possibly be measured in financial terms' (Porritt, 2007, p170).

Nevertheless, for tourism destinations and, indeed, tourism businesses, human capital is most appropriately seen, as defined above, as the supply and capability of individuals to contribute to the production and delivery of touristic services and experiences. In other words, depending on levels of skills, education, motivation and innovation, not all the available pool of labour within a destination community might be included in the stock of tourism human capital. Furthermore, tourism development should reflect existing human capital in terms of knowledge, skills and ability, both directly in tourism and in associated industries, or appropriate investment in human capital should be made to enable the destination to take advantage of market opportunities. For example, tourism in general, and farm diversification in particular, have increasingly been considered an effective catalyst of rural development and regeneration, especially in peripheral regions in Europe, North America and elsewhere. However, some of the challenges facing the development of rural and farm-based tourism are human capital-related. People who have traditionally worked in the agrarian sector may not possess appropriate business or marketing skills whilst research has found that not only do many farmers experience difficulty in adapting from a productivist to a service provider role (Fleischer and Pizam, 1997; Sharpley and Vass, 2006), but there is also no clear evidence that farmers possess the appropriate entrepreneurial skills to diversify into the service/tourism sector. Thus, greater emphasis in public sector funded investment in training may be a prerequisite to the successful and widespread development of rural tourism.

At the same time, tourism may be (and is) utilized in a more social development role as a means of enhancing the life chances of human capital destination areas. In particular, pro-poor tourism policies, as discussed briefly in Chapter 3, focus on distributing the benefits of tourism more widely to those excluded from, or unable to gain access to, the formal tourism sector (www.propoortourism.org.uk). In this case, interventions on the part of the state or external actors, such as non-governmental organizations (NGOs), into the working of the market are required. Therefore, the relationship between tourism development policy and human capital should reflect the needs and objectives of destination communities with respect to human capital.

Environmental capital

Environmental capital is frequently seen to be synonymous with the concept of natural capital, which can be defined as any naturally occurring stock of assets that yields valuable goods and services (Porritt, 2007, p149). In other words, environmental or natural capital can be thought of generally as the eco-system's natural resources, although Costanza and Daly (1992) suggest that natural resources can be deconstructed into two separate elements, namely: natural capital, such as stocks of trees or fish, and natural income, which represents 'a flow or annual yield of trees or fish, a flow that can be sustainable year after year' (Costanza and Daly, 1992, p38). Thus, the exploitation of natural resources that reduces either the natural capital or natural income (for example, where natural income is 'harvested' by human activity) can be viewed as a 'cost' that should be borne by those benefiting from natural goods and services. Hence economists have long suggested that, to meet the objectives of sustainable development, a monetary value should be placed on the natural environment so that the exploitation or degradation of natural resources can be paid or compensated for by those to whom benefits flow from their use (Pearce et al, 1989). Consequently, a simple example could be air passengers contributing to carbon offset schemes to compensate for their share of a flight's carbon emissions.

There are three elements of natural capital: natural resources, some of which may be renewable, such as timber, and some of which are non-renewable, in particular fossil fuels; natural sinks, that absorb or recycle waste, such as the atmosphere absorbing the pollution generated from the use of fossil fuels; and the services that the ecosystem provides, such as climate regulation. Thus, as Porritt (2007, p148) summarizes, 'natural capital is therefore ... the basis for all production in the human economy and the provider of services without which human society could not sustain itself'. Consequently, there have been calls for the development of so-called 'natural capitalism', or the adoption of business practices that recognize the value of natural capital and, hence, follow four principles (Lovins et al, 1999): an increase in the productivity of natural resources through more effective manufacturing processes; a shift in focus from quantity to quality; the re-use of natural materials or wastes; and investment to sustain or enhance the stock of natural resources.

For tourism destinations, the natural environment is, as discussed at length in the preceding chapter, core to the tourism product and experience.

Therefore, sustaining natural resources within the environmental needs and perceptions of destination communities is a prerequisite to tourism planning and development. Indeed, it could be argued that 'natural capitalism' should be a fundamental objective for an economic sector that interacts with and depends upon natural resources and services. However, the concept of environmental capital can be interpreted more widely to also include the built environment. The environmental attraction of a destination frequently lies not only in its natural capital (the climate, the marine environment, natural landscapes and so on) but in its building and other structures which, directly or indirectly, add value to the tourism product and, hence, are assets from which returns may be generated. Of course, the distinction between built environmental capital in general and, as considered above, specific forms of cultural capital, such as historic monuments, is a little fuzzy. Nonetheless, defining environmental capital broadly to include the built environment serves to focus attention on a stock of assets, such as redundant industrial buildings or even particular urban areas – the emergence of Rio de Janeiro's favellas as tourist attractions being a notable example (see Jaguaribe and Hetherington, 2004) – that could be transformed into tourism assets; equally, it identifies 'negative' assets, or those structures that diminish the tourism experience, such as working industrial plants or slum urban areas, and which must therefore be addressed in tourism planning and development.

Financial capital

Financial capital, or money, is not strictly a form of capital in the sense of capitals as productive assets. As previously discussed, it is essentially a medium of exchange, a common value equivalent for products and services that are traded on markets. Thus, financial capital is, in effect, the oil that keeps the engine of capitalism running smoothly and efficiently.

In reality, of course, the situation is significantly more complex. For example, whilst producers of goods and services may earn profits that can be retained and re-invested in the business, more commonly finance must be obtained from the financial markets, the nature of the finance usually determined by the amounts required, the timescale and its purpose. Therefore, longer-term capital to grow a business might be acquired through a share issue or venture capital, whilst short-term cash flow requirements might draw on a bank overdraft facility. At the same time, financial products, such as shares or currencies, are traded in financial markets, the aim being to generate a profit from investing in forms of financial capital that are anticipated to increase in value. The effective operation of these financial markets is fundamental to capitalism, as demonstrated by the wider impacts of the financial crisis of 2008 where, essentially, a lack of available credit fuelled the subsequent global economic recession.

Tourism development quite evidently requires financial capital, whether for infrastructural projects (airports, harbours, roads, power/water supply and so on), the development of specific facilities and attractions, investment in supporting businesses and industries and for 'day-to-day' operations, from street-cleaning to destination marketing and information provision. Thus, the nature and extent of tourism development (and whether it is private or public sector led) will be determined by availability of or access to financial capital in both the private and public sectors. This, in turn, is determined by factors such as the availability of finance on domestic markets, government revenues and budget priorities, the potential for international investment and the extent to which the 'profits' from tourism at a destinational level are generated by, for example, arrival or departure taxes, sales taxes imposed on tourism-related businesses, import duties on goods utilized by the tourism sector or an overt tourist tax on tourism enterprises. In less developed countries in particular, the role of the state is critical in both funding tourism development and/or establishing attractive conditions for international investment. However, in some instances, such as in The Gambia, the tourism sector itself may be seen as a source of general government revenues rather than as an asset to be invested in (Sharpley, *forthcoming*).

Political capital

Tourism has long been viewed from a political perspective (Richter, 1983; Matthews and Richter, 1991). Generally, tourism is inherently political; as a powerful economic and social force, it can be both used and manipulated for political purposes. More specifically, the nature and extent of government intervention in tourism is central to the analysis of tourism planning, the state being inextricably linked, in one form or another, with the development of tourism (Elliott, 1997; Hall, 2000), whilst a dominant theme within the political economic study of tourism has been, and remains, the largely unequal and asymmetric power relations between actors, institutions and geographic regions within the tourism system, in particular in the context of core-periphery relations within a global/globalized economy (Britton, 1982; Bianchi, 2002). Nonetheless, less attention has been paid to political structures and institutions within destinations or, more specifically, to the extent to which destination societies – or identifiable groups within destination societies – are endowed with political power or capital.

Political capital is, perhaps, a nebulous concept. It may, for example, be considered a social institution and, hence, a constituent element of social capital whilst, more pragmatically, politicians may equate political capital with the levels of support they enjoy amongst the electorate. According to Baumann and Sinha (2001, p1), however, political capital (within a sustainable liveli-hoods framework) can be defined as 'the ability to use power in support of political or economic positions and so enhance livelihoods; it refers to both the *legitimate* distribution of rights and power as well as the *illicit* operation of power' [emphasis in original]. In other words, political capital is an asset in as much as, in general, it links individuals and groups with what Baumann (2000, p20) refers to as 'power structures and policy' outside their immediate community and, in particular, it gives access to rights and assets. In tourism, such rights and assets are the ability to participate in and influence both tourism planning and development and the tourism production process within the destination.

For Baumann (2000), who criticizes its omission in SLA models, an analysis of political capital is essential because:

- access to assets (capitals) depends upon the political capital of individuals and groups. 'It is therefore critical to understand how rights are constituted at the local level and the dynamic interrelation between political capital and other assets' (Baumann, 2001, p21);
- the location of political capital is important because the state may lack legitimacy;
- political negotiations and processes may not always be transparent; an analysis of political capital may enhance transparency;
- an understanding of political capital may reveal potential support or resistance to change implemented by those entrusted or endowed with political power.

For tourism destinations, therefore, political capital is an important concept as it provides a basis for exploring and understanding: the extent to which different stakeholder groups are able to access or benefit from other tourism assets or capitals within the destination or are excluded from the formal tourism sector; the ways in which tourism planning and development reflects the power or influence of particular groups within the destination; the extent to which external policies and influences may be challenged or resisted; the form and structure of the power relationship between the destination community as a whole and external sources of political power and influence; and the potential means of overcoming inequalities in political capital both within the destination (that is, between those able to access and benefit from tourism, whether through ownership of assets, formal employment in the sector or the ability to influence or direct tourism development policies and those unable to do so) and beyond, between the destination and centres of political capital within the wider tourism system.

Technological capital

Strictly speaking, technology, as with finance, is not a type of capital in the traditional sense of the word. That is, technological equipment, specifically that related to information and communication (computer hardware and software, as well the technological networks that enable computers to communicate with each other through, for example, the internet), arguably does not directly generate income and profits. Rather, it enables organizations and businesses to operate more efficiently and quickly in markets, to market or supply their products and services more widely and to provide customers with access to (and a means of paying for) those products and services. Thus, although financial investment is required in technology equipment, it enables markets for goods and services (including tourism) to function efficiently.

Nevertheless, information and communication technology has become increasingly pervasive within the tourism sector (WTO, 2001; Buhalis, 2002). Technology has not only become critical to both the day-to-day operations and the strategic functions of tourism businesses, enabling them to operate more efficiently for example, through e-ticketing in the airline sector or yield management systems, balancing capacity with prices, in tour operations or the accommodation sector, and to remain competitive. It has also revolution-ized tourism markets or, more simply, the relationship between producers and consumers. Tourists increasingly expect to be able to access informa-tion, products, services or complete holidays through the internet, and also to be able to pay for them online. Therefore, for businesses and destinations to operate within the tourism market, to be able to promote and sell their products and services, not only must they have an 'online presence' but they must also possess the appropriate skills and knowledge to optimize their use of information and communication technology. In short technological capital (that is, access to, ownership of and skill in the use of technology) is an essential requirement for tourism destinations and, hence, a fundamental consideration in tourism development and planning. Indeed, Buhalis (2005) refers to the 'eDestination', where technology-based destination management systems have been established to integrate the entire tourism supply at the destination. As a minimum, these provide full information of available products and services, along with limited reservation facilities, although some offer 'fully functional websites that can support the entire range of customer purchasing requirements' (Buhalis, 2005, p242). A logical progression, according to Buhalis, is the development of so-called Destination Integrated Computerized Information Reservation Management Systems; that is, systems that will meet all the needs and services required by tourists and tourism businesses at specific destinations. Of course, such systems are not appropriate for all destinations. Nevertheless, technological equipment and high levels of skill in its use and application has, in recent years, become an indispensible destination capital.

To summarize, then, this chapter has argued that tourism is, first and fore-most, a manifestation of capitalistic endeavour. Tourism businesses in both generating and destination regions produce and supply tourism products, services and experiences to meet the demands of tourist consumers and in the expectation of generating a profit. Similarly, destinations are in the business of tourism; they seek to generate benefits from producing and selling tourism products and services, the potential returns or 'profit' being income, employment and economic growth. In fact, as suggested in earlier chapters, 'development' is not an inevitable outcome of tourism; the extent to which the economic returns from tourism translate into wider development is dependent on a variety of local factors. Thus, in order to optimize those benefits, it is necessary, in turn, to make the most appropriate use of capitals to compete effectively in tourism markets whilst meeting local needs. At the same time, and as the following case study of tourism in Cyprus demonstrates, an analysis of capitals may reveal potential destination management challenges. Therefore, as the next chapter suggests, destination capitals should form the basis of tourism development.

Case study: Tourism and destination capitals in Cyprus

In 1960, Cyprus achieved independence from British rule and began to develop its tourism sector. Over the following 40 years, the island evolved into a major mass tourism destination and, by the early years of the new millennium, not only were tourists visiting the island in record numbers – in 2001, for example, almost 2.7 million arrivals were recorded – but tourism had also become the engine driving the local economy. It accounted for a quarter of all employment on the island, total receipts of CY£1,272 million in that year contributed around 21 per cent of gross domestic product (GDP) and represented 40 per cent of exports of goods and services, and the wider tourism economy accounted for 31 per cent of GDP. More recently, however, the tourism sector in Cyprus has faced a number of significant challenges. Not only have tourist arrival figures been erratic and, overall, exhibited a downward trend, but tourist receipts have also fallen (even in some years when an increase in arrivals has been experienced). More significantly, tourism's contribution to GDP has decreased dramatically. Latest figures suggest that in 2007 tourism accounted for around 14 per cent of GDP, a not insignificant contribution when compared with many other countries but, nevertheless, evidence of a rapid decline in its position in the Cypriot economy. On the one hand, this points, perhaps positively, to less economic dependence on tourism but, on the other hand, it suggests that the tourism sector faces an uncertain future. In particular, the fall in value of sterling against the Euro in early 2009 suggests that Cyprus, always a relatively expensive destination, may become prohibitively so for the British market which has consistently provided about half of all tourist arrivals on the island. Thus, the 'story' of tourism in Cyprus is one of dramatic success followed by a relatively rapid decline in the sector's fortunes, both of which can be explained, to an extent, by considering the island's tourism 'capitals'. First, however, a brief review of the development of tourism will provide the framework for that analysis.

As widely discussed in the literature, tourism development in Cyprus has occurred in two distinct phases (Andronikou, 1987; Ayers, 2000; Sharpley, 2001, 2003).

Phase 1: 1960–1974
From 1960, as the focus of tourism shifted from the traditional hill resorts of the Troodos mountains to the coast, tourism grew rapidly. Annual arrivals, which totalled just 25,700 in 1960, exceeded 264,000 by 1973, representing an average annual growth rate of over 20 per cent, whilst tourist receipts grew at an annual average of 22 per cent (Table 6.3). Tourism development reflected a pattern of the rapid development of coastal resorts typical of many Mediterranean destinations; by 1973, Kyrenia and Famagusta accounted for 58 per cent of accommodation and 73 per cent of arrivals on the island, demand was highly seasonal and the UK had already emerged as the principal market.

This first period of tourism development coincided with the rapid expansion of the island's economy: 'in the 14 years after independence... Cyprus, with

Table 6.3 *Tourism growth rates in Cyprus 1960–1973*

	Arrivals/earnings				Rates of growth (%)		
	1960	1966	1971	1973	1960–66	1966–73	1960–73
Tourist arrivals ('000s)	25.7	54.1	178.6	264.1	13	25	20
Foreign exchange earnings (CY£m)	1.8	3.6	13.6	23.8	12	31	22
Contribution of earnings to GDP (%)	2.0	2.5	5.2	7.2			

Source: PIO, 1997, p251; Ayers, 2000

a free enterprise economy based on trade and agriculture, achieved a higher standard of living than any of its neighbours, with the exception of Israel' (Brey, 1995, p92). Tourism's contribution to GDP also increased from around 2.0 per cent in 1960 to 7.2 per cent in 1973 whilst, by the end of the period, some 3.8 per cent of the working population were employed in the sector.

Phase 2: 1974–2000

The Turkish invasion in 1974 had a devastating impact on the island's economy in general and on the tourism sector in particular (Andronikou, 1979; Lockhart, 1993). The great majority of existing and planned accommodation, situated in the northern part of the island, was lost, along with the island's international airport at Nicosia and many other tourist facilities. As a consequence, in 1975 arrivals in the Republic of Cyprus in 1975 amounted to just 47,000.

However, from 1975 onwards the Cypriot tourism sector again witnessed remarkable growth. Between 1976 and 1989, for example, annual arrivals increased by some 700 per cent, whilst the receipts from tourism also grew rapidly. Indeed, the 1973 figure of CY£23.8 million was re-attained by 1977 and, during the 1980s as a whole, tourism receipts grew at an average annual rate of 23 per cent. From 1990, arrivals and receipts figures became somewhat erratic. Nevertheless, over 2.6 million arrivals were recorded in 2000, generating CY£1,194 million in receipts (see Table 6.4). Such overall dramatic growth reflected the island's rapid emergence as a major Mediterranean summer sun destination, in particular since the mid-1980s when overseas charter airlines were first permitted to operate to Cyprus. This, in turn, was driven by the equally rapid growth in accommodation facilities, primarily in the coastal resorts of Paphos, Limassol, Agia Napa and Paralimni, the latter two resorts accounting for over 40 per cent of the island's accommodation stock and attracting 32 per cent of all arrivals in 2000.

Inevitably, during this period tourism assumed an increasingly important role in the Cypriot economy. Its contribution to GDP, at just over 2 per cent of GDP in 1975, increased to over 20 per cent in 2000, whilst other sectors, particularly construction, financial services, communications and transport,

Table 6.4 *Tourism in Cyprus 1975–2007: Key indicators*

Year	Arrivals ('000s)	Receipts (CY£mn)	Average tourist spending (CY£)	Tourism receipts as % of GDP	Total licensed bed spaces
1975	47	5	n.a.	2.1	5685
1980	349	72	200	9.4	12,830
1985	770	232	299	15.7	30,375
1986	828	256	308	16.0	33,301
1987	949	320	334	18.0	45,855
1988	1,112	386	344	19.4	48,518
1989	1,379	490	350	21.7	54,857
1990	1,561	573	364	23.4	59,574
1991	1,385	476	343	18.4	63,564
1992	1,991	694	351	23.8	69,759
1993	1,841	696	379	21.4	73,657
1994	2,069	810	389	22.3	76,117
1995	2,100	810	383	20.5	78,427
1996	1,950	780	382	19.0	78,427
1997	2,088	843	393	20.4	84,368
1998	2,222	878	380	20.2	86,151
1999	2,434	1,025	400	22.0	84,173
2000	2,686	1,194	445	21.7	85,303
2001	2,697	1,272	472	21.1	91,422
2002	2,418	1,132	468	18.4	94,466
2003	2,303	1,015	441	16.2	95,185
2004	2,349	982	419	15.1	96,535
2005	2,470	1,006	406	14.8	95,648
2006	2,401	1,027	428	14.8	93,957
2007	2,416	1,087	449	14.7	92,952

Source: CTO Reports; Department of Statistics and Research and author's calculations

benefited from the growth in tourism, as did agriculture and manufacturing from the increasing number of arrivals who boosted demand for a wide range of locally produced products' (Ayers, 2000). Thus, as noted above, by 2000 the wider tourism economy in Cyprus contributed almost 31 per cent of GDP. Tourism also became the dominant source of employment on the island. In 2000, 40,500 people were directly employed in tourism, around 18,000 of whom worked in the hotels sector whilst, overall, some 25 per cent of the working population were directly and indirectly dependent on the tourism sector.

As is evident from Table 6.4, since 2000 the Cypriot tourism sector has experienced a period of volatility and uncertainty. Following record numbers in 2001, arrivals fell back in 2002 and, despite some growth in 2004–2005, continue to fluctuate. Indeed, latest figures suggest a decline to 2,403,750 arrivals in 2008. Initially, the decline in 2002 was attributed to increased tensions in the Middle East (specifically the invasion of Iraq) and capacity reductions on the part of tour operators following the events of 11 September 2001. At the same time, however, the 'Agia Napa' factor was also significant. That is, the popularity of Agia Napa as one of the Mediterranean's premier clubbing/nightlife centres had been a major contributor to the growth in arrivals in Cyprus from 1999 to 2001 but, by early 2002, bookings for the resort were some 40 per cent down on the previous year. Not only had its popularity as a nightlife centre proved to be short-lived but also the family market had been deterred by extensive negative publicity surrounding the resort's clubbing image.

However, the continuing problems facing the Cypriot tourism industry point to more fundamental challenges which, along with the preceding success story, can be summarized within a capitals framework. Of course, whilst each capital, reflecting those outlined earlier in this chapter, is considered here separately, in practice it is sometimes difficult to delineate between them. As will be seen, for example, the balance of political power or capital within the tourism sector has undoubtedly been a defining characteristic of tourism development in Cyprus, yet this cannot be separated from either human or socio-cultural capital as a fundamental force behind the nature and scale of tourism development on the island. Similarly, those human and socio-cultural capitals are, in many ways, inter-related. Nevertheless, the following framework provides a basis for identifying the key capitals from which the benefits (and dis-benefits) of tourism have flowed.

Cyprus: Tourism capitals

Socio-cultural capital To a great extent, the socio-cultural capital of the Cypriots, reflecting a combination of an Eastern Mediterranean lifestyle, 'island-ness', Greek culture in general and 'philoxenia' (welcoming to all guests) in particular, a long and varied history and institutions and practices resulting from the past political relationship with Britain (English is widely spoken as a second language, cars drive on the left and, until the recent adoption of the Euro following accession to the European Union in 2004, the local currency was the Cypriot Pound) was, and remains, a principal attraction of Cyprus, particularly for the British market which still accounts for over half of all tourist arrivals on the island (Table 6.5). In other words, in addition to the environmental capital of Cyprus (see below), the local population, its culture and its undoubted hospitality is a significant capital underpinning the success of tourism on the island. At the same time, however, and linked to human capital

Table 6.5 *Arrivals from major markets 1990–2007 (% of total)*

	1990	1995	2000	2005	2006	2007
UK	44.3	41.5	50.7	56.3	56.6	53.1
Scandinavia	17.6	10.9	9.8	7.9	8.6	9.5
Germany	6.4	11.2	8.7	7.4	6.4	5.7
Greece	4.5	3.1	3.7	5.3	5.3	5.8
Russia/E. Europe	–	4.5	7.7	6.6	7.9	10.0

Source: author's calculations from Republic of Cyprus, 2007, p56

discussed next, a specific characteristic of Cypriot society is that the ownership of land is valued both for the status it conveys and for its potential economic return. More specifically, many Cypriots wish to pass on land to their children as no inheritance tax is payable on it. As a consequence, the sale of land provided opportunities for rapid financial gain through hotel development or to buy more land as an investment. This, in turn, has contributed to the over-development of tourism facilities as more people seek to share in the wealth and status of land ownership and development.

Human capital Although the Cypriot government was a principal actor in the post-1974 redevelopment of tourism, according high priority to the tourism sector in terms of financial incentives, training and the provision of infrastructure, the ambition and drive of the Cypriot people was a significant factor. As Andronikou (1979, p245) observes, 'the ideology and value system [in Cyprus] attach great importance to individual achievement and are generally responsive to innovations, new ideas and opportunities'. Moreover, 'a competitive spirit is encouraged at an early stage, and upward socioeconomic striving is highly valued' (1979, p246). Free enterprise and individualism are thus valued and respected and, in short, the entrepreneurial spirit of Cypriot 'human capital' was a major driver in the successful and rapid development of tourism. However, that entrepreneurial spirit has, arguably, contributed to excessive development in general and an over-supply of accommodation in particular; simply stated, too many hotels have been built, creating a tour-operators' 'buyers' market'. At the time, as the island has become more developed the population has become better educated; many younger Cypriots are over-qualified and foreign workers have been required to fill vacancies in hotels and restaurants, sometime resulting in a decline in service levels.

Environmental capital The principal attraction of Cyprus is its climate – from May to October, the island enjoys virtually uninterrupted sunshine. Perhaps surprisingly for a major sun-sea-sand destination, however, it is not well endowed with beaches; the best ones are to be found in the (Turkish-controlled) northeast, although there are beaches in the resorts in the southwest (Paphos) and southeast (Agia Napa). The island's natural capital includes a fertile central plain and, to the west, the forested Troodos massif and Mount Olympus (1957m), the island's highest point and a popular day trip destination. Numerous small, traditional villages are located in the hinterland, some of which have become the focus of agri-tourism developments, whilst evidence of the island's long and varied history is to be found in its castles, churches, monasteries and other historical structures. Thus, the island boasts significant built capital, although it remains largely incidental to its overall attraction as mass summer sun destination.

It is generally accepted that there has been 'unprecedented pressure on the natural environment of the island due to the uncontrolled expansion of tourism' (Kammas, 1993, p81), to the extent that the resource capacity of the island has been exceeded. Much of the coastline has been developed or earmarked for development (although the Akamas peninsula in the northwest is protected by national park designation) with some resorts suffering from architecturally polluting ribbon development. Nonetheless, local infrastructural development, such as roads, sewage systems or public spaces, has not kept pace with the rate of accommodation development, whilst land, sea and air pollution is a growing problem. Moreover, water shortages during the summer are an increasing problem exacerbated by the growth of tourism. Conversely, important cultural sites, such as Kolossi Castle and the Roman ruins at Kourion, have been protected and tourism has been the driving force behind the preservation and renovation of historic villages, such as Kakopetria on the northern slopes of Troodos, and Nicosia old town. Thus, tourism has, in a sense, been a mixed blessing, although the overdevelopment of much of the coastline has left few options for future development.

Financial capital Although Cyprus has enjoyed rapid economic growth since the 1980s, in the immediate aftermath of the 1974 invasion limited private sector finance was available for investment in tourism. Thus, from the outset, the government was obliged to invest in the development of tourism, not only building new airports (at Larnaca and, subsequently, at Paphos) and other necessary infrastructure, but also in stimulating private sector investment through, for example, the provision of low-interest loans, free land for hotel construction and duty-free imports of materials and equipment for the accommodation sector (Ioannides, 1992). After an initial period of rapid growth, the private sector became financially self-sustaining and expansion of coastal hotel development continued. Therefore, government subsidy was directed towards meeting tourism development objectives, such as high quality resort hotels and the construction of smaller, family-run hotels in inland villages. The agri-tourism project, designed to spread the benefits of tourism away from the coast to traditional villages, has also benefited from public subsidy though these developments have had little impact on the overall patterns of tourism on the island.

Political capital Since 1969, during the first phase of tourism development in Cyprus, responsibility for the organization and promotion of tourism on the island has been delegated to the Cyprus Tourism Organisation (CTO), a semi-autonomous body that is funded by direct government subsidy and by income from licensing and other commercial activities it undertakes. Nevertheless, the CTO's role is, to a great extent, framed by a series of Five Year Plans which, since 1975, have guided national tourism development policy. Moreover, despite its formal position within the Cypriot tourism sector, the CTO has had limited success in translating its policies and plans for tourism development into practice, largely reflecting the patterns of political capital in Cyprus. Hence, it enjoys relatively little political influence either internally within the island's tourism sector or with external players.

Three factors are of particular relevance. Firstly, not only is there a lack of formal structures for the implementation of policy at the national level, but also a multi-layered, democratic system of government, with frequent elections at different levels in the system, limits longer-term planning and focuses political power at the local level. Consequently, many decisions, such as planning permission for hotel development, are made according to local short-term, as opposed to national, interests. Secondly, sectoral bodies, such as the Cyprus Hotels Association, have been able to exert considerable influence on tourism policy; the decision to open up Cyprus to charter flights along with a policy to restrict seat-only sales was driven by the need for the hotel sector to attract increasing numbers of visitors to fill the rapidly expanding stock of accommodation. Thirdly, trade unions have long enjoyed political power in Cyprus. Following the successful growth of tourism during the 1980s and consequential minimal levels of unemployment, the unions were able to negotiate generous wage settlements which, over time, served to raise costs – for example, the average cost of labour in hotels rose by 94 per cent between 1992 and 1997 – and to reduce employment (and, hence, levels of service) in the hotel sector. Moreover, the increasing recruitment of overseas staff is likely to dilute the traditional hospitality for which Cyprus is renowned, further diminishing the island's competitiveness. Thus, a number of challenges currently facing the tourism sector in Cyprus are grounded in the 'ownership' of political capital in Cyprus.

Overall, then, it is evident that both the successful development of tourism in Cyprus and the more recent challenges faced by the island's tourism sector can be explored from a capitals perspective, which may also point to solutions for the future development of tourism on the island.

7
Destination Capitals: An Alternative Framework for Tourism Development

The purpose of this book has been twofold. Firstly, it set out to challenge what was referred to in the introduction as the 'status quo' of sustainable tourism development. In other words, it set out to argue that, despite maintaining its position in both academic and tourism policy circles as the dominant tourism development paradigm, sustainable tourism development has failed to deliver. Not only is there little, if any, evidence of 'true' sustainable tourism development in practice – there are, of course, numerous examples of small-scale, local projects that conform to the principles of sustainability yet these are, to paraphrase a well-used argument, micro responses to macro issues – but also the significant attention paid to the concept in the academic literature has resulted in neither a consensus with regards to definitions and theoretical underpinnings, nor a translation of its principles into a viable set of practices for developing tourism 'on the ground'. In short, it is time to recognize that the concept of sustainable tourism development, both as a subject of academic debate and as an approach to tourism development, has reached an impasse; it is time to move on and consider tourism development 'beyond sustainability'. Indeed, there is some evidence that this is beginning to occur (Lim and Cooper, 2009).

Consequently, the second purpose of the book has been to propose an alternative approach to tourism development which addresses the tourism–development–environment nexus unencumbered by the idealism of sustainable tourism development and its typically prescriptive, managerialist and, arguably, western-centric principles. More specifically, it has argued that tourism is, fundamentally, an economic activity, a significant and valuable sector of the global capitalist economy that has the potential to bring a variety of economic benefits to destination areas, as well as to those countries that are generators of international tourism. Therefore, recognizing that tourism is, in essence, a form of capitalistic endeavour manifested in the market-led production and consumption of tourism products, services and experiences, it has been suggested that a 'destination capitals' perspective provides the most appropriate framework for optimizing the economic benefits of tourism to the destination. That is, like any business operating within a capitalist system, destinations seek to exploit their resources or assets in order to make a 'profit'. Thus, tourism development should be based on the exploitation of those assets in a manner which reflects and respects local needs and meets the demands of potential tourists.

The previous chapter related tourism to the defining characteristics of capitalism before going on to propose a number of different capitals that, individually and collectively, are exploited to produce the outputs of the tourism production system. In other words, it identified the productive assets possessed by destinations that contribute to the production of goods and services consumed by tourists and, hence, to a flow of economic benefits that, generated by tourism spending, accrue to the destination. In this final chapter, these destination capitals form the basis of an alternative framework for the development of tourism, a framework that focuses upon the needs and productive assets of destinations and their interaction with opportunities and challenges external to the destination. Drawing on a number of case studies, it then suggests how such an approach may prove to be more effective in optimizing tourism's benefits – within environmental parameters as defined by the destination – than overarching sets of principles such as those that characterize the concept of sustainable tourism development.

As noted previously, it is not the purpose here to propose a set of principles or guidelines for the development of tourism; to do so would be simply to re-place one universal approach (sustainable tourism development) with another. Nor is it to detail the tourism destination planning process, which is considered extensively in the literature (for example, Dredge and Jenkins, 2006; Hall, 2007b). Rather, it is to propose a more pragmatic approach to tourism development that, in offering an alternative to the comfortable or, as described in Chapter 3, the hypocritical and delusional idealism of sustainable tourism development, provides a platform for more vigorous debate and further research into some of the issues identified in this book. At the same time, it may go some way to building a bridge between academic discourse of tourism development and the practical challenges facing destinations. Firstly, however, it is useful to review briefly some of the key points raised in this book that justify a 'destination capitals' model of tourism development.

The story so far

As its title suggests, the principal focus of this book is on the relationship between tourism, its developmental role and the environment within which it occurs. More specifically, it focuses primarily on how to optimize the benefits of tourism within environmental parameters, the fundamental argument being that, in order to do so, it is necessary to progress beyond the restrictive concept of sustainable tourism development. Immediately, then, three broad questions emerge: What is tourism? What are the benefits that flow from tourism development? And what is the tourism environment? These have all been considered in the preceding chapters and they now provide useful headings for summarizing the main themes and issues that have been discussed in the book so far.

What is tourism?

In Chapter 1, it was suggested that the term 'tourism' may be defined in three ways, namely: as the movement of people or, more generally, a social phenomenon; as an economic sector; and as an interacting system of people, places and processes. Tourism is, of course, all of these; each definition simply reflects either a different way of looking at tourism or a different disciplinary framework for its analysis. Nevertheless, each definition also points to key issues that underpin the argument for a 'destination capitals' approach to tourism development.

In particular, although the term 'tourism' is most frequently associated with specific manifestations of travel as categorized, for example, by the World Tourism Organization (now United Nations World Tourism Organization or UNWTO) (WTO, 1994), such is the variety and scope of travel-related activity with respect to purpose and behaviour that it is almost impossible to distinguish between tourism and mobility more generally. However, both tourism and most forms of mobility, or movements of people, by definition involve going *from* places *to* places; thus, the only common feature of tourism/mobility, other than that it involves travel, is the destination. Nonetheless, 'the destination' itself is almost infinitely variable. Although typically domestic, or within the tourist's own country (the great majority of tourist trips are domestic, supporting the arguments that tourism, though occurring globally, is not a globalized phenomenon), destinations vary from specific facilities or attractions to urban centres, resorts (landlocked or coastal) and rural or wilderness areas. Thus, each destination is unique with respect to its environmental, socio-cultural, political and economic characteristics and, consequently, its potential to benefit from tourism. This, in turn, suggests that tourism development can only be considered from the perspective of the destination, not within 'one-size-fits-all', top-down planning frameworks.

From the economic sector perspective, tourism is revealed as a complex, multi-layered and multi-sectoral production system. In other words, it comprises innumerable businesses and organizations, the great majority of which are small to medium, private sector and, hence, profit-motivated enterprises. Universal policies, guidelines, codes of practice, regulations or other forms of intervention in the day-to-day operations are, therefore, impossible to implement and contradict the very basis of market-led capitalistic economic systems of which tourism is a notable example. Certainly, there are several industry-wide initiatives, such as the International Tourism Partnership (www.tourismpartnership.org) which encourages socially and environmentally responsible business practices amongst travel and tourism businesses, and various accreditation schemes that similarly recognize and promote such practices, as well as numerous examples of individual businesses engaging in responsible business activity. Many airlines and tour operators, for example, are proactive in seeking ways of minimizing the negative social and environ-mental consequences of their businesses. However, corporate social responsib-ility cannot be imposed upon all sectors and all businesses across the tourism production system. Therefore, the destination again represents the most ap-propriate context for considering tourism development from the perspective of the industry, as local planning restrictions and so on may be imposed to reflect local environmental and social conditions. Equally, when viewing tourism as a complex interacting system, it becomes evident that it is difficult to delineate tourism clearly from other social and economic systems, thus reinforcing the arguments that the destination is the most appropriate 'unit of analysis' for tourism development.

What are the benefits that flow from tourism development?

For reasons that are well known and widely discussed in the literature, tourism has long been, and still is, considered an effective vehicle of development. However, an argument central to this book is that 'development' as currently conceptualized does not inevitably or automatically flow from tourism. As dis-cussed in Chapter 2, development is a rather slippery, ambiguous and broad term that defies precise definition, embracing as it does both measurable indicators (wealth, literacy levels, access to education, child mortality rates and so on) and less tangible objectives, such as self-reliance and freedom (Sen, 1999). It is, therefore, unclear how a direct causal relationship can be established between tourism and development, in particular sustainable development. Indeed, although it is suggested by the UNWTO and others that tourism, in all its manifestations, should be developed according to the principles of sustainable development, this book has demonstrated that such a marriage is, in reality, unworkable.

In other words, tourism does not necessarily lead to development. It does, however, possess the potential to generate economic benefits that derive from the expenditure of tourists on products, services and experiences. It also, of course, has the potential to generate costs, either directly in the form of, for example, leakages (the cost of importing goods and services into the local economy to meet the needs of the tourism sector), or indirectly as what economists refer to as 'externalities'. For destinations, the net benefits of tourism development are, in effect, the 'profit', or the value of tourism once the costs have been taken into account (including, perhaps, environmental costs). Therefore, tourism is, essentially, a catalyst of economic growth. Moreover, the extent to which that economic growth both occurs and also translates into wider development is dependent on a combination of economic, socio-cultural, political and environmental factors particular to each destination. Thus, different types of tourism development generate different benefits; high volume-lower yield tourism (that is, 'mass' tourism), for example, may provide wider (though perhaps lower quality) employment opportunities but relatively less income, whereas low volume-high yield 'quality' tourism (the objective of many destinations) may have the opposite effect, along with more limited environmental and social impacts. In either case, however, the immediate benefits that flow from tourism are economic. It is, therefore, logical that tourism development should be considered as an economic activity. This, in turn, suggests that the capitalistic nature of tourism production and consumption should be both recognized and embraced as the basis for planning tourism, hence the focus on destination capitals.

What is the tourism environment?

There is no single tourism environment. As discussed at length in Chapter 5, not only is each destination unique with respect to its physical resource base, but that resource base may be perceived differently by different groups and stakeholders both within and external to the destination. In other words, even within particular destinations numerous environments potentially exist. Nevertheless, the important and, perhaps, contentious point to emerge from this discussion is that, by and large, destination environments 'belong' to the destination. Certain environmental resources and services, such as the oceans, the atmosphere and the climate system, are of course globally shared assets which require a shared global responsibility for their upkeep. However, resources which are specific to the destination are owned by, and understood and perceived in ways particular to, the destination. Therefore, decisions as to what resources should be exploited for tourism and to what extent they should remain the responsibility of the destination or, more specifically, should reflect indigenous environmental knowledge, custom and needs rather than being guided by exogenous, ideologically grounded conceptualizations of conservation and resource use, should be made by the destination.

Quite evidently, this is not a new argument. The idea of community-based tourism development was first proposed some 25 years ago (Murphy, 1983; 1985), subsequently evolving into a key, yet contested, pillar of sustainable tourism (Scheyvens, 2002). More specifically, enabling indigenous involvement, particularly within a free market context, is thought to contribute to more effective and sustainable resource use (Hulme and Murphree, 1999; Southgate and Sharpley, 2002) whilst, more generally, self-reliance and grassroots decision-making are key elements of contemporary interpretations of development. However, what this means in the context of this book is that destinations should be able to develop and promote forms of tourism that best meet their economic and development needs and objectives, whether it be traditional sun-sea-sand mass tourism, as is common around the Mediterranean and elsewhere, low volume-high value cultural tourism as in the case, for example, of Bhutan where the development objective remains 'Gross National Happiness' (GNH) as opposed to gross domestic product (GDP), or even the dramatic and, in some ways, extreme forms of development such as those described in the case study of Dubai later in this chapter. That is, although certain types of (usually mass) tourism might be criticized for being unsustainable (Hickman, 2007), the right of destinations to follow such a path should be respected.

Based upon these points and arguments, the following section proposes a model of tourism development based upon destination capitals. In so doing, it provides a framework for developing tourism in all types of destinations, the fundamental premise being that the concept of destination capitals is applicable to any tourism development context, whether domestic or international, large or small scale, urban, coastal or in natural environments. The key elements of the model are then explored within the context of a number of case studies.

Inevitably, the inherent emphasis within the model on tourism as a capitalistic activity and its consequential economic benefits may attract criticism, in particular as an apparent return to a neo-classical, modernization perspective on development and all that implies. However, the focus on destination capitals provides a basis for optimizing the benefits of tourism and internalizing its costs whilst both reflecting destinational needs and tourism development opportunities.

Tourism development: A destination capitals model

A tourism destination may be thought of, somewhat simplistically, as a sort of business or, more precisely, as a corporation comprising numerous business units. In other words, all the facilities, attractions and other organizations that collectively supply tourist services and experiences in the destination are, in a sense, different divisions within the overall destination business. There are, of course, significant differences between destinations and corporations, not least that, generally, there is no formal organizational structure, chain of command or common ownership within a destination. Nevertheless, corporations (including those in the travel and tourism sector) typically follow a strategic management process that seeks to achieve 'fit' between their resources and the external environment in order to remain competitive and profitable (Figure 7.1).

Figure 7.1 *A basic model of strategic management*

In simple terms, organizations typically undertake an internal audit of their resources, capabilities, knowledge and core competencies, plus an external analysis of the competitive environment, as a basis for establishing their strategic direction (Grant, 2002; Evans et al, 2003). In the following model, a similar process is proposed with, in particular, the analysis of destination capitals providing the basis of the 'internal audit' of the destination (Figure 7.2).

To a great extent, the model in Figure 7.2 is self-explanatory. It depicts a logical process of need identification followed by an analysis of destination

Figure 7.2 *A destination capitals model of tourism development*

resources or capitals which, when related to market opportunities and external forces or restrictions, provides a basis for developing tourism development plans and processes. Central to the process is the identification and inter-relationship of destination capitals as described in the previous chapter. This establishes what resources or assets should be exploited for tourism, the extent to which they might generate a flow of benefits to the destination and, through the analysis of political capital in particular, who has access to and control over the use of these capitals. It is also significant in that, when compared with other models and concepts of tourism development, it focuses the respons-ibility for resource or asset use on the destination. It is the destination that establishes, within the parameters of local knowledge, custom and culture, how resources, whether environmental, human or socio-cultural, are utilized. As a consequence, sustainability, as defined by the destination, is inherent within the destination capital process as opposed to being an externally imposed ideo-logical concept.

Inevitably, this raises the question as to who is responsible for assessing destination capitals or for the process through which decisions are made with respect to resource use for tourism development. In other words, 'the destina-tion' has been referred to here largely in abstract terms, but the destination capitals approach requires appropriate decision-making processes. Typically, the answer lies in the prevailing political systems, institutional structures and patterns of political capital in the destination, both generally and in relation to tourism in particular. In some instances, open democratic processes may be in evidence. For example, in the case study of Blackpool below, it is the local authority (the public sector) that, ostensibly possessing political capital, has the potential to lead the tourism development process, though only in partnership with the owners of other capitals (the private sector). Conversely, as discussed in the Dubai case study, political capital and, to a great extent, financial capital is concentrated in the hands of the ruling elite. However, in both cases political and institutional structures are but one element of a destination's capitals. Again in Dubai, it is the concentrated political capital that has been a significant factor in the rapid and, arguably, successful development of tourism in the emirate. Thus, planning and decision-making processes are, just as sustainability is, inherent in the model.

Looking at the model in more detail, as with all forms of tourism planning and development processes, the first stage in the process is the identification of the goals and objectives of tourism development – in a sense, the destination's mission statement. Typically, these are seen to embrace four distinct goals: enhanced visitor satisfaction; resource sustainability; improvements to the local economy and businesses; and effective integration of tourism into the destination's economy and communities (Gunn, 1994, pp11–18). However, for destinations, tourism is a means to an end. The principal objective of developing tourism is to meet local or, in some cases, national needs and, therefore, the destination capitals approach commences with establishing what benefits are sought from tourism development with respect to these needs. Such needs vary from one destination to another, and may include economic diversification to reduce dependency on an existing economic sector, economic regeneration where other sectors are in decline, or more specific income, foreign exchange or employment generation requirements. In some cases, the objective may be broader, such as acting as a vehicle for attracting investment in other sectors. Generally, however, the benefits sought from tourism are economic in character and frequently reflect regional or national development policy. In the UK, for example, national tourism policy has varied over time, reflecting shifts in government priorities from employment creation to the redevelopment of the regions.

Consequently, the analysis of destination capitals, or the 'internal audit' of the destination, is framed and guided by the objectives of tourism development. That is, the potential contribution of destination capitals, both individually and collectively, to generate a flow of benefits to the destination is assessed according to the desired outcomes of tourism development. That is, it is those assets which, when exploited through tourism, have the potential to optimize the returns to the destination that should form the basis of tourism development. At the same time, however, the exploitation of those assets should evidently also reflect what are referred to in Figure 7.2 as tourism development opportunities. These include particular markets (that is, particular countries or tourist generating areas, or particular segments within markets, such as the family market or the youth market) and particular products, such as adventure tourism, ecotourism, sun-sea-sand tourism or cultural/heritage tourism, or even more specialized products, such as medical tourism. For example, Cuba possesses extensive and highly trained 'medical capital' as a subgroup of its human capital. In other words, Cuba has a highly regarded (and relatively cheap) health service which is attracting increasing numbers of international 'medical' tourists (Connel, 2006). Other opportunities include international investment by multinational corporations and the support of international agencies, non-government organizations (NGOs) and other organizations. For example, for those destinations with significant human capital that, for one reason or another, remains excluded from the formal economy, pro-poor tourism initiatives supported by the UNWTO and other agencies represent a vital opportunity for enhancing income and employment amongst the local community.

It is also important to recognize external factors that may restrict or otherwise influence the nature and extent of resource exploitation in destinations. Such factors may emanate from the national context within which destinations are located: for example, land-use planning laws or employment regulations and other legislative controls, such as licensing or gaming laws, may all facilitate or hinder the destination's ability to utilize fully its capitals for tourism development. Equally, more general political, economic and environmental policies at the national level also need to be taken into consideration whilst a variety of international factors, such as air transport regulations, environmental accords, trade agreements, bi-lateral visa arrangements and so on may also be relevant. Nevertheless, the destination capitals framework allows destinations to plan for and develop tourism of a nature and scale that meets local needs and makes best use of local resources to optimize the flow of benefits from tourism. In other words, as the following case studies now demonstrate, destinations may follow significantly different tourism development paths dependent upon their needs/objectives and capitals.

Case Study A: Tourism and economic diversification in Dubai

The development of Dubai over the last four decades has been, by any stretch of the imagination, remarkable. Once 'one of the least developed countries in the world' (Shihab, 2001, p249), this small city-state located in the desert in the southwestern corner of the Arabian Gulf has transformed itself over a short period of time from a small economy based on fishing and trade into a global centre for shipping, communications, finance and, most significantly, tourism. Not only has Dubai been, since the early 1990s, one of the world's fastest growing tourism destinations (Henderson, 2006), achieving an average annual increase in arrivals of almost 14 per cent (Table 7.1), but it has also created for itself an image of luxury, opulence and dramatic and innovative architecture (manifested, in particular, in the iconic Burj al Arab hotel) that has placed it firmly on the global tourism map.

Although the rapid development of Dubai as a centre for both tourism and business more generally has occurred relatively recently, the foundations of its growth can be traced back, according to Matly and Dillon (2007), to the early 1970s. The United Arab Emirates (UAE), of which Dubai is one of seven constituent members, was established in 1971 following the withdrawal of the so-called Trucial Agreements with Britain. The capital of the UAE is Abu Dhabi, the largest and richest of the emirates and contributing some 80 per cent of the federal budget. The ruler of Abu Dhabi is constitutionally the

Table 7.1 *Dubai international tourist arrivals 1985–2006*

Year	Arrivals	Growth rate (annual %)	Year	Arrivals	Growth rate (annual %)
1985	422,383	–	1998	2,544,088	20.3
1990	632,903	–	1999	3,026,734	19.0
1991	716,642	13.2	2000	3,420,209	13.0
1992	944,350	31.8	2001	3,626,625	6.0
1993	1,087,733	15.2	2002	4,756,280	31.1
1994	1,238,934	13.9	2003	4,980,228	4.7
1995	1,600,847	29.2	2004	5,420,724	8.8
1996	1,918,471	19.8	2005	6,160,003	13.6
1997	2,114,895	10.2	2006	6,441,670	4.6
			2007	6,950,500	7.9

Source: compiled DTCM reports

UAE's president although each emirate institutes its own development policies, including tourism development, free from federal interference. Abu Dhabi also possesses the largest oil reserves in the region and, as a consequence, accounts for over 90 per cent of the UAE's total oil production.

In comparison, at the time of the formation of the UAE, Dubai's oil and gas reserves amounted to less than one-twentieth of those of Abu Dhabi. Recognizing that these would run out by around 2010, the then ruler of Dubai, Sheikh Rashid Al Maktoum (the father of the current ruler, Sheikh Mohammed Bin Rashid Al Maktoum) realized that there was a need even then to diversify the emirate's economy in order to ensure its economic health and survival in the post-oil era. Therefore, building on Dubai's history as a trading nation, he set out to establish Dubai as the region's trade and service hub by developing facilities for sea and air communications. Most notably, the Jebel Ali Port, located some 35km southwest of the city, was completed in 1979; as Davis (2006) observes, Dubai was the logical shipping centre for the UAE as a whole and so the federation's earnings from the first 'oil shock' helped to finance the construction of what became the world's largest man-made port. Interestingly, this project also perhaps set the tone for subsequent world-leading developments, such as the construction of the world's tallest building, the Burj Dubai, which, it is claimed, 'is a shining symbol – an icon of the new Middle east: prosperous, dynamic, and successful' (www.burjdubai.com). Dubai's airport, originally commissioned by Sheikh Rashid in 1959 and opened in 1960, also benefited from upgrading in the 1970s. It currently handles over a third of all air traffic in the region and has recently undergone further expansion to enable the handling of the new A380 'super jumbo' aircraft. A new international airport at Jebel Ali is also under construction. When completed (by 2017) it will be one of the world's largest airports. Another of Sheikh Rashid's initiatives was the construction of the Dubai World Trade Centre. Completed in 1979, it was then the tallest building in the Middle East and is now a core element of the largest exhibition centre in the region. Thus, by the end of the 1970s, the stage was set for the subsequent expansion and diversification of Dubai's economy.

In the early 1980s, Dubai's economy was reliant on oil production which, at that time, accounted for two-thirds of GDP; by 2006, the oil and gas sector contributed just 5 per cent of GDP. Conversely, tourism was at that time limited to business travel, with arrivals in 1985 totalling just 422,000. However, the need to diversify the economy to compensate for dwindling oil reserves resulted in tourism being seen as a catalyst for direct foreign investment and wider business development rather than being established as a sector itself. As a consequence, initial efforts focused on marketing Dubai to business travellers in two core markets – western Europe and neighbouring Gulf Cooperation Council (GCC) countries – supported by transport and infrastructural developments, including: the establishment in 1985 of the state-owned Emirate Airlines under the leadership of the then Crown Prince Sheikh Ahmed Bin Rashid Al Maktoum; the setting up of the Dubai Commerce and Tourism Promotion Board (DCTPB) as a government body responsible for the promotional activities of various bodies involved in tourism, including Emirates Airlines; and the on-going development of high quality hotels, again under government control. As early as 1985, 26 out of 42 Dubai hotels were in the deluxe/first class segment.

This initial strategy resulted in steady growth in tourism; by 1996, annual tourist arrivals had reached 1.9 million and the supply of accommodation facilities had increased to around 18,000 rooms (Ellson, 1999). However, within the framework of a national strategic development plan, the development of tourism then entered a new phase which, initially, focused on expanding the supply of accommodation and increasing the number of leisure tourism visitors. As part of this process, the state-owned Jumeirah Group was established to develop and operate luxury hotels in the emirate, including the Burj Al Arab and the Bab Al Shams luxury desert spa resort. As can be seen from Table 7.2, both the number of hotels/hotel rooms and hotel guests have increased steadily since the late 1990s, the high occupancy rates pointing to a match between supply and demand and potential for further growth in the accommodation sector. Indeed, the figures in Table 7.2 do not include hotel apartments which, if added

Table 7.2 *Dubai hotel data 1998–2007*

	Hotels	Hotel rooms	Hotel guests	Average length of stay (days)	Average room occupancy (%)
1998	258	17,040	2,184,292	2.49	58.72
1999	254	18,630	2,480,821	2.36	59.04
2000	265	20,315	2,835,638	2.51	61.21
2001	264	21,428	3,064,701	2.34	60.90
2002	272	23,170	4,107,236	2.18	70.19
2003	271	25,571	4,342,341	2.37	72.36
2004	276	26,155	4,724,543	2.60	81.01
2005	290	28,610	5,294,485	2.53	84.57
2006	302	30,850	5,473,509	2.56	82.00
2007	319	32,617	5,863,509	2.72	84.40

Source: adapted from DCTM Hotel Statistics 1998–2007 (www.dubaitourism.ae)

to the stock of hotel rooms, increase the total room supply in 2007 to 50,386. Moreover, if current projects are taken into account, total accommodation supply is expected to reach more than 63,000 rooms by 2010 and 100,000 rooms by 2016. At the same time, an ambitious target of 15 million tourist arrivals by 2015 has been set: that is, more than double the number of arrivals in 2007. However, whether this will be achieved remains to be seen.

As Matly and Dillon (2007, p4) note, 'with hotels and luxury resorts in place, the next challenge was to create attractions for tourists'. Events such as the Dubai Shopping Festival were established to attract visitors and to reduce seasonality, but perhaps the most evident (and publicized) outcome of the development of tourism in Dubai has been the dramatic and continuing increase in the supply of accommodation facilities, attractions and other infrastructural developments, the most notable being the 'Palm' developments, 'The World', an 'attempt to re-create Earth in the form of three hundred artificial islands four kilometres out to sea' (Hickman, 2007, p35), and Ski Dubai, a 400m indoor ski slope located in the Mall of the Emirates, itself the largest shopping mall outside the US. September 2008 witnessed the opening of the 1539-room Atlantis Hotel on Palm Jumeirah, an attraction in its own right as much as an hotel, whilst current projects include Dubai Festival City, the Dubai Waterfront Project and Dubailand which, when completed (scheduled to be between 2015 and 2018), will be larger than Disneyland and Disneyworld combined and will attract an estimated 200,000 visitors daily.

The rapid growth of the tourism sector in Dubai since the early 1990s has attracted inevitable criticism. The development of grandiose schemes is seen by some as resulting in irreversible impacts upon fragile marine and desert environments (Hickman, 2007) – for example, there is already evidence of rapid algae growth and sewage pollution in the waters around the Palm islands – whilst the generation of power and desalination of water to feed the growing city is itself seen to be unsustainable. Moreover, the conditions under which the large migrant workforce live and work have attracted significant negative publicity. Additionally, some commentators point to challenges that the future development of tourism in the emirate may face, such as increased competition, excessive supply, the lack of repeat visits and potential political instability (Henderson, 2006). Nevertheless, the development of tourism in Dubai is in many ways a success story. Not only has the tourism sector evolved in a country with few natural attractions other than sunshine, but it has also underpinned the rapid and successful diversification of the economy, contributing to the image of Dubai as a modern, vibrant, innovative commercial centre and, hence, to increasing foreign investment. More specifically, some tourism developments have had a beneficial environmental impact. For example, the Al Maha Desert Resort Spa, though a luxury 'Bedouin style' resort (each suite benefits from a private plunge pool), funds and maintains the nearby Dubai Desert Conservation Reserve, an 225sq km national park where Arabian oryx and gazelles have been successfully reintroduced.

In other words, as a result of the successful exploitation of its capitals, the development of tourism in Dubai is undoubtedly achieving national objectives, underpinning the economic diversification and development of the emirate whilst meeting the needs of specific tourist markets. In particular, the success of Dubai has been underpinned by political capital and financial capital, both of which lie primarily in the hands of the ruling family of the emirate. Dubai is increasingly referred to as 'Dubai Inc' and the Dubai Strategic Plan as 'the biggest business plan in the world' (AME Info, 2006). Similarly, Sheikh Mohammed has been labelled the 'CEO of Dubai' (Hickman, 2007, p36). That is to say, the emirate is largely owned by the royal family, either directly or through government-owned organizations. Thus, despite the existence of relevant departments, such as the Department of Tourism and Commerce Marketing and their tourism-related policies, it is evident that the Sheikh acts as an entrepreneur and is largely responsible for the successful development of tourism in Dubai – it is he who has developed the vision, taken risks, invested capital and, through the structures he has created, directed and managed the development of tourism. To put it another way, what Davis (2006) describes as 'feudal absolutism' has been dressed up as 'enlightened corporate administration'; there is little or no distinction between political leadership and commercial management and 'the state ... is almost indistinguishable from private enterprise' (Davis, 2006).

In short, the financial and political capital owned by the royal family has been the driving force in the development of tourism in Dubai. Expatriate human capital has been 'bought in' to provide labour for the extensive building projects and also to manage the growing tourism sector (just 17 per cent of the 1.4 million population are UAE nationals), as has technological capital, whilst the environmental capital of Dubai, other than the climate and the attractions of the desert, has been created through significant investment and bold visions. Nevertheless, such developments could not, perhaps, have occurred without the socio-cultural capital of Dubai. The emirate has a long history of trade with Europe, the Middle East and South Asia and, unlike some of its neighbours, is more open to the people and customs of other cultures (Matly and Dillon, 2007). This has enabled the indigenous population to work with expatriates, to accept and tolerate the needs and expectations of western tourists and to integrate the tourism sector more closely into the economic and social fabric of Dubai than might otherwise have been the case, thereby contributing to the development of arguably its most significant capital – its image as an innovative, futuristic, dynamic and luxury destination where anything is possible.

Case Study B: Resort regeneration – Blackpool

Imagine the coldest water that you have ever waded into... Imagine wind-driven sand that stings your cheeks, dusts your hair, and leaves you feeling, at the end of the day, like a newly stuccoed house. Imagine noise that hits you like a car crash and coloured lights that jangle your senses. Imagine paying good money for this. Imagine enjoying it. Welcome to Blackpool. (Bryson, 1998, p38)

Blackpool, on England's northwest coast and within easy reach of the country's old northern industrial cities, is undoubtedly one of the best-known, and certainly the most successful, seaside resort in Britain. As Walton (1998, p1) introduces his seminal history of the town, 'Its fame as Britain's largest, brashest, busiest and best-publicized popular resort is long-established, unchallenged and has practically passed into folklore'. Famed for its three piers, its tower which, at 158m high, is a half-size replica of Paris' Eiffel Tower, its 'Golden Mile' of amusement arcades, its illuminations and its 'Pleasure Beach' theme park, it has maintained its position as the country's most popular working-class resort for more than 150 years. Even during the 1970s and 1980s when, as will be discussed in more detail below, many of Britain's seaside resorts entered a period of decline, Blackpool demonstrated what Walton (1998, p164) describes as its 'recurrent ability to make Houdini-like escapes from what seem to be dead ends in the resort cycle'. Indeed, between 1972 and 1988, the annual number of visits to the resort increased to the extent that it was claimed that, with 17 million day visitors in 1987, more British people holidayed in Blackpool than in Greece, Italy, Turkey and Yugoslavia combined (ETB, 1988).

In more recent years, however, tourism to Blackpool declined significantly – for example, latest figures from an Omnibus survey suggest that, since 1989, total annual visits have declined by more than 40 per cent, falling from 12 million to 7.13 million in 2007. Moreover, as a central pillar of the local economy, the problems facing the tourism sector have undoubtedly had wider social and economic consequences; for example, unemployment rates, teenage pregnancies and suicide rates are higher than the national average, net household earnings are 85 per cent of the national average and the town's overall population has declined (Blackpool Council, n.d.; ReBlackpool, 2007). Such trends have not, of course, gone unaddressed. Since 2005, a regeneration company, ReBlackpool, funded by Blackpool Council and the North West Regional Development Agency, has been implementing a master plan for the town, much of which focuses on redeveloping its tourism infrastructure, whilst it was announced in 2008 that Blackpool was one of three coastal towns in England to receive up to £4 million funding under the government's *Sea Change* programme which seeks to encourage economic regeneration through investment in specific culture and heritage projects. Indeed, it is recognized that Blackpool's core function is as a tourist resort and, hence, the regeneration of Blackpool is dependent upon the revitalization of its tourism sector (ReBlackpool, 2007, p4). This case study, therefore, briefly reviews the rise and decline of Blackpool before identifying the key destination capitals that might underpin its regeneration.

As with seaside resorts more generally in Britain, Blackpool's origins as a tourism destination lie in the 18th century fashion for 'taking the waters' at the seaside. In 1753, one Dr Richard Russell had published a paper extolling the supposed recuperative powers of sea water – bathing and even drinking sea water was seen to be good for the health – and, as a consequence, a number of resorts, such as Brighton, Southport and Scarborough, were well established by the end of the 1700s. Blackpool, however, was a late starter. Although described in the *Blackburn Mail* in 1795 as 'the first watering place in the Kingdom, whether we consider the salubrity of the air, the beauty of the scenery, the excellence of the accommodation or the agreeable company', there were just four main hotels providing accommodation for well-to-do visitors and it attracted far fewer tourists than other resorts. In 1841, for example, the town's population was just 1000 and at the height of the summer could accommodate no more than 3000 tourists (Walton, 1998, p2). Thus, for its first 80 years or so, Blackpool was, in effect, an exclusive, up-market resort.

Again as with other seaside resorts, it was the advent of the railways that provided the catalyst for the rapid expansion of Blackpool as a destination, along with its subsequent emergence as a mass, working-class resort. The railway to Blackpool opened in 1846 although, at that time, tourist facilities and amenities remained limited – its first pier, the North pier, was not opened until 1863. Nevertheless, by the mid-1860s rail passenger arrivals numbered more than 285,000 a year and, according to Walton (1998), over 25,000 tourists stayed in the town at peak periods. However, it is the period from 1880 through to the start of the First World War that witnessed Blackpool's fastest expansion. The town's population, for example, grew from around 20,000 in 1890 to over 58,000 by 1911, whilst visitor numbers increased from 850,000 in 1873 to 3,850,000 in the year before the outbreak of war (Walton, 1998, p47). It is also during this period that many of the town's facilities and attractions were opened, including the Opera House (1889), Victoria (now South) Pier (1893) and the Tower (1894), whilst the promenade was constructed between 1902 and 1905, during which time the foundations of the present Pleasure Beach were also laid. The Blackpool Illuminations were first switched on in 1912 and, though discontinued between 1914 and 1925 and 1939 and 1948, have since evolved into one of the resort's major attractions, extending the tourist season into late October.

Blackpool's growth as a tourist resort continued during the inter-war years; the town's population moved towards 140,000 whilst, during the 1930s, an estimated 7 million visitors travelled to the resort annually. The main source markets for tourists were and, to a great extent, remain, the industrial cities of Lancashire and Yorkshire, whilst Blackpool also became a popular destination for visitors from Scotland. This pattern continued during the 1950s and 1960s, with demand for tourism in Blackpool remaining buoyant. In the early 1970s, for example, some 16 million visits were made by 6 million visitors, though this hinted at an emerging problem, namely, that the resort was becoming increasingly dependent on repeat visits made by an ageing clientele. In other words, Blackpool, in common with other seaside resorts in Britain, was struggling to attract new markets although, as noted earlier, it managed to maintain its tourism sector reasonably successfully during a period when other resorts in the country were suffering a decrease in visitor numbers.

More specifically, by the late 1960s, British seaside resorts accounted for 75 per cent of all British holidays (Middleton, 1989, p5.2). Over the next 20 years, however, many entered a period of decline, experiencing a loss in the volume of tourists and market share. Table 7.3 summarizes these trends.

Table 7.3 *Seaside resorts' market share of English tourism 1973–1988 (%)*

	1973	1980	1986	1988
% of all trips	30	28	24	24
% of all nights	40	38	33	32
% of all expenditure	45	41	34	33

Source: Middleton, 1989, p5.5

This decline in the fortunes of the resorts, explored at some length in the literature (for example, Shaw and Williams, 1997) is largely attributable to factors both within and beyond their control. Certainly, the rapid growth in overseas travel, particularly the boom in summer sun package holidays to the Mediterranean, had a major impact. During the 1980s, for example, the number of overseas holidays taken by Britons rose from 8 to 20 million a year, though with little overall growth in the British holiday market. At the same time, new domestic destinations and attractions were being developed, such as heritage towns, theme parks and purpose-built inland holiday centres, further eroding the seaside resorts' traditional markets. Moreover, the resorts also experienced a shift in demand from one- and two-week summer holidays to short breaks and day visits, whilst staying visitors tended to spend fewer nights in the resorts. Even Blackpool, which increased its number of staying visitors between 1972 and 1988, experienced a 15 per cent decline in tourist nights.

In short, the resorts faced increasing competition from both overseas and newer domestic destinations. Importantly, however, it was competition that they were ill-prepared for. As Owen (1990, p191) observed, 'it seems our seaside resorts have remained frozen in a 1950's insularity, as though not yet free of post-war rationing and austerity'. In other words, the resorts had experienced significant erosion in the quality of their core tourism environment relative to the competition. In part, this was due to the fact that, built in the Victorian and Edwardian eras, the resorts were unable effectively to accommodate ever increasing numbers of cars and, in many cases, the beach had been dissected from the town by busy roads. At the same time, however, a lack of investment on the part of the private sector in attractions and amenities, as well as a lack of strategic planning and investment in infrastructure and public facilities by local authorities, meant that the resorts were unable to provide the range and quality of attractions necessary to attract new markets whilst also becoming less appealing places to visit for existing markets. Consequently, they moved down-market into a vicious circle of lower profit margins and, hence, continued lower investment.

Initially, Blackpool, along with a small number of other resorts, bucked this trend. By 1987, 12.36 million visits were made, generating some £306 million for the town. Subsequently, a national survey found that, in 1989, a total of over 16 million visits were made to Blackpool, generating an estimated £445 million in spending. Whilst some caution is necessary in accepting the latter figure (it differs significantly from the Omnibus survey results in Table 7.4 below) there is no doubt that Blackpool was able to maintain its visitor numbers, albeit with fewer nights spent in the town, as a result of its longer season (curiously, the 1987 English Tourist Board (ETB) survey revealed that the highest hotel occupancy was achieved in September and October, during the Illuminations season), and diversifying its markets, particularly the gay market. By 1991, there were, according to Walton (1998, p146) 'perhaps 150 guest houses catering mainly for gays', whilst the gay night-club scene was also thriving.

Nevertheless, since 1989, tourism to Blackpool has demonstrated a consistent decline (Table 7.4). Of particular note, the total number of visits has

Table 7.4 *Estimated visits to Blackpool 1989–2007 (millions)*

	1989	1999	2001	2003	2005	2006	2007
British residents making at least one trip to Blackpool	6.62	6.09	6.31	7.10	5.58	5.12	4.23
Great Britain: all adult visits	12.01	11.05	10.81	10.72	9.94	9.67	7.13
Overnight stay	3.00	3.32	4.11	4.50	2.68	3.19	–
Overnight stay (% of total)	25.0	30.0	38.0	42.0	27.0	33.0	–

Source: Blackpool Council, 2009

declined, despite some rises in numbers of people visiting, indicating that the number of repeat visits has, on average, fallen. This is a particular challenge for Blackpool given its high dependence on repeat business. A survey in 2005, for example, found that 92 per cent of those questioned were repeat visitors compared with 81 per cent in 2003 (Blackpool Council, 2006). Whilst this may indicate a high level of satisfaction amongst regular visitors to the resort, more significant is its apparent inability to attract new visitors.

Thus, in order to revitalize the tourism sector, new markets must be sought within the overall objective of maintaining Blackpool's competitive position as a mass, though modern, contemporary and appealing tourism destination. This, in turn, requires the redevelopment of the resort and its facilities in a manner which, on the one hand, maintains and rebuilds the traditional character of Blackpool, implying, perhaps, the need to reconnect the town with the beach and sea, these being an essential element of the natural capital of the destination (Blackpool's history and image as a seaside resort also being a powerful element of its cultural capital). On the other hand, it also requires the upgrading and diversification of the built environment to meet the needs and expectations of new markets. Beyond some key structures, such as the Tower and the piers, Blackpool may currently be considered to possess limited built environmental capital that may be successfully exploited, although existing projects, such as a £78 million scheme to rebuild the resort's sea defences as well as providing additional public spaces for events and improved access to the beach, go some way to addressing this problem. Social capital may also be considered to be limited, in as much as the tourism sector is fragmented and diverse, comprising a few large businesses and numerous small businesses which collectively (and not surprisingly) focus on short-term survival and profit rather than the longer-term development of the resort. Therefore, a central role exists for the local authority (which it is currently fulfilling) exploiting its political capital to take a lead in directing the regeneration of the resort, working with and encouraging the private sector to strive towards agreed objectives for the resort, at the same time as seeking external funding opportunities and liaising with appropriate regional and national agencies. Certainly, the successful regeneration of Blackpool as a tourist destination is largely dependent on the ability of the local authority to use its political capital to drive through the necessary changes and developments.

Case Study C: Bhutan – Tourism and 'Gross National Happiness'

The Kingdom of Bhutan, located towards the eastern end of the Himalayan mountain range, is a small landlocked country sharing a 470km border with Tibet to the north and a 605km border with India to the south. Called Druk Yul, or 'Land of the Thunder Dragon', by the Bhutanese (hence the name of the national airline, Druk Air), the country covers a total land area of approximately 47,000sq km, ranking it 135th out of 230 states globally by size. However, with an altitude differential of almost 7400m between its sub-tropical lowlands and its Himalayan peaks – its highest mountain is Gangkhar Puensum at 7570m – it is claimed to be 'one of the most topographically diverse countries in the world' (Brunet at al, 2001). It is usually described as comprising three distinctive geographical zones: the lowlands and foothills, rising to 1500m, the middle mountains, rising to 5000m, and the high mountains rising up to 7500m or more. Some 65 per cent of the land area is forested, almost 7 per cent is alpine pasture and just 8 per cent is suitable for agriculture. Nevertheless, around 70 per cent of the population of almost 700,000 live in rural areas and depend upon subsistence farming and animal husbandry.

According to the World Bank (2008), Bhutan's GDP in 2007 amounted to US$1.2 billion, of which 20.9 per cent was accounted for by agriculture (down from 37.7 per cent in 1987), 36.3 per cent by services (including tourism) and over 40 per cent by industry, much of the latter representing the generation and export of hydroelectric power to neighbouring India. Indeed, recent growth in GDP, averaging 8.2 per cent between 1997 and 2007 and a remarkable 19.1 per cent in 2007 alone, making it the second fastest growing economy in the world that year, has resulted from significant increases in the export of hydro-electricity. In particular, the commissioning of the giant Tala hydroelectric project in the west of the country in March 2007, the entire output of which is exported to India, has further increased the economic contribution of power generation which, even before the Tala project came on stream, accounted for more than 45 per cent of the country's gross revenues (Power-technology.com, 2009). As a consequence, per capita GDP in Bhutan has risen significantly in recent years, reaching US$1400 by 2007. Nevertheless, 32 per cent of the Bhutanese population live in poverty; moreover, over 40 per cent of the rural population are poor compared with just over 4 per cent of the urban population. It is for this reason that the development of ecotourism is seen as a potential means of encouraging economic growth amongst rural communities in particular (Gurung and Seeland, 2008) whilst, since it was first established in Bhutan in 1974, tourism more generally has been developed 'with the primary objective of generating revenue, especially foreign exchange' (Dorji, 2001, p84).

Importantly, however, the development of tourism in Bhutan has not only been driven by economic need; it has also been underpinned and shaped by a political imperative: to maintain and promote its culture to both enhance national identity and to strengthen its international political legitimacy (Reinfeld, 2003). This political imperative has, in turn, emerged from the country's more recent political history. As Reinfeld (2003) describes, for most of the first six decades of the 20th century, the Royal Government of Bhutan followed a policy of isolationism, focusing on gradual independent modernization. However, faced with potential aggression from China in the late 1950s, Bhutan turned to its southern neighbour, India, for development assistance, remaining dependent on that country throughout the 1960s and 1970s (see Priesner, 1999 for more detail). Nonetheless, following India's annexation of Sikkim in 1973 and sensing its own autonomy was again under threat, Bhutan sought to protect its national identity and political sovereignty by electing through one means or another – including the development of tourism – to preserve and enhance it unique traditional culture, fundamental to which is the concept of what has come to be known as 'Gross National Happiness'.

According to Priesner (1999), although the term 'Gross National Happiness' (GNH) was coined by the then King of Bhutan in the late 1980s, it is in fact the popularization of the Bhutanese perception of the purpose of development or, more specifically, the 'translation of a cultural and social consciousness into development priorities' (Priesner, 1999, p27). Broadly focusing upon happiness and emotional well-being rather than simply economic prosperity, GNH embraces four key elements, namely: (economic and political) self-reliance; human development; cultural preservation; and environmental preservation. Thus, although economic growth is a core requirement of development in Bhutan, it is not an end in itself but a means to an end: 'the enhancement of human wellbeing, not merely the acquisition of material wealth' (Reinfeld, 2003, p8).

International tourists first arrived in Bhutan in 1974 to witness the coronation of King Jigme Singye Wanchuk, who remained the ruler of the country until his abdication in late 2005. His son, Jigme Khesar Namgyel Wanchuk, was crowned King of Bhutan in 2008, though he enjoys less influence than his father did: many administrative powers having been transferred to the elected government under a new 2005 constitution. The country has evident and unique attractions – often portrayed as a Shangri-La, it possesses a rich and diverse natural and cultural heritage; it is home to a number of rare Himalayan species, boasts spectacular scenery and has a vibrant culture manifested in distinctive architecture and spectacular festivals. Initially, however, few tourists visited the country, as both gaining the necessary visas and actually travelling to Bhutan (with no airport at that time, the only way to reach the country was by road from India) was a complex and lengthy process. As Brunet et al (2001, p252) observe, 'in the early days only a few hardy "adventurers" chose to visit the kingdom'. Moreover, the government soon established a quota of just 200 tourists a year, with visitors being required to travel in groups of six or more and paying a set price of US$130 per day although, somewhat controversially, visitors from India were, and still are, not required to pay the daily rate and are allowed to enter Bhutan without a visa and to travel without restriction around the country. As a consequence, no records of Indian tourist arrivals in Bhutan are kept, though some estimate that up to 15,000 tourists from India now visit the country each year (SASEC, 2004). Thus, from the outset, a policy of 'high value-low volume' tourism was adopted, the purpose being to optimize revenue from tourism at the same time as protecting its cultural and natural heritage.

Throughout the 1970s and early 1980s, annual arrivals figures remained low. However, following the opening of the airport at Paro in 1983 and, in particular, the extension of the runway in 1990 allowing Druk Air to operate international flights, tourism to Bhutan entered a new phase, with the number of tourists visiting the country increasing year by year. By 1989, arrivals had reached 1480 (still insignificant in international terms) generating US$1.95 million for the government which, at that time, controlled all tourism to the country through its agency, the Bhutan Tourism Corporation. Tourist arrivals figures for Bhutan are presented in Table 7.5.

From Table 7.5, it is evident that constant growth in arrivals has been achieved since the early 1990s, with particularly marked increases since 2004. The significant decline in arrivals in 2001 and 2002, following the events of '9/11', reflects the traditional dependence of Bhutan on the North American market which, in 2000, accounted for 40 per cent of all tourist arrivals in the country. By 2006, the North American share had fallen to 32 per cent, with European tourists accounting for almost 41 per cent.

The growth in tourism in Bhutan since the early 1990s is largely attributable to the effective privatization of the tourism sector in 1991, followed by a subsequent relaxation on the restrictions on the number of licences issued to local tour operators. Numerous private companies were set up which, though having to abide by standard tourist rates (which, since 1991, have been US$200 per day in the high season and US$165 per day in the low season: a recent planned increase to US$250 has been postponed owing to the global economic downturn) and other government regulations and processes, are

Table 7.5 *Tourist arrivals and receipts Bhutan 1989–2006*

	Arrivals	Receipts ($mn)		Arrivals	Receipts ($mn)
1989	1480	1.95	1998	6203	7.98
1990	1538	1.91	1999	7158	8.88
1991	2106	2.30	2000	7559	10.49
1992	2763	2.99	2001	6393	9.19
1993	2984	3.30	2002	5599	7.98
1994	3971	3.97	2003	6267	8.32
1995	4765	6.00	2004	9249	12.45
1996	5138	6.51	2005	13,626	18.54
1997	5363	6.50	2006	17,365	23.92

Source: adapted from Dorji, 2001; SASEC, 2004; www.exodusbhutan.com/Factaboutbhutan.htm

able to operate as profit-making businesses (Brunet et al, 2001). Nevertheless, although the government lifted its original restriction on tourist numbers, arrivals were limited by local capacity constraints. By the late 1990s, some 75 licences had been issued, rising to 133 by 2003; currently, there are some 200 private tourist operators in Bhutan. All operators charge the set rate of US$200 per person per day for groups of three or more tourists. From this, 10 per cent commission is paid to overseas agents, 35 per cent (US$65) is paid to the government as a royalty and a further 2 per cent tax is deducted, leaving operators with approximately US$112 to cover costs and make a profit.

There are two important characteristics of tourism in Bhutan that, to an extent, limit its contribution to GNH. Firstly, it remains markedly seasonal, the high season being March to May and September to November, coinciding with the main *tshechus*, or seasonal religious festivals (Gurung and Seeland, 2008). Up to 80 per cent of tourists visit the country during these six months, with the result that during the low season hotels, restaurants, transport and other tourist services are underutilized and there is limited work for those whose income is dependent on tourism, such as hotel staff or guides. In 2001, there were approximately 1000 people employed in hotels, 224 cultural guides and 87 trekking guides (SASEC, 2004). Secondly, as shown in Table 7.6, the great majority of tourists engage in cultural activities/tours rather than in trekking, the proportion of those participating in the latter declining steadily. This reflects, in part, the ending of a reduced daily rate for those on trekking holidays and, in part, the profile of tourists to Bhutan, a majority of whom represent the 'silver market' – older, often retired people from wealthier countries who would find high altitude trekking difficult (Gurung and Seeland, 2008). Thus, in addition to being highly seasonal, tourist activity (and, hence, the benefits of tourism) tends to be restricted to the western part of the country around Thimpu, the capital.

More recently, the high value-low volume objective of tourism development in Bhutan has been replaced by a high value-low impact objective; that is, to focus on increasing income, foreign exchange earnings and employment

Table 7.6 *Tourism: Purpose of visit 1996–2006*

	1996	1997	1998	1999	2000	2001	2002	2003	2004	2005	2006
Tour, culture	3287	4617	4860	6328	6633	5025	5242	5823	8742	13,013	16,576
Trekking	1851	746	1343	830	926	468	357	438	507	613	766

Source: adapted from SASEC, 2004; www.exodusbhutan.com/Factaboutbhutan.htm

in the sector through diversifying the product, encouraging private sector engagement in the industry, facilitating greater community participation and promoting a value-for-money image, though maintaining close control over the environmental consequences of tourism development. Most recent figures suggest that the growth in arrivals is continuing, with over 21,000 arrivals recorded in 2007. The extent to which such growth can be sustained, however, very much depends upon capacity constraints – hotels are full during the peak season and Druk Air, with a monopoly on flights into Bhutan, also operates at full capacity during these periods. Moreover, although total tourist arrivals are small by international standards, it is likely that increasing environmental and socio-cultural impacts will be experienced. Nevertheless, the case of tourism development in Bhutan is both fascinating and relevant to the context of destination capitals, in that the country's environmental and socio-cultural capitals are being exploited within limits determined by the culturally-determined objective of GNH, whilst the promotion of the country's cultural capital in particular as a tourist attraction is based upon the broader political objective of protecting and strengthening that capital. At the same time, of course, the government has also utilized its political capital to ensure that tourism contributes significantly to its revenues. Thus, Bhutan exemplifies explicitly the value of exploring tourism development within a destination capitals framework.

Some concluding thoughts

Although it may be so, this book did not set out to be deliberately provocative. Certainly, its aim has been to argue that the concept of sustainable tourism development does not represent a viable approach to tourism development, to demonstrate that tourism cannot conform to or be developed according to the principles of sustainable development as generally defined or understood. In particular, despite its inherent focus on community- or people-centred tourism development, sustainable tourism development remains, somewhat contradictorily, an overarching, top-down and prescriptive approach to tourism that is unable to embrace the diversity of destination contexts, hence the need for an alternative perspective that starts, as this book has proposed, with the destination.

However, this is not to say that the objectives of sustainable development, whether generally or in the specific context of tourism, are not valid or desirable. The world undoubtedly faces significant developmental challenges, such as those targeted in the Millennium Development Goals (MDGs). Furthermore, such specific goals are unlikely to be achieved until broader issues, such as the highly inequitable distribution of wealth both within and between all countries, the inequitable access to and use of resources, economic development policies that, at least in the developed world, promote already excessive levels of consumption, and a global political system which permits the continued existence or malfunctioning of so-called failed states, are addressed. At the same time, the (environmental) sustainability imperative cannot be denied. Excessive demands are being placed upon the global ecosystem's source, sink and service functions and, consequently, there is a pressing need to ensure the sustainability of those functions.

Equally, in many ways tourism contributes to these challenges. The very existence of fossil fuel-based land, sea and air travel on a mass scale is environmentally unsustainable, whether in terms of its contribution to greenhouse gas (GHG) emissions or to the depletion of non-renewable supplies of oil, whilst tourism development more generally is 'resource-hungry'. Without careful management, it has the potential to be environmentally destructive – and there are, of course, numerous examples of these destructive tendencies – whilst under certain circumstances it may enhance, rather than reduce, inequalities between people and societies. Thus, it is not surprising that some would suggest the only form of sustainable tourism is 'no tourism'.

Such an option is quite evidently unrealistic. Not only is tourism, in all its forms, an integral element of contemporary life in many societies, but it is a vital and, for some destinations, the only source of employment, income and economic growth. In that sense, it is no different from any other economic activity or sector. Although the presence and activities of tourists 'on site' in the destination may potentially spread the economic benefits (and, of course, costs) more widely or deeply, tourism is, as argued in this book, fundamentally a form of capitalistic endeavour similar to any other economic sector. The point is, therefore, that tourism is no more likely to offer the solution to local/global developmental challenges than any other economic sector. At the same time, travel and tourism organizations are no more likely to adopt responsible business practices than those in other sectors, and nor is the consumption of tourism more likely to be influenced by environmental values than the consumption of other goods and services. In other words, the adoption of the principles of sustainability in the production and consumption of tourism in particular is unlikely to occur until such a time that there is a more widespread and general shift in values towards more sustainable production and consumption in general. Therefore, as this book has suggested, in the meantime a more pragmatic approach is required that, rather than intervening in the production and consumption of tourism in ways that may limit the flows of benefits of tourism to destinations, provides a framework for optimizing those benefits within locally determined environmental parameters. It is hoped that the destination capitals approach proposed here provides such a framework, as well as stimulating further debate and research into tourism 'beyond sustainability'.

References

Adams, W. (2001) *Green Development: Environment and Sustainability in the Third World, 2nd Edition*. London: Routledge

Adler, P. and Kwon, S. (2002) 'Social capital: prospects for a new concept'. *Academy of Management Review* 27(1), 17–40

Akis, S., Peristianis, N. and Warner, J. (1996) 'Resident attitudes to tourism development: the case of Cyprus'. *Tourism Management* 17(7), 481–494

Albright, H. and Cahn, R. (1985) *The Birth of the National Park Service*. Salt Lake City, UT: Howe Brothers

Alvord, K. (2000) *Divorce Your Car! Ending the Love Affair with the Automobile*. Gabriola Island, British Columbia: New Society Publishers

AME Info (2006) 'Dubailand to double Dubai hotel rooms', *AME Info Middle East*. Available on: www.ameinfo.com/84720.html (accessed May 2006)

Andronikou, A. (1979) 'Tourism in Cyprus'. In E. de Kadt (ed) *Tourism: Passport to Development?* New York: Oxford University Press, 237–264

Andronikou, A. (1987) *Development of Tourism in Cyprus: Harmonisation of Tourism with the Environment*. Nicosia: Cosmos

Archer, B. (1977) 'Tourism multipliers: the state of the art'. *Bangor Occasional Papers in Economics 11*. Cardiff: University of Wales Press

Ayers, R. (2000) 'Tourism as a passport to development in small states: the case of Cyprus'. *International Journal of Social Economics* 27(2), 114–133

Bah, A. and Goodwin, H. (2003) 'Improving access for the informal sector to tourism in The Gambia', PPT Working Paper No.15, London: Pro-poor Tourism Partnership

Baldicchino, G. (2006) Editorial: 'Islands, island studies', *Island Studies Journal* 1(1), 3–18

Barke, M., Towner, J. and Newton, M. (1996) *Tourism in Spain: Critical Issues*. Wallingford: CAB International

Baumann, P. (2000) 'Sustainable livelihoods and political capital: arguments and evidence from decentralisation and natural resource management in India'. ODI Working Paper 136. London: Overseas Development Institute

Baumann, P. and Sinha, S. (2001) 'Linking development with democratic processes in India: political capital and sustainable livelihoods analysis'. *ODI Natural Resource Perspectives* 68, June. London: Overseas Development Institute

Becken, S. and Hay, J. (2007) *Tourism and Climate Change: Risks and Opportunities*. Clevedon: Channel View Publications

Becken, S. and Simmons, D. (2005) 'Tourism, fossil fuel consumption and the impact on the global climate'. In C.M. Hall and J. Higham (eds) *Tourism, Recreation and Climate Change*. Clevedon: Channel View Publications, 192–206

Beckerman, W. (2002) *A Poverty of Reason: Sustainable Development and Economic Growth*. Oakland: The Independent Institute

Berno, T. and Bricker, K. (2001) 'Sustainable tourism development: the long road from theory to practice'. *International Journal of Economic Development* 3(3), 1–18

Bianchi, R. (2002) 'Towards a new political economy of global tourism'. In R. Sharpley and D. Telfer (eds) *Tourism and Development: Concepts and Issues*. Clevedon: Channel View Publication, 265–299

Bigano, A., Hamilton, J., Lau, M., Tol, R. and Zhou, Y. (2007) 'A global database of domestic and international tourist numbers at national and subnational level'. *International Journal of Tourism Research* 9(3), 147–174

Blackpool Council (2006) *Destination Blackpool: Benchmarking Survey 2005*. Blackpool Council

Blackpool Council (2009) *Summary of Blackpool Omnibus Visitor Surveys*. Figures provided by Blackpool Council (J. Patterson, Research and Intelligence Officer: personal communication)

Blackpool Council (n.d.) *A Strategy for Blackpool's Visitor Economy 2006–2010*. Blackpool Council. Available on: www.visitblackpool.com/?OBH=80&ID=77&OBT=14&AC=5 (accessed 05.02.09)

Boulding, K. (1992) 'The economics of the coming spaceship earth'. In A. Markandya and J. Richardson (eds) *The Earthscan Reader in Environmental Economics*. London: Earthscan, 27–35

Bourdieu, P. (1986) 'The forms of capital'. In J. Richardson (ed) *Handbook of Theory and Research for the Sociology of Education*. New York: Greenwood, 241–258

Bramwell, B. and Lane, B. (1993) 'Sustainable tourism: an evolving global approach'. *Journal of Sustainable Tourism* 1(1), 1–15

Bramwell, B. and Lane, B. (2000) *Tourism Collaboration and Partnerships: Politics, Practice and Sustainability*. Clevedon: Channel View Publications

Brendon, P. (1991) *Thomas Cook – 150 Years of Popular Tourism*. London: Secker & Warburg

Brey, H. (1995) 'A booming economy'. In H. Brey and C. Muller (eds) *Cyprus*. London: APA Publications (HK) Ltd, 92–93

Britton, S. (1982) 'The political economy of tourism in the Third World'. *Annals of Tourism Research* 9(3), 331–358

Britton, S. (1991) 'Tourism, dependency and place. Towards a critical geography of tourism development'. *Environment and Planning D: Society and Space* 9, 451–478

Brockington, D., Duffy, R. and Igoe, J. (2008) *Unbound Nature: Conservation, Capitalism and the Future of Protected Areas*. London: Earthscan

Brohman, J. (1996a) *Popular Development: Rethinking the Theory and Practice of Development*. Oxford: Blackwell

Brohman, J. (1996b) 'New directions in tourism for Third World development'. *Annals of Tourism Research* 23(1), 48–70

Brougham, J. and Butler, R. (1981) 'A segmentation analysis of resident attitudes to the social impact of tourism'. *Annals of Tourism Research* 8(4), 569–590

Brown, F. (1998) *Tourism Reassessed: Blight or Blessing?* Oxford: Butterworth-Heinemann

Brown, T. (1999) 'Antecedents of culturally significant tourist behaviour'. *Annals of Tourism Research* 26(3), 676–700

Brunet, S., Bauer, J., De Lacy, T. and Tshering, K. (2001) 'Tourism development in Bhutan: tensions between tradition and modernity'. *Journal of Sustainable Tourism* 9(3), 243–263

Bryson, B. (1998) 'Blackpool'. *National Geographic* 193(1), 37–51

Budowski, G. (1976) 'Tourism and environmental conservation: conflict, coexistence or symbiosis?' *Environmental Conservation* 3(1), 27–31

Buhalis, D. (2002) *eTourism*. London: Pearson Education

Buhalis, D. (2005) 'Information and communication technologies for tourism'. In L. Pender and R. Sharpley (eds) *The Management of Tourism*. London: Sage Publications, 232–245

Bull, A. (1995) *The Economics of Travel and Tourism, 2nd Edition*. Harlow: Longman

Burns, P. and Holden, A. (1995) *Tourism: A New Perspective*. Hemel Hempstead: Prentice Hall International

Butler, R. (1990) 'Alternative tourism: pious hope or Trojan horse?' *Journal of Travel Research* 28(3), 4–45

Butler, R. (1993) 'Tourism – an evolutionary perspective'. In J. Nelson, R. Butler and G. Wall (eds) *Tourism and Sustainable Development: Monitoring, Planning, Managing*. Department of Geography Publication Series No.37, University of Waterloo: Canada, 27–43

Butler, R. (1998) 'Sustainable tourism – looking backwards in order to progress?' In C.M. Hall and M. Lew (eds) *Sustainable Tourism: A Geographical Perspective*. Harlow: Longman, 25–34

CAA (2008) *Recent Trends in Growth of UK Air Passenger Demand*. London: Civil Aviation Authority. Available on www.caa.co.uk/docs/589/erg_recent_trends_final_v2.pdf (accessed 08.10.08)

Carney, D. (2002) *Sustainable Livelihoods Approaches: Progress and Possibilities for Change*. London: Department for International Development

Carrier, J. and Macleod, D. (2005) 'Bursting the bubble: the socio-cultural context of eco-tourism'. *Journal of the Royal Anthropological Institute* 11(2), 315–334

Cater, E. (1987) 'Tourism in the least developed countries'. *Annals of Tourism Research* 14(2), 202–226

Cater, E. (1995) 'Environmental contradictions in sustainable tourism'. *The Geographical Journal* 161(1), 21–28

Cater, E. (2006) 'Ecotourism as a Western construct'. *Journal of Ecotourism* 5(1&2), 23–39

Cavaco, C. (1995) 'Rural tourism: the creation of new tourist spaces'. In A. Montanari and A. Williams (eds), *European Tourism: Regions, Spaces and Restructuring*. Chichester: John Wiley & Sons, 129–149

Clancy, M. (1999) 'Tourism and development: evidence from Mexico'. *Annals of Tourism Research* 26(1), 1–20

Clarke, J. and Critcher, C. (1985) *The Devil Makes Work: Leisure in Capitalist Britain*. Basingstoke: Macmillan

Cohen, E. (2002) 'Authenticity, equity and sustainability in tourism'. *Journal of Sustainable Tourism* 10(4), 267–276

Coleman, J. (1988) 'Social capital in the creation of human capital'. *The American Journal of Sociology* 94, S95–S120

Coles, T., Duval, D. and Hall, C.M. (2004) 'Tourism, mobility and global communities: new approaches to theorising tourism and tourist spaces'. In W. Theobald (ed) *Global Tourism*. Oxford: Heinemann, 463–481

Collier, P. (2007) *The Bottom Billion*. Oxford: Oxford University Press

Connel, J. (2006) 'Medical tourism: sun, sea, sand … and surgery'. *Tourism Management* 27(6), 1093–1110

Costanza, R. and Daly, H. (1992) 'Natural capital and sustainable development'. *Conservation Biology* 6(1), 37–46

Cowen, M. and Shenton, R. (1996) *Doctrines of Development*. London: Routledge

Cox, R. (1991) 'The global political economy and social choice'. In D. Drache and M. Gertler (eds) *The New Era of Global Competition: State Policy and Market Power*. Montreal and Kingston, Ontario: McGill-Queens University Press, 335–350

Creative Research (2002) *Cumbria Tourism Survey 2002: Report of Findings*. London: Creative Research

Croall, J. (1995) *Preserve or Destroy: Tourism and the Environment*. London: Calouste Gulbenkian Foundation

Cronin, L. (1990) 'A strategy for tourism and sustainable developments'. *World Leisure and Recreation* 32(3), 12–18

Culler, J. (1981) 'Semiotics of tourism'. *American Journal of Semiotics* 1(1–2), 127–140

Daly, H. and Cobb, C. (1989) *For the Common Good*. Boston: Beacon Press

Davies, H. (1968) 'Potentials for tourism in developing countries'. *Finance and Development* 5(4), 34–39

Davis, M. (2006) 'Fear and money in Dubai'. *New Left Review* 41, 47–68

de Kadt, E. (1979) *Tourism: Passport to Development?* New York: Oxford University Press

de Rivero, O. (2001) *The Myth of Development: The Non-viable Economies of the 21st Century*. London: Zed Books

Din, K. (1982) 'Tourism in Malaysia: competing needs in a plural society'. *Annals of Tourism Research* 16(4), 453–480

Dobb, M. (1946) *Studies in the Development of Capitalism*. London: George Routledge & Sons

Dorji, T. (2001) 'Sustainability of tourism in Bhutan'. *Journal of Bhutan Studies* 3(1), 84–104

Dowling, R. (1992) 'Tourism and environmental integration: the journey from idealism to realism'. In C. Cooper and A. Lockwood (eds) *Progress in Tourism, Recreation and Hospitality Management (Vol 4)*. London: Belhaven Press, 33–46

Dredge, D. and Jenkins, J. (2006) *Tourism Planning and Policy*. Chichester: John Wiley & Sons

Dresner, S. (2002) *The Principles of Sustainability*. London: Earthscan

DSTC (2005) *The Gambia Tourism Development Master Plan: The Challenges for 2005–2010 and the 2020 Vision*. Banjul: Department of State for Tourism and Culture

Duffy, R. (2002) *A Trip Too Far. Ecotourism, Politics and Exploitation*. London: Earthscan

Eagles, P. and McCool, S. (2002) *Tourism in National Parks and Protected Areas: Planning and Management*. Wallingford: CABI Publishing

Eber, S. (1992) *Beyond the Green Horizon: Principles for Sustainable Tourism*. Godalming: WWF

EC (1993) *Taking Account of Environment in Tourism Development*. DG XXIII Tourism Unit, Luxembourg: European Commission

Edwards, M. (1996) 'How relevant is development studies?'. In F. Schuurman (ed) *Beyond the Impasse: New Direction in Development Theory*. London: Zed Books, 77–92

Edwards, M. and Hulme, D. (eds) (1995) *Non-Governmental Organisations. Performance and Accountability: Beyond the Magic Bullet*. London: Earthscan

Ehrlich, P. (1972) *The Population Bomb*. London: Ballantine

Ekins, P. (2000) *Economic Growth and Environmental Sustainability: The Prospects for Green Growth*. London: Routledge

Elliot, J. (1999) *An Introduction to Sustainable Development*. London: Routledge

Elliott, J. (1997) *Tourism: Politics and Public Sector Management*. London: Routledge

Ellson, C. (1999) 'Oil change'. *Conference and Incentive Travel*. December, 59–66

Erisman, H. (1989) 'Tourism and cultural dependency in the West Indies'. *Annals of Tourism Research* 10(3), 337–361

Escobar, A. (1997) 'The making and unmaking of the Third World through development'. In M. Rahnema and V. Bawtree (eds) *The Post Development Reader*. London: Zed Books, 85–93

Espino, M. (2000) 'Cuban tourism during the Special Period'. *Cuba in Transition, Vol 10*. Miami: Association for the Study of the Cuban Economy, 360–373

Esteva, G. and Prakash, M. (1997) 'From global thinking to local thinking'. In M. Rahnema and V. Bawtree (eds) *The Post Development Reader*. London: Zed Books, 277–298

ETB (1988) *Blackpool Visitor Survey*. London: English Tourist Board

ETB (1991) *The Green Light: A Guide to Sustainable Tourism*. London: English Tourist Board

Evans, N. (2002) 'Travel and tourism economics'. In R. Sharpley (ed) *The Tourism Business: An Introduction*. Sunderland: Business Education Publishers, 368–396

Evans, N., Campbell, D. and Stonehouse, G. (2003) *Strategic Management for Travel and Tourism*. Oxford: Butterworth Heinemann

Farrell, B. and Twining-Ward, L. (2004) 'Reconceptualising tourism'. *Annals of Tourism Research* 31(2), 274–295

Fayos-Solà, E. and Bueno, A. (2001) 'Globalization, national tourism policy and international organizations'. In S. Wahab and C. Cooper (eds) *Tourism in the Age of Globalisation*. London: Routledge, 45–65

Fleischer, A. and Pizam, A. (1997) 'Rural tourism in Israel'. *Tourism Management* 18(6), 367–372

Forsyth, T. (1995) 'Business attitudes to sustainable tourism: self-regulation in the UK outgoing tourism industry'. *Journal of Sustainable Tourism* 3(4), 210–231

Forum for the Future (2009) *The Five Capitals Framework*. Available on: www.forumforthefuture.org/our-approach/tools-and-methodologies/5capitals (accessed 20.01.09)

Frank, A. (1967) *Capitalism and Underdevelopment in Latin America*. London: Monthly Review Press

Garrod, B., Worrell, R. and Youell, R. (2006) 'Re-conceptualising rural resources as countryside capital: the case of rural tourism'. *Journal of Rural Studies* 22(1), 117–128

Gerrard, B. (1989) *Theory of the Capitalist Economy*. Oxford: Basil Blackwell

Ghani, A. and Lockhart, C. (2008) *Fixing Failed States: A Framework for Rebuilding a Fractured World*. Oxford: Oxford University Press

Ghimire, K. (2001) *The Native Tourist: Mass Tourism within Developing Countries*. London: Earthscan

Godfrey, K. (1996) 'Towards sustainability? Tourism in the Republic of Cyprus'. In L. Harrison and W. Husbands (eds) *Practising Responsible Tourism: International Case Studies in Tourism Planning, Policy and Development*. Chichester: John Wiley & Sons, 58–79

Goldsworthy, D. (1988) 'Thinking politically about development'. *Development and Change* 19(3), 505–530

González, Prof. M. (2007) Personal Communication, University of Havana

Goodland, R. (1992) 'The case that the world has reached its limits'. In R. Goodland, H. Daly, S. Serafy and B. von Droste (eds) *Environmentally Sustainable Economic Development: Building on Brundtland*. Paris: UNESCO, 15–27

Gössling, S. (2002) 'Human-environmental relations with tourism'. *Annals of Tourism Research* 29(4), 539–556

Gössling, S. (2006) 'Iceland'. In G. Baldacchino (ed) *Extreme Tourism: Lessons from the World's Cold Water Islands*. Oxford: Elsevier, 115–127

Goulet, D. (1968) 'On the goals of development'. *Cross Currents* 18, 387–405

Grant, D. and Sharpley, R. (2005) 'The law and tourism'. In L. Pender and R. Sharpley (eds) *The Management of Tourism*. London: Sage Publications, 150–160

Grant, M. (2002) *Contemporary Strategy Analysis, 4th Edition*. Oxford: Blackwell Publishing

Grihault, N. (2007) 'Travel and tourism: Cuba'. *Travel & Tourism Analyst*, August. London: Mintel International

GTA (2003) *Peace, Stability and Growth*. The Gambia: Gambia Tourism Authority

GTA (2007) *Arrivals Data: 2005–2007*. The Gambia: Gambia Tourism Authority

Gunn, C. (1994) *Tourism Planning: Basics, Concepts, Cases*. London: Taylor and Francis

Gursoy, D. and Rutherford, D. (2004) 'Host attitudes towards tourism: an improved structural model'. *Annals of Tourism Research* 31(3), 495–516

Gurung, D. and Seeland, K. (2008) 'Ecotourism in Bhutan: extending its benefits to rural communities'. *Annals of Tourism Research* 35(2), 489–508

Hall, C.M. (2000) *Tourism Planning: Policies, Processes and Relationships*. Harlow: Pearson Education Ltd.

Hall, C.M. (2005) *Tourism: Rethinking the Social Science of Mobility*. Harlow: Pearson Education

Hall, C.M. (2007a) Editorial: 'Pro-poor tourism: do "tourism exchanges benefit primarily the countries of the South"?' *Current Issues in Tourism* 10(2&3), 111–118

Hall, C.M. (2007b) *Tourism Planning: Policies, Processes and Relationships, 2nd Edition*. Harlow: Prentice Hall

Hall, C.M. and Higham, J. (2005) *Tourism, Recreation and Climate Change*. Clevedon: Channel View Publications

Hall, J. (2006) 'Is Iceland facing meltdown?' *Daily Telegraph*, 18 March. Available on: www.telegraph.co.uk/finance/2934589/Is-Iceland-facing-meltdown.html (accessed 01.12.08)

Hamilton, J., Maddison, D. and Tol, R. (2005) 'The effects of climate change on international tourism'. *Climate Research* 29, 245–254

Hannam, K., Sheller, M. and Urry, J. (2006) Editorial: 'Mobilities, immobilities and moorings'. *Mobilities* 1(1), 1–22

Harrigan, J. and Mosley, P. (1991) 'Evaluating the impact of World Bank structural adjustment lending'. *Journal of Development Studies* 27(3), 63–94

Harrison, D. (1988) *The Sociology of Modernisation and Development*. London: Routledge

Harrison, D. (2008) 'Pro-poor tourism: a critique'. *Third World Quarterly* 29(5), 851–868

Harvey, D. (1989) *The Condition of Postmodernity*. Oxford: Blackwell

Held, D., McGrew, A., Goldblatt, D. and Perraton, J. (1999) *Global Transformations*. Cambridge: Polity Press

Held, D. and McGrew, A. (2000) 'The great globalization debate: a review'. In D. Held and A. McGrew (eds) *The Global Transformations Reader*. Cambridge: Polity Press

Henderson, J. (2006) 'Tourism in Dubai: overcoming barriers to destination development'. *International Journal of Tourism Research* 8(2), 87–99

Henson, R. (2008) *The Rough Guide to Climate Change*. London: Rough Guides

Hettne, B.(1995) *Development Theory and the Three Worlds*. New York: Longman

Hickman, L. (2007) *The Final Call: In Search of the True Cost of our Holidays*. London: Eden Project Books

Hiernaux-Nicolas, D. (1999) 'Cancún bliss'. In D. Judd and S. Fainstein (eds) *The Tourist City*. New Haven, CT: Yale University Press, 124–139

Hillery, M., Nancarrow, B., Graham Griffin, G. and Syme, G. (2001) 'Tourist perception of environmental impact'. *Annals of Tourism Research* 28(4), 853–867

Hirst, P. and Thompson, G. (1999) *Globalization in Question, 2nd Edition*. Cambridge: Polity Press

Hoggart, K., Buller, H. and Black, R. (1995) *Rural Europe: Identity and Change*. London: Arnold

Høivik, T. and Heiberg, T. (1980) 'Centre-periphery tourism and self-reliance'. *International Social Science Journal* 32(1), 69–98

Holden, A. (2000) *Environment and Tourism*. London: Routledge

Howie, F. (1990) Editorial: 'The conference and its theme: sustainable tourism development'. In F. Howie (ed) *Proceedings of the Sustainable Tourism Development Conference*. Edinburgh: Queen Margaret College, 3–4

Høyer, K. (2000) 'Sustainable tourism or sustainable mobility? The Norwegian case'. *Journal of Sustainable Tourism* 8(2), 147–160

Hudson, S. (2000) *Snow Business: A Study of the International Ski Industry*. London: Cassell

Hulme, D. and Murphree, M. (1999) 'The "new conservation" in Africa'. In D. Hulme and M. Murphree (eds) *African Wildlife and Livelihoods: The Promise and Performance of Community Conservation*. London: James Currey, 1–15

Hultsman, J. (1995) 'Just tourism: an ethical framework', *Annals of Tourism Research* 22(3) 553–567

Hunter, C. (1995) 'On the need to re-conceptualise sustainable tourism development'. *Journal of Sustainable Tourism* 3(3), 155–165

IATA (2008) 'Scheduled passengers carried'. Available on: www.iata.org/ps/publications/wats-passengers-carried.htm (accessed 14.10.08)

IFTO (1994) *Planning for Sustainable Tourism: The ECOMOST Project*. Lewes: International Federation of Tour Operators

Inskeep, E. and Kallenberger, M. (1992) *An Integrated Approach to Resort Development: Six Case Studies*. Madrid: World Tourism Organisation

Ioannides, D. (1992) 'Tourism development agents: the Cypriot resort cycle'. *Annals of Tourism Research* 19(4), 711–731

IPCC (2007) *Climate Change 2007: Synthesis Report. Summary for Policymakers*. Intergovernmental Panel on Climate Change. Available on: www.ipcc.ch/pdf/assessment-report/ar4/syr/ar4_syr_spm.pdf (accessed 08.01.09)

ITB (2005) 'Tourism in Iceland'. Available on: www.visiticeland.com/upload/files/STATISTICS_2005.pdf (accessed 23.11.08)

IUCN (1980) *World Conservation Strategy: Living Resources Conservation for Sustainable Development*. Gland, Switzerland: World Conservation Union

Jafari, J. (1989) 'Sociocultural dimensions of tourism: an English language literature review'. In J. Bystrzanowski (ed) *Tourism as a Factor of Change: A Sociocultural Study*. Vienna: Vienna Centre, 17–60

Jaguaribe, B. and Hetherington, K. (2004) 'Favella tours: indistinct and mapless representations of the Real Rio de Janeiro'. In M. Sheller and J. Urry (eds) *Tourism Mobilities: Places to Play, Places in Play*. London: Routledge, 155–166

Jeffries, D. (2001) *Governments and Tourism*. Oxford: Butterworth-Heinemann

Jóhannesson, G., Huijbens, E. and Sharpley, R. (forthcoming) 'Icelandic tourism: past directions and future challenges', *Tourism Geographies*

Jónsson, A. (2006) *The Icelandic Economic Miracle. Where Does the Money Come From?* Reykjavik: Kaupthing Bank. Available on: www.kaupthing.is/lisalib/getfile. aspx?itemid=6897 (accessed 10.11.08)

Kammas, M. (1993) 'The positive and negative influences of tourism development in Cyprus'. *Cyprus Review* 5(1), 70–89

Kantor, B. (1995) *Understanding Capitalism: How Economies Work*. London: Bowerdean Publishing Co. Ltd and Marion Boyars Publishers

Karlsson, G. (2000) *Iceland's 1100 Years: History of a Marginal Society*. London: Hurst & Company

Kastenholz, E. (2000) 'The market for rural tourism in north and central Portugal. A benefit segmentation approach'. In G. Richards and D. Hall (eds) *Tourism and Sustainable Community Development*. London: Routledge, 268–284

Kemp, R., Parto, S. and Gibson, R. (2005) 'Governance for sustainable development: moving from theory to practice'. *International Journal of Sustainable Development* 8(1&2), 12–30

Khrushchev, S., Henthorne, T. and Latour, M. (2007) 'Cuba at the crossroads: the role of the US hospitality industry in Cuban tourism initiatives'. *Cornell Hotel and Restaurant Administration Quarterly* 48(4), 402–415

King, B., Pizam, A. and Milman, A. (1993) 'Social impacts of tourism: host perceptions'. *Annals of Tourism Research* 20(4), 650–665

Kinnaird, V. and Hall, D. (1994) *Tourism: A Gender Analysis*. Chichester: John Wiley & Sons

Knowles, T., Diamantis, D. and El-Mourabi, J. (2001) *The Globalisation of Tourism: A Strategic Perspective*. London: Continuum

Kousis, M. (2000) 'Tourism and the environment: a social movements perspective'. *Annals of Tourism Research* 27(2), 468–489

Krippendorf, J. (1987) *The Holiday Makers. Understanding the Impact of Leisure and Travel*. Oxford: Heinemann

Lane, B. (1990) 'Sustaining host areas, holidaymakers and operators alike'. In F. Howie (ed) *Proceedings of the Sustainable Tourism Development Conference*. Edinburgh: Queen Margaret College, 9–16

Law, C. (2002) *Urban Tourism: The Visitor Economy and the Growth of Large Cities, 2nd Edition*. London: Continuum

Lea, J. (1988) *Tourism and Development in the Third World*. London: Routledge

Leiper, N. (1979) 'The framework of tourism'. *Annals of Tourism Research* 6(1), 390–407

Lekachman, R. and Van Loon, B. (1981) *Capitalism for Beginners*. London: Writers and Readers Publishing Cooperative

Lélé, S. (1991) 'Sustainable development: a critical review'. *World Development* 19(6), 607–621

Lett, J. (1989) 'Epilogue to touristic studies in anthropological perspective'. In V. Smith (ed) *Host and Guests: The Anthropology of Tourism, 2nd Edition*. Philadelphia: University of Pennsylvania Press, 265–279

Levy, A. and Scott-Clark, C. (2008) 'Country for sale'. *The Guardian, Features and Comment*, 26 April, 30

Lim, C. and Cooper, C. (2009) 'Beyond sustainability: optimising island tourism development'. *International Journal of Tourism Research* 11(1), 89–103

Liu, Z. (2003) 'Sustainable tourism development: a critique'. *Journal of Sustainable Tourism* 11(3), 459–475

Lockhart, D. (1993) 'Tourism and politics: the example of Cyprus'. In D. Lockhart, D. Drakakis-Smith and J. Schembri (eds) *The Development Process in Small Island States*. London: Routledge, 228–246

Lomborg, B. (2001) *The Skeptical Environmentalist: Measuring the Real State of the World*. Cambridge: Cambridge University Press

Lovins, A. Lovins, H. and Hawken, P. (1999) 'A road map for natural capitalism'. *Harvard Business Review*, May–June, 145–158

Lowe, P. and Rüdig, W. (1986) Review article: 'Political ecology and the social sciences'. *British Journal of Political Science* 16, 513–550

Mabogunje, A. (1980) *The Development Process: A Spatial Perspective*. London: Hutchinson

MacCannell, D. (1989) *The Tourist: A New Theory of the Leisure Class, 2nd Edition*. New York: Shocken Books

Macnaghten, P. and Urry, J. (1998) *Contested Nature*. London: Sage Publications

Mann, M. (2000) *The Community Tourism Guide*. London: Earthscan

Marshall, J. and Walton, J. (1981) *The Lake Counties from 1830 to the Mid-20th Century*. Manchester: Manchester University Press

Mason, P. and Cheyne, J. (2000) 'Resident attitudes to proposed tourism development'. *Annals of Tourism Research* 27(2), 391–411

Mathieson, A. and Wall, G. (1982) *Tourism: Economic, Physical and Social Impacts*. Harlow: Longman

Matly, M. and Dillon, L. (2007) 'Dubai strategy: past, present, future'. *Harvard Business School*. Available on: www.belfercenter.ksg.harvard.edu/files/matly_paper1.pdf (accessed 03.02.09)

Matthews, H. and Richter, L. (1991) 'Political science and tourism'. *Annals of Tourism Research* 18(1), 120–135

McCormick, J. (1995) *The Global Environmental Movement*. Chichester: John Wiley & Sons

McKercher, B. (1993) 'Some fundamental truths about tourism: understanding tourism's social and economic impacts'. *Journal of Sustainable Tourism* 1(1), 6–16

McNamee, K. (1993) 'From wild places to endangered species: a history of Canada's national parks'. In P. Dearden and R. Rollins (eds) *Parks and Protected Areas in Canada: Planning and Management*. Toronto: Oxford University Press

Meadows, D.H., Meadows, D.L., Randers, J. and Behrens, W. (1972) *Limits to Growth*. London: Pan Books

Mebratu, D. (1998) 'Sustainability and sustainable development: historical and conceptual review'. *Environmental Impact Assessment Review* 18, 493–520

Meyer-Arendt, K. (2004) 'Tourism and the natural environment'. In A. Lew, C.M. Hall and A. Williams (eds) *A Companion to Tourism*. Oxford: Blackwell Publishing, 425–437

Middleton, V. (1989) 'Market profile: seaside resorts'. *Insights*. London: English Tourism Board, 5.1–5.19

Mieczkowski, Z. (1995) *Environmental Issues of Tourism and Recreation*. Lanham, MD: University Press of America

Mihalič, T. (2002) 'Tourism and economic development issues'. In R. Sharpley and D. Telfer (eds) *Tourism and Development: Concepts and Issues*. Clevedon: Channel View Publications, 81–111

Mill, R. and Morrison, A. (1998) *The Tourism System: An Introductory Text*. Dubuqu, Iowa: Kendall Hunt Publishing

Millward, D. and Starmer-Smith, C. (2008) 'Thousands of flights scrapped by airlines'. *Daily Telegraph: Telegraph Travel*, 11 October, T4

Milman, A. and Pizam, A. (1988) 'Social impacts of tourism on Central Florida'. *Annals of Tourism Research* 15(2), 191–204

Mishan, E. (1969) *The Costs of Economic Growth, 2nd Edition*. Harmondsworth: Penguin

Molz, J. (2004) 'Playing online and between the lines: round-the-world websites as virtual places to play'. In M. Sheller and J. Urry (eds) *Tourism Mobilities: Places to Play, Places in Play*. London: Routledge, 169–180

Mowforth, M. and Munt, I. (2003) *Tourism and Sustainability: Development and New Tourism in the Third World, 2nd Edition*. London: Routledge

Mowl, G. (2002) 'Tourism and the environment'. In R. Sharpley (ed) *The Tourism Business: An Introduction*. Sunderland: Business Education Publishers, 219–242

Müller, H. (1994) 'The thorny path to sustainable development', *Journal of Sustainable Tourism* 2(3), 131–136

Murphy, P. (1983) 'Tourism as a community industry: an ecological model of tourism development'. *Tourism Management* 14(3), 180–193

Murphy, P. (1985) *Tourism: A Community Approach*. London: Routledge

Mydral, G. (1963) *Economic Theory and Under-Developed Regions*. London: University Paperbacks

Nash, D. (1981) 'Tourism as an anthropological subject'. *Current Anthropology* 22(5), 461–481

Nash, D. (1989) 'Tourism as a form of imperialism'. In V. Smith (ed) *Hosts and Guests: The Anthropology of Tourism, 2nd Edition*. Philadelphia: University of Pennsylvania Press, 37–52

Nicholson, N. (1963) *Portrait of the Lakes*. London: Robert Hale Limited

OECD (1981) *The Impact of Tourism on the Environment*. Paris: Organisation for Economic Co-operation and Development

Opperman, M. (1993) 'Tourism space in developing countries', *Annals of Tourism Research* 20(3), 53–556

Opperman, M. and Chon, K. (1997) *Tourism in Developing Countries*. London: International Thomson Business Press

Orams, M. (1999) *Marine Tourism: Development, Impacts, Management*. London: Routledge

O'Reilly, K. (2003) 'When is a tourist? The articulation of tourism and migration in Spain's Costa del Sol'. *Tourist Studies* 3(3), 301–317

O'Riordan, T. (1981) *Environmentalism, 2nd Edition*. London: Pion

Ousby, I. (1990) *The Englishman's England: Taste, Travel and the Rise of Tourism*. Cambridge: Cambridge University Press

Owen, C. (1990) 'Better days at the seaside: can UK resorts learn from European experience?' *Tourism Management* 11(3), 190–194

Padilla, A. and McElroy, J. (2007) 'Cuba and Caribbean tourism after Castro'. *Annals of Tourism Research* 34(3), 649–672

Pearce, D., Barbier, E. and Markandya, A. (1990) *Sustainable Development: Economics and the Environment in the Third World*. London: Earthscan

Pearce, D., Markandya, A. and Barbier, E. (1989) *Blueprint for a Green Economy*. London: Earthscan

Pearce, P. (2005) *Tourist Behaviour: Themes and Conceptual Schemes*. Clevedon: Channel View Publications

Peston, R. (2008) 'The new capitalism'. *BBC News*. Available on: www.bbc.co.uk/blogs/thereporters/robertpeston/newcapitalism.pdf (accessed 08.12.08)

Pieterse, J. (1998) 'My paradigm or yours? Alternative development, post-development, reflexive development'. *Development and Change* 29, 343–373

Pigram, J. (1990) 'Sustainable tourism: policy considerations'. *Journal of Tourism Studies* 1(2), 2–9

PIO (1997) *The Almanac of Cyprus 1997*. Nicosia, Press and Information Office

Poirier, R. (1995) 'Tourism and development in Tunisia'. *Annals of Tourism Research* 22(1), 157–171

Poon, A. (1993) *Tourism, Technologies and Competitive Strategies*. Wallingford: CAB International

Porritt, J. (2007) *Capitalism As If The World Matters*. London: Earthscan

Portes, A. (1998) 'Social capital: its origins and applications in modern sociology'. *Annual Review of Sociology* 24, 1–24

Power-technology.com (2009) 'Tala Hydroelectric Project, Bhutan'. Avaliable on: www.power-technology.com/projects/tala (accessed 05.02.09)

Preston, P. (1996) *Development Theory: An Introduction*. Oxford: Blackwell

Priesner, S. (1999) 'Gross National Happiness – Bhutan's vision of development and its challenges'. Thimpu: Centre for Bhutan Studies. Available on: www.bhutanstudies.org.bt/admin/pubFiles/GNH_Ch3_Priesner.pdf (accessed 27.01.09)

Putman, R. (1995) 'Bowling alone: America's declining social capital'. *Journal of Democracy* 6(1), 65–78

Rahnema, M. (1992) 'Poverty'. In W. Sachs (ed) *The Development Dictionary: A guide to Knowledge as Power*. London: Zed Books, 158–176

Rahnema, M. (1997) 'Towards post-development: searching for signposts, a new language and new paradigms'. In M. Rahnema and V. Bawtree (eds) *The Post Development Reader*. London: Zed Books, 377–404

ReBlackpool (2007) 'Sea Change'. *365: Blackpool's Regeneration Magazine*, Summer, 4–7

Redclift, M. (1987) *Sustainable Development: Exploring the Contradictions*. London: Routledge

Reid, D. (2003) *Tourism, Globalization and Development: Responsible Tourism Planning*. London: Pluto Press

Reinfeld, M. (2003) 'Tourism and the politics of cultural preservation: a case study of Bhutan'. *Journal of International and Public Affairs*. Available on: www.princeton.edu/~jpia/pdf2003/Ch%207%Bhutan-Reinfeld-JPIA%202003.pdf (accessed 7.02.09)

Reisinger, Y. and Turner, L. (2003) *Cross-cultural Behaviour in Tourism: Concepts and Analysis*. Oxford: Butterworth-Heinemann

Renner, M. (2003) 'Vehicle production inches up'. *Vital Signs*. Available on: www.worldwatch.org/brain/media/pdf/pubs/vs/2003_cars.pdf (accessed 24.09.08)

Republic of Cyprus (2007) *Tourism Statistics 2007*. Nicosia: Republic of Cyrpus Statistics Section

Republic of The Gambia (2003) *First National Millennium Development Goals Report*. Available on: http://planipolis.iiep.unesco.org/upload/Gambia/Gambia%20MDG%20Report%202003.pdf (accessed 12.12.08)

Responsible Travel (2008) *Responsible Travel and Responsible Tourism*. Available on: www.responsibletravel.com/Copy/Copy100259.htm (accessed 07.11.08)

Richter, L. (1983) 'Tourism, politics and political science: a case of not so benign neglect'. *Annals of Tourism Research* 10(3), 313–335

Robbins, T. (2008) 'Are you being greenwashed?' *The Guardian*, 6 July. Available on: www.guardian.co.uk/travel/2008/jul06/green.ethicalholidays (accessed 26.11.08)

Robinson, J. (2004) 'Squaring the circle? Some thoughts on the idea of sustainable development'. *Ecological Economics* 48(4), 369–384

Robison, L., Schmid, A. and Siles, M. (2000) 'Is social capital really capital?' Available on: www.eclac.cl/prensa/noticias/comunicados/3/7903/robison-siles2409.pdf (accessed 16.01.09)

Rogers, P., Jalal, K. and Boyd, J. (2008) *An Introduction to Sustainable Development*. London: Earthscan

Rojek, C. (1993) *Ways of Escape*. Basingstoke: Macmillan

Rosenthal, E. (2008) 'Air travel and carbon on increase in Europe'. *Stop Global Warming*. Available on: www.stopglobalwarming.org/sgw_read.asp?id=1148066222008 (accessed 02.09.08)

Rostow, W. (1967) *The Stages of Economic Growth: A Non-Communist Manifesto, 2nd Edition*. Cambridge: Cambridge University Press

Russell, A. and Wallace, G. (2004) Editorial: 'Irresponsible ecotourism'. *Anthropology Today* 20(3), 1–2

Sachs, W. (1992) 'Introduction'. In W. Sachs (ed) *The Development Dictionary: A Guide to Knowledge and Power*. London: Zed Books, 1–6

SASEC (2004) *Analysis of SASEC Tourism*. South Asia Subregional Economic Co-operation. Available on: www.adb.org/Documents/Reports/SASEC/Tourism-Development/chap3.pdf (accessed 9.02.09)

SATC (2007) *Design Guidelines for Sustainable Tourism Development*. Adelaide: South Australian Tourism Commission

Saunders, P. (1995) *Capitalism: A Social Audit*. Buckingham: Open University Press

Sautter, E. and Leisen, B. (1999) 'Managing stakeholders: a tourism planning model'. *Annals of Tourism Research* 26(2), 312–328

Scheyvens, R. (2002) *Tourism for Development: Empowering Communities*. London: Prentice Hall

Scheyvens, R. (2007) 'Exploring the tourism-poverty nexus'. *Current Issues in Tourism* 10(2&3), 231–254

Scholte, J. (2002) 'What is globalisation? The definitional issue – again'. *Working Paper No.109/02*, University of Warwick: Centre for the Study of Globalisation and Regionalisation. Available on: www2.warwick.ac.uk/fac/soc/pais/staff/brassett/teaching/scholte-globalization.pdf (accessed 04.12.08)

Scholte, J. (2005) *Globalization: A Critical Introduction, 2nd Edition (Revised)*. Basingstoke: Palgrave Macmillan

Schuurman, F. (1993) 'Introduction: development theory in the 1990s'. In F. Schuurman (ed) *Beyond the Impasse: New Direction in Development Theory*. London: Zed Books, 1–48

Seabrook, J. (1993) *Victims of Development: Resistance and Alternatives*. London: Verso

Seaton, A. V. and Alford, P. (2001) 'The effects of globalization on tourism promotion'. In S. Wahab and C. Cooper (eds) *Tourism in the Age of Globilisation*. London: Routledge, 97–122

Seers, D. (1969) 'The meaning of development'. *International Development Review* 11(4), 2–6

Seers, D. (1977) 'The new meaning of development'. *International Development Review* 19(3), 2–7

Sen, A. (1994) 'Development; which way now?' In R. Kanth (ed) *Paradigms of Economic Development*. New York: M.E. Sharpe, 211–231

Sen, A. (1999) *Development as Freedom*. New York: Anchor Books

Sharp, R. (2008) 'Heritage site in peril: Angkor Wat is falling down'. *The Independent*. Available on: www.independent.co.uk/news/world/asia/heritage-site-in-peril-angkor-wat-is-falling-down-795747.html (accessed 08.01.09)

Sharpley, R. (1998) *Island Tourism Development: The Case of Cyprus*. Sunderland: Business Education Publishers

Sharpley, R. (2000a) 'Tourism and sustainable development: exploring the theoretical divide'. *Journal of Sustainable Tourism* 8(1), 1–19

Sharpley, R. (2000b) 'The influence of the accommodation sector on tourism development: lessons from Cyprus'. *International Journal of Hospitality Management* 19(3), 275–293

Sharpley, R. (2001) 'Tourism in Cyprus: challenges and opportunities'. *Tourism Geographies* 3(1), 64–85

Sharpley, R. (2003) 'Tourism, modernization and development on the island of Cyprus: challenges and policy responses'. *Journal of Sustainable Tourism* 11(2&3), 246–265

Sharpley, R. (2004) 'The impacts of tourism'. In D. Hind and J. Mitchell (eds) *Sustainable Tourism in the English Lake District*. Sunderland: Business Education Publishers, 207–242

Sharpley, R. (2006a) 'Ecotourism: a consumption perspective'. *Journal of Ecotourism* 5(1&2), 7–22

Sharpley, R. (2006b) 'In defence of (mass) tourism'. In M. Robinson, J. Swarbrooke, N. Evans, P. Long and R. Sharpley (eds) *Environmental Management and Pathways to Sustainable Tourism*. Sunderland: Business Education Publishers, 269–284

Sharpley, R. (2007a) 'A tale of two islands: sustainable resort development in Cyprus and Tenerife'. In S. Agarwal and G. Shaw (eds) *Managing Coastal Tourism Resorts: A Global Perspective*. Clevedon: Channel View Publications, 112–133

Sharpley, R. (2007b) 'Tourism in The Gambia – 10 years on'. In J. Tribe and D. Airey (eds) *Developments in Tourism Research*. Oxford: Elsevier: 49–61

Sharpley, R. (2008) *Tourism, Tourists and Society, 4th Edition*. Huntingdon: Elm Publications

Sharpley, R. (forthcoming) 'Tourism and development challenges in the Least Developed Countries: the case of The Gambia'. *Current Issues in Tourism*

Sharpley, R. and Craven, B. (2001) 'The 2001 Foot and Mouth crisis – rural economy and tourism policy implications. A comment'. *Current Issues in Tourism* 4(6), 527–537

Sharpley, R. and Knight, M. (2009) 'Tourism and the state in Cuba: from the past to the future'. *International Journal of Tourism Research* 11(3), 241–254

Sharpley, R. and Vass, A. (2006) 'Tourism, farming and diversification: an attitudinal analysis'. *Tourism Management* 27(5), 1040–1052

Shaw, G. and Williams, A. (1997) *The Rise and Fall of British Coastal Resorts: Cultural and Economic Perspectives*. London: Pinter

Sheehan, J. and Ritchie, J. (2005) 'Destination stakeholders: exploring identity and salience'. *Annals of Tourism Research* 32(3), 711–734

Sheller, M. and Urry, J. (2004) 'Places to play, places in play'. In M. Sheller and J. Urry (eds) *Tourism Mobilities: Places to Play, Places in Play*. London: Routledge, 1–10

Shields, R. (1991) *Places on the Margin: Alternative Geographies of Modernity*. London: Routledge

Shihab, M. (2001) 'Economic development in the UAE'. In P. Hellyer and I. Al-Abed (eds) *The United Arab Emirates: A New Perspective*. London: Trident Press Ltd., 249–259

Silver, I. (1993) 'Marketing authenticity in Third World countries'. *Annals of Tourism Research* 20(2), 302–318

Sinclair, T. and Stabler, M. (1997) *The Economics of Tourism*. London: Routledge

Skidmore, J. (2008) 'Britons: more mean than green'. *Daily Telegraph: Telegraph Travel*, 14 June, T4

Smeeding, T. (2005) 'Public policy, economic inequality, and poverty: the United States in comparative perspective'. *Social Science Quarterly* 86, 956–983

Smith, J. (2007) 'Tourist invasion threatens to ruin glories of Angkor Wat'. Available on: www.discoveryof.com/eZine/NewsArticles/_2007/_02/20070225-005.pdf (accessed 08.01.09)

Smith, V. (ed) (1977) *Hosts and Guests: The Anthropology of Tourism, 1st Edition*. Philadelphia: University of Pennsylvania Press

Smith, V. and Eadington, W. (eds) (1992) *Tourism Alternatives: Potentials and Problems in the Development of Tourism*. Philadelphia: University of Pennsylvania Press

Southgate, C. and Sharpley, R. (2002) 'Tourism, development and the environment'. In R.Sharpley and D. Telfer (eds) *Tourism and Development: Concepts and Issues*. Clevedon: Channel View Publications, 231–262

Spenceley, A. (ed) (2008) *Responsible Tourism: Critical Issues for Conservation and Development*. London: Earthscan

Stabler, M. and Goodall, B. (1996) 'Environmental auditing in planning for sustainable island tourism'. In L. Briguglio, B. Archer, J. Jafari and G. Wall (eds) *Sustainable Tourism in Islands and Small States: Issues and Policies*. London: Pinter, 170–196

Starmer-Smith, C. (2008) 'Christmas sales start early for travellers'. *Daily Telegraph: Telegraph Travel*, 1 November

Statistics Iceland (2008) *Tourist Industry*. Available on: www.statice.is/Statistics/Tourism,-transport-and-informati/Tourist-industry (accessed on 12.11.08)

Taylor, I. (2008) 'Trade out of step on climate, study finds'. *Travel Weekly*, 4 July, 3

Tearfund (2002) *Worlds Apart: A Call to Responsible Global Tourism*. Teddington: Tearfund

Telfer, D. (1996) 'Food purchases in a five-star hotel: a case study of the Aquila Prambanan Hotel, Yogyakarta, Indonesia'. *Tourism Economics* 2(4), 321–38

Telfer, D. (2002a) 'The evolution of tourism and development theory'. In R. Sharpley and D. Telfer (eds) *Tourism and Development: Concepts and Issues*. Clevedon: Channel View Publications, 35–78

Telfer, D. (2002b) 'Tourism and regional development issues'. In R. Sharpley and D. Telfer (eds) *Tourism and Development: Concepts and Issues*. Clevedon: Channel View Publications, 112–148

Telfer, D. and Sharpley, R. (2008) *Tourism and Development in the Developing World*. London: Routledge

The Beach War (n.d.) Available on: www.uq.edu.au/~pggredde/beach/overview.html (accessed 18.12.08)

Thomas, A. (2000a) 'Meaning and views of development'. In T. Allen and A. Thomas (eds) *Poverty and Development into the 21st Century*. Oxford: Oxford University Press, 23–48

Thomas, A. (2000b) 'Poverty and the "end of devlopment"'. In T. Allen and A. Thomas (eds) *Poverty and Development into the 21st Century*. Oxford: Oxford University Press, 3–22

Throsby, D. (1999) 'Cultural capital'. *Journal of Cultural Economics* 23, 3–12

Todaro, M. (2000) *Economic Development, 7th Edition*. Harlow: Addison-Wesley

Tohamy, S. and Swinscoe, A. (2000) *The Economic Impact of Tourism in Egypt*. Working Paper No. 40, Egyptian Centre for Economic Studies. Available on: www.eces.org.eg/Publications/Index2.asp?L1=4&L2=1&L3=1 (accessed 10.12.08)

Torres, R. (2003) 'Linkages between tourism and agriculture in Mexico'. *Annals of Tourism Research* 30(3), 546–566

Tosun, C. and Jenkins, C. (1998) 'The evolution of tourism planning in Third-World countries: a critique'. *Progress in Tourism and Hospitality Research* 4(2), 101–114

Towner, J. (1996) *An Historical Geography of Recreation and Tourism in the Western World 1540–1940*. Chichester: John Wiley & Sons

Toye, J. (1993) *Dilemmas of Development*. Oxford: Blackwell

Turner, L. and Ash, J. (1975) *The Golden Hordes: International Tourism and the Pleasure Periphery*. London: Constable

Twining-Ward, L. and Butler, R. (2002) 'Implementing STD on a small island: development and use of sustainable tourism development indicators in Samoa'. *Journal of Sustainable Tourism* 10(5), 363–387

UN (2001) *Outcome of the High Level Meeting on Tourism in the Least Developed Countries*. Third United Nations Conference on the Least Developed Countries. Available on: www.unohrlls.org/UserFiles/File/SIDS%20documents/A-CONF_%2019-_BP-4.pdf (accessed 15.11.08)

UN (2008) *The Criteria for the Identification of the LDCs*. United Nations OHRLLS. Available on: www.un.org/special-rep/ldc/ldc%20criteria.htm (accessed 20.04.08)

UNCTAD (2001) 'Tourism and development in the Least Developed Countries'. *Third UN Conference on the Least Developed Countries*, Las Palmas, Canary Islands

UNDP (2006) *Human Development Report 2006*. New York: United Nations Development Programme. Available on: www.undp.org (accessed 20.04.08)

UNDP (2007) *Human Development Report 2007*. New York: United Nations Development Programme. Available on www.undp.org (accessed 10.12.08)

UNEP/WTO (2005) *Making Tourism More Sustainable: A Guide for Policy Makers*. Paris/Madrid: United Nations Environment Programme/World Tourism Organization

UNWTO (2008a) 'Historical perspective of world tourism: international tourist arrivals'. World Tourism Organization. Available on: www.unwto.org/facts/eng/pdf/historical/ITA_1950_2005.pdf (accessed 22.08.08)

UNWTO (2008b) Home page: World Tourism Organization: www.unwto.org/index.php (accessed 22.08.08)

UNWTO (2008c) *Tourism Highlights 2008 Edition*. www.unwto.org (Facts & Figures Section), (accessed 16.10.08)

UNWTO (2008d) 'Conceptualisation of sustainable tourism development'. World Tourism Organization. Available on: www.unwto.org/sdt/mission/en/mission.php (accessed 12.11.08)

UNWTO (2008e) *Sustainable Tourism-Eliminating Poverty: the 7 mechanisms*. World Tourism Organisation. Available on: www.unwto.org/step/mechanisms/en/ms.ph (accessed 14.11.08)

UNWTO (2009) 'International Tourism Arrivals / Receipts 1950-2005'. World Tourism Organization. Available on: www.unwto.org/facts/eng/pdf/historical/ITA_1950_2005.pdf (accessed 22.01.09)

UNWTO/UNEP (2008) *Climate Change and Tourism – Responding to Global Challenges*. Madrid: World Tourism Organization/United Nations Environment Programme

UNWTO-UNEP-WMO (2007) *Davos Declaration: Climate Change and Tourism – Responding to Global Challenges*. World Tourism Organization-United Nations Environment Programme-World Meteorological Organization. Available on: www.unwto.org/pdf/pr071046.pdf (accessed 14.01.09)

Urry, J. (1994) 'Cultural change and contemporary tourism'. *Leisure Studies* 13(4), 233–238

Urry, J. (2002) *The Tourist Gaze, 2nd Edition*. London: Sage Publications

USAID (2005) *USAID and Sustainable Tourism: Meeting Development Objectives*. United States Agency for International Development. Available on: http://pdf.usaid.gov/pdf_docs/PNADE710.pdf (accessed 15.06.08)

Vellas, F. and Bécherel, L. (1995) *International Tourism: An Economic Perspective*. Basingstoke: Macmillan

Viner, D. (2006) Editorial: 'Tourism and its interactions with climate change'. *Journal of Sustainable Tourism* 14(4), 317–322

Viner, D. and Agnew, M. (1999) *Climate Change and its Impacts on Tourism*. Report prepared for WWF–UK. University of East Anglia: Climatic Research Unit. Available on: www.wwf.org.uk/filelibrary/pdf/tourism_and_cc_full.pdf (accessed 08.01.09)

VisitBritain (2008) *Key Tourism Facts*. Available on: www.tourismtrade.org.uk/MarketIntelligenceResearch/KeyTourismFacts.asp (accessed 26.09.08)

Wahab, S. and Cooper, C. (2001) 'Tourism, globalisation and the competitive advantage of nations'. In S. Wahab and C. Cooper (eds.) *Tourism in the Age of Globilisation*. London: Routledge, 3–21

Wall, G. (1993) 'International collaboration in the search for sustainable tourism in Bali, Indonesia'. *Journal of Sustainable Tourism* 1(1), 38–47

Wall, G. and Mathieson, A. (2006) *Tourism Change, Impacts and Opportunities*. Harlow: Pearson Prentice Hall

Wallerstein, I. (1979) *The Capitalist World Economy*. Cambridge: Cambridge University Press

Walton, J. (1998) *Blackpool*. Edinburgh/Lancaster: Edinburgh University Press/Carnegie Publishing

WCED (1987) *Our Common Future*. Oxford: Oxford University Press

Weaver, D. (2004) 'Tourism and the elusive paradigm of sustainable development'. In A. Lew, C.M. Hall and A. Williams (eds) *A Companion to Tourism*. Oxford: Blackwell Publishing, 510–521

Welch, R. (1984) 'The meaning of development. Traditional views and more recent ideas'. *New Zealand Journal of Geography* 76, 2–4

Wheeller, B. (1990) 'Is sustainable tourism appropriate?' In F. Howie (ed) *Proceedings of the Sustainable Tourism Development Conference*. Edinburgh: Queen Margaret College, 61–63

Wheeller, B. (1991) 'Tourism's troubled times: responsible tourism is not the answer'. *Tourism Management* 12(2), 91–96

Wilkinson, P. (1989) 'Strategies for island micro-states'. *Annals of Tourism Research* 16(2), 153–177

Williams, A. and Hall, C.M. (2000) 'Tourism and migration: new relationships between production and consumption'. *Tourism Geographies* 2(1), 5–27

Williams, S. and Shaw, G. (1998) *Tourism and Economic Development: European Experiences, 3rd Edition*. Chichester: John Wiley & Sons

Willis, K. (2005) *Theories and Practices of Development*. London: Routledge

Winter, T. (2007) 'Rethinking tourism in Asia'. *Annals of Tourism Research* 34(1), 27–44

Wong, P. (2004) 'Environmental impacts of tourism'. In A. Lew, C.M. Hall and A. Williams (eds) *A Companion to Tourism*. Oxford: Blackwell Publishing, 450–461

Wood, K. and House, S. (1991) *The Good Tourist: A Worldwide Guide for the Green Traveller*. London: Mandarin

Woodhouse, A. (2006) 'Social capital and economic development in regional Australia: a case study'. *Journal of Rural Studies* 22, 83–94

World Bank (2005) Classification of economies. Available on: www.worldbank.org/data/aboutdata/errata03/ Class.htm (accessed 01.04.05)

World Bank (2008) *Bhutan at a Glance*. Available on: www. devdata.worldbank.org/AAG/btn_aag.pdf (accessed 7.02.09)

WSSD (2002) *Report of the World Summit on Sustainable Development*. New York: United Nations

WTO (1980) *Manila Declaration on World Tourism*. Madrid: World Tourism Organization

WTO (1993) *Sustainable Tourism Development: A Guide for Local Planners*. Madrid: World Tourism Organization

WTO (1994) *Recommendations on Tourism Statistics*. Madrid: World Tourism Organisation

WTO (1998) *Tourism – 2020 Vision: Influences, Directional Flows and Key Influences*. Madrid: World Tourism Organization

WTO (2001) *eBusiness for Tourism. Practical Guidelines for Destinations and Businesses*. Madrid: World Tourism Organization

WTO/UN (1994) *Recommendations on Tourism Statistics*. Madrid: World Tourism Organization

WTO/WTTC (1996) *Agenda 21 for the Travel & Tourism Industry: Towards Environmentally Sustainable Development*. Madrid: World Tourism Organization/World Travel & Tourism Council

WTTC (2007a) *Cuba Travel and Tourism: Navigating the Path Ahead*. World Travel and Tourism Council. Available on: www.wttc.travel/bin/pdf/original_pdf_file/cuba.pdf (accessed 20.01.08)

WTTC (2007b) *Progress and Priorities 2007/08*. World Travel and Tourism Council. Available on: www.wttc.org/eng/About_WTTC/Annual_Reports (accessed 26.09.08)

WTTC (2008) 'Tourism impact data and forecasts'. World Travel and Tourism Council. Available on: www.wttc.org/eng/Tourism_Research/Tourism_Economic_Research (accessed 15.09.08)

Young, G. (1973) *Tourism: Blessing or Blight?* Harmondsworth: Penguin

Index